We Exist, Our Own Hierarchy

VICTORIA CARISIMO

Copyright © 2025 by Victoria Carisimo

All rights reserved.

No part of this book may be reproduced or transmitted in any form or by any means, electronic or mechanical, including photocopying, recording, or by any information storage and retrieval system, without permission in writing from the copyright owner.

Book Cover Design By Vicki Grech/Carisimo
Edited by Vicki Grech/Carisimo
www.atthechameleonturn.com

ISBN: 978-1-7640866-0-8 (paperback)
ISBN: 978-1-7640866-1-5 (ebook)

Typeset by Westchester Publishing Services

TABLE OF CONTENTS

Introduction	1
In the Beginning was the Word	5
Questions and Answers	9
Final Words	265
Ariel's Prayer	266
Ariel's Prayer Explained	267

The wound is the place where the light enters you.

—*Rumi*

INTRODUCTION

Imagine you are trying-out a new form of meditation—eyes open, focused on the flame of a candle while sitting comfortably on a rug. When, out of the blue, BOOM! Like a news flash interrupting a peaceful track of music, you hear a voice not your own; both within your head and announcing itself in the space surrounding you. A voice which—*you know*—in no way belongs to you, with a message that makes no sense, using words unfamiliar to your manner of speaking...

"SAY WHAT!?"

This may not have been the most appropriate response, but it was what—in shock—I had blurted back. To my further astonishment, the message was promptly repeated.

"Whoa! What in the...?"

I immediately stood and wrote down what I had heard—puzzled, and frankly quite shaken.

"What just happened!?"

I read the message several times. Two of the words—Hierarchy and Chameleon—though I knew them, were not part of my everyday vocabulary; consequently, I had misspelt them. This, I speedily corrected when, without hesitation, in an endeavour to shed some light upon what I'd received, I went in search of a dictionary.

It was the mid-nineties, so mobile phones were scarce, and not the mini-computers they are today; the dictionary became an especially close friend to me, thereafter.

What unfolded over the years was an intense, heuristic, and introspective search. I was hooked. I needed to know more, and though I had asked to audibly hear anew from this invisible source, I received no further broadcasts—not like the initial revelation. Nonetheless, a nonintrusive manner of communication, and relationship developed.

I like to think of this gracious stimulus as my *mentors or guides, teachers, and companions.*

Eventually imparting that *they* are a council of four, although in truth, One, *they* have shared that, together—when I "listen," and am not distracted by my conditioned beliefs and delusions—we are all an Us, a Unified state of Spirit or Consciousness. *They* have also informed me that the word, Spirit, can be viewed as an acronym, and enabler of this Unified state, which is not only available to me but to everyone—

Supreme **P**resence **I**nspiring **R**eal **I**nner **T**uition.

Our exchanges came by way of what I intuitively knew was acceptable and comfortable for me, which I came to dub as "Turns." As in turning a short, unremarkable phrase or sentence—made distinctively noticeable to me—into a 2, 3- or 4- page, meaningful composition. These became my weekly lessons which, though they always conveyed the same simple precepts, floored me by how they would emerge.

My guides—or if you prefer—mode of guidance, has seen me through many trials over the years. The guidance is always present. *Always* there for me. However, only available when I remember to Trust, Let Go, and Allow; in other words: get out of my own way . . .

My fictional book: *At the Chameleon, Turn,* was a result of some of what I had gleaned and learnt to date, passed on in a manner that could invite curiosity, would entertain, and which I felt deeply driven to express. The statement I received that life-changing day is comprised within its pages—the concluding words of the astonishing announcement, being said title.

Incredibly simple, the book's core message is not easy to implement when in the grip of one's doubts or fears . . . I know this; I have failed to apply its directive many times, and yet discovered more of my true self with each seeming stumble. I say seeming because falls can bring us closer to the ground, as in, the ground of being.

The guidance inevitably took on a new format where I was encouraged to ask questions, to which the answers were given in a simple but curious way. A way in which I was urged to expand my literal way of thinking by using a more lateral approach. This required not only a good dose of intuition, but some deeply soul-searching honesty.

This book: *We Exist, Our Own Hierarchy*, was the first part of the message I received that day, followed by, *At the Chameleon, Turn*.

Since the writing of my fictional book, *At the Chameleon, Turn*, I have been guided to share my *Turned* compositions on "X" (formerly known as Twitter) and post 365 inspired messages on Instagram, regarding the Chameleon and when to Turn. For example: *'At the Chameleon, Turn.' At the constant voice of doubt, Turn: Trust that life is guiding you in the right direction.*

For those wishing to view these on "X" my profile name is: Victori4ALL, while the messages on Instagram are similarly under the name: victori4all.

IN THE BEGINNING WAS THE WORD

And the Word was made flesh. Or rather, matter… Words matter!

Have you ever stopped to consider the importance of words and how their meanings, along with the subtle or evident allusions we individually give them, affect how we feel? Words are our current medium of exchange, as in, our present way of communicating, of exchanging or trading ideas. Words are a form of currency in this realm; they are the means we use to create sentences, a series of words cogitated or thought, that due to the charge we have endowed them with, go on to generate and construct another form of sentence: a ruling judgement that either sentences us to a life of drudgery, suffering and punishment or one of gratitude, joy and peace, and everything in between.

God is a word. What kind of charge does the word God hold for you? Think about it. Have you ever been asked if you believe in God? If so, your response—rather than a yes or no—would best be: "That all depends on what you mean by the word God…" For me, if the questioners' sense of the word God is a masculine entity that lives in the clouds and passes judgement down on everybody, then, absolutely not. No thank you. That definition of the word God sentences one to the gallows, if you get my drift. But, if the word God represents the All in all, the Great Mystery that many of us are endeavouring to grasp and intimately know, the presence within us that inspires and lifts us through acts of love to be all that we can, the life force that flows though and unites the whole kit and caboodle; the driving dynamism supplying all its miraculous creations with unlimited free will, allowing them, thereafter, to learn from their errors and foibles, or not learn. If the questioners' sense of the word God can be interchanged with the words Source, Spirit, Love, Unity, Awareness or Presence because these are indicative of Consciousness, which is fundamental to all we feel, observe, contemplate and experience, then yes, I do believe in God.

So, then, if words matter, what do the words in the title of this book: *"We Exist, Our Own Hierarchy,"* mean? When I first heard these words, they blew a few circuits. To say their announcement was astounding is an understatement. I had no idea what or who was trying to reach me, let alone why or what the words they had delivered meant. For a very long time I believed that the word Hierarchy—as it is typically known—signified some sort of ranking order, and that whoever *this* particular Hierarchy were, they were letting me know they *existed* and that I should pay attention to them because they were from a Higher Echelon. This was true in a sense; however, as time went on this grouping of words transformed into more than their initial implication to me. I eventually began to see that the, *We Exist,* referred not only to the source that transmitted the message, but also to me, to us, to all. We Exist! We Live! We Experience! We Are! And, our own Hierarchy, referred to our own level of knowledge or progress within this Existence: this realm or world we are currently experiencing. Wow! Words hey? They matter, literally and laterally, that is to say, sometimes in an imaginative, creative, allegorical or metaphorically sense.

To top things off, the source from which these words came, subsequently made it known to me that the word, Hierarchy, contained two significant root words: Hiero, from the Greek language, meaning Sacred, Divine or Holy and Archos, also derived from Greek, meaning Ruler or in this case Prime Rules. *Sacred Rules.* We Exist, Our Own Sacred Rules. Therefore, who's Sacred Rules was I going to follow: the *seemingly* sacred to me, though more accurately defined: established rules imprinted on my person through the collective social conditioning of my past indoctrination, etc., or the supportive, principled, peace-loving rules this beneficent source was endeavouring to teach me?

Words became my new friends and tutors, their rich etymologies often leading me—as with the word Hierarchy— down a heuristic path I hadn't considered or expected. Take the words: *Unified Kingdom's Currency*, at first glance the mind will associate the words with its past experience or comprehension of each word's literal significance; however, what if through *introspection* the words convey an esoteric meaning, a meaning that unless delved into, meditated upon and given a new underlying impression, can transmit a whole other way of seeing and experiencing things?

In this book you will find that a Unified Kingdom refers to a state of coherence between our Spirit, Mind and Body, and that Currency, as alluded to before, refers to our energy and medium of exchange: our current stream of currency, or present flow of vitality; our existing good feelings or lack thereof, and their powerful, potential influence on us depending on whichever way we choose to use or decipher them. In other words, the words, or stories we tell ourselves and others either consciously or unconsciously (habitually or automatically), which unbeknown to many, create our reality. Of course, if your Kingdom is Unified, then the narrative would be conscious and therefore the currency: current of energy you are intermingling with and expressing, would be malleable, adaptable, and as a consequence, able to generate a desired or better outcome.

The words we consume everyday by way of our thoughts, are undeniably life enhancing or disabling. Much of the mental cogitation we perpetually feed on is like a broken record that only changes tracks when it is bumped, that is to say, something in our life gives us a shake, shove or wakeup call. The message I received many years ago: *"We exist, our own Hierarchy. At the Chameleon, Turn,"* was my wakeup call. Not to say that I am now an enlightened being by any stretch of the imagination; however, I am by far more enlightened than I was.

Consider the word enlightened for a moment… In light… It not only signifies to be within the light, which is synonymous with clarity, truth, brightness and consciousness, therefore being cognizant, but it also means to be less burdened. Lighter. Happier. What else but encumbering words that construct limiting, misleading and disabling tales allowed free-range in us due to lack of awareness or ignorance—lack of light—can weigh us down?

The key here is Light, Consciousness, Awareness, Presence, God, if you will. For without the ever-present sentience that allows us to plainly know and acknowledge our irrefutable existence, who or what are we: animals running on instinct, unwittingly ruled by our suppressed and unaddressed fears, ignorantly driven by habitual thoughts and the subsequent emotions they swamp and overwhelm us with? We Exist, so let's start truly appreciating the fact. Let's start using that wonderous power that conveys this very real, *very, very obvious* fact to us every glorious day, and not so brilliant moment, with every single breath we take. Let's remain as acutely and astutely *Conscious* as we possibly can of every word we think, feel, speak, and put into action.

QUESTIONS AND ANSWERS

This current book is written in a dialogue form, using:

V: For when I speak, and **A:** For the answer I received.

I have also used parentheses to further explain a word or expression, and was intuitively guided to use capitals to emphasize words that need particular attention paid to them.

Though the answers I received were for my benefit, I've been made aware that they refer to the human condition in general, and though some questions are personal and perhaps embarrassing due to my ignorance, I felt strongly guided to share them. My mentors' answers have helped me to understand myself on a deeper level as well as cope with many difficult, everyday situations and emotions, therefore I hope you, dear reader, may also recognize yourself in my human frailties and glean what is relevant for you.

Please let me apologise for any questions that, because of my many doubts, were repeated; however, in saying that, repetition is how we learn. And believe me when I say, I am not the quickest learner, but then again, the Chameleon is exceedingly deceptive, and navigating this earthly realm is difficult for the best of us. The good thing is my mentors always gave me the answer I needed, regardless, and never seemed displeased, no matter what I asked.

I would like to point out that the language they use can sound cryptic sometimes, but I urge you to read a passage several times if at first it doesn't make sense to you; the meaning will penetrate if you sit with it and allow it to soak in . . .

A further small aside, dear reader, is that I occasionally allude to sections of a prayer throughout the discourse that was given to me by this source, and which I refer to as Ariel's prayer, or simply the prayer. For access to the entire prayer and an explanation of it, please flick through to the last couple of pages.

So, let us begin.

31st August 2022

V: What would you like to discuss today?

A: Being benign, nonthreatening, compassionate. Being gentle, mild, of kind disposition, as this is favourable and emerges forth from Consciousness, from being Aware. Any worthless matter that you defend, misrepresents and disguises Truth. This fails to fulfill. Flush these masquerades out from their cover, drive these veneers out from their ununified polarity.

V: Any hints on how to recall all this when I am triggered?

A: As a beginner or novice, treasure the benign, for thus one lives in fresh, pure Consciousness. And cull. Select quality over false and misleading idols.

V: How do you think I am going?

A: One's capacity is of great quantity, like all here. Rely, place one's trust and confidence upon Our peal: Our prolonged sonorous vibration. We appeal to the fair, just and honest, directly.

4th September 2022

V: Hi. Is there anything you would like to talk about?

A: We are beside one to undertake that which explains, represents, or symbolizes ideas; thus, one can anew, become afresh.

V: Yes, and I am grateful for the many times you have done this for me.

A: Together We dismantle the dismal, the devoid of joy, one's Badlands (internal programs) which, cut by erosion, are capable of being reformed.

We corroborate with one to strengthen and support, to confirm one's conviction, thus produce a large pure bloom.

5th September 2022

V: Day by day by day by day . . . ?

A: Be Present. Say I am here now . . . I am going Home.

V: I feel like I am stagnant.

A: This assessment: *I feel like I am stagnant*, imposes a burden on one. The remedy for all dis-eases is the second coming of Christ (Conscious Awareness), one's nobility and agency of communication, the way to vary and modify one's rhythm, and henceforward remove this weight and affliction.

8th September 2022

V: I lost my shit at David, my husband, today. Working together at our jewellery store isn't always fun. But, I think it needed to happen, and I feel okay now. I let him have it concerning how critical he can be sometimes and rebuked him about how he over stresses. I think I needed to explode, however I was *aware* that I needed to remain *present*, so I did realize I should follow his advice more closely. I also realized it was foolish of me not to, as I would only suffer his inevitable annoyance, and so, in a sense, I am actually inviting or inciting his criticism. What do you think?

A: A Unified Kingdom (optimal state of coherence between Spirit, Mind and Body) is the common wealth of nations.

V: Well, he did appear to be listening to me.

A: Upon being seized by one's battle cry.

V: Yeah, well I did throw a bit of a fit. His constant stress wears me down sometimes.

A: To oppose with an equal force is a counterweight of expression, it is a communication and outward manifestation of thought which, having a pivotal point—a nucleus around which other concepts gather—pulls, draws, or removes ideas from a natural or fixed place; thus, they can improve in stability and security.

V: So, it was a good thing? What surprised me was that I was able to understand his frustration with me, and while I loudly and forcefully voiced my exasperation with him, I was able to let go of my initial anger very quickly.

A: One sealed the deal, one established peace, and finally settled via a soft, gentle directive.

9th September 2022

V: What would you like to talk about today?

A: Let Us (Unified state) talk about going beyond the stellar.

V: Okay.

A: To excel, look upon one's new willingness to improve, with respect and deference. Beside the booming bark of one's old will, lies one' new will; thus, through the act of association, the old connects via relation to the new, creating fresh neuro pathways; hence, regardful ideas and feelings.

V: Therefore, I should honour my new will?

A: One's new will is the energy conductor that sends messages to one to reclaim one's willingness, aiding the process of balancing one. Willingness hears, audits, examines, adjusts and certifies; hence, together we agree with the Covenant: the promise of God (Consciousness, Awareness, Knowledge) to bless those who fulfil this condition. Willingness imparts and makes known a way to Turn (Transcend) with a counterpoise: an equal power, force, or influence.

V: So, by paying attention to my new will, which is essentially to know the truth of things, I am effectively venerating it and going beyond stellar.

A: It is a counterbalance: a power equally opposing another. And, much like Homeopathy, it is a system of therapy using minute doses that produce symptoms of dis-ease for organic equilibrium, as the tendency of an organism is to maintain a uniform and beneficial physiological stability within and between its parts.

V: As in small doses of upset? Small disturbances?

A: Which assist.

V: And the counterbalance to this would be?

A: To exonerate. To free from all accusation or blame. To unburden from the record (memory, program) kept by the depositor—Oneself.

V: Hmm... I did do that with David during our argument yesterday, didn't I?

A: One was prepared to exchange one's assumed necessities.

V: I did feel something shift.

A: A hidden inner secret.

V: Yes. I kept yelling, in an arrogant manner, that I must be stupid otherwise I would follow his guidelines. But I was saying it to be hurtful and make him feel bad. And then it dawned on me that there was sadly some truth to what I was saying.

A: An official announcement communally shared.

V: Yes! Did I have some sort of break through?

A: One grew better. One improved. One thrived via the tracing of the word *stupid* from its original form and past meaning to one.

V: The erroneous, hidden belief that I am stupid, put there by incompetent teachers throughout my school years. I think David had a breakthrough too, as he was really attentive today.

A: One's battle cry is bearing the fruit of a purifying experience. The emergency calling one to the immediate action of losing one's shit, as said, came about in order to retire from active service, the hidden, false claim that one is stupid, which emerged and came to light, becoming apparent.

V: Let me get this straight. Because of this old, deeply buried, deceptive belief that I am stupid, I subconsciously act in foolish or unproductive ways so that others are forced to get annoyed with me. I then get upset because it seems they've made me feel like I am stupid or useless, however, this is really my programming trying to prove my belief (mind lie) which I vehemently fight or resist, so I can never truly see it?

A: This is the foundation one built as a child, one's supreme law structure, which was written hastily and carelessly. It is extremely irrational; in fact, it is insane. Childhood is its virgin genesis, its origin. To remove this belief (mind lie) from active participation, one pronounced and delivered it solemnly. One proclaimed it.

V: I did! It was like a light suddenly came on. Does that mean I am free of it now?

A: Like a door admitting light, this amplifies one's voice to a higher level, where one can approve and express a choice to exchange a constitution in one, hence, the state of being glad or joyous can be constant.

V: Thank you.

10th September 2022

V: Is there anything I can do to help quicken my spiritual progress?

A: Free oneself from the burdening load that one's vehicle (body) carries. One who is a student of higher learning always has assistance, thus can easily make crumble or pulverize the dogmatic orders (beliefs) that are tarnished or corrupted.

V: Always has assistance?

A: Direction.

V: Direction?

A: When one is thrown into confusion, this discolouration (chaotic influence) attaches an attribute, condition or consequence that is designed to improve and strengthen one.

V: I'm not sure I know what you mean?

A: When one's Prime Consciousness is free from the faults of the old testament (old programming), the elimination of the blameworthy helps to yield and weave the highest crop.

V: So, to quicken, I need to be free of all my burdens, as in the things I blame?

A: That branch out as the outgrowths from the trunk—offshoots.

V: Anything that is not good, that is not of God? (Pure Consciousness).

A: One is populated with inhabitants: set, unbalanced beliefs and customs used disparagingly, similar to simians (apes, animal nature).

V: I am trying.

A: One thing gives place to another. See claims, stories, opinions, beliefs, as rumours, as unfounded reports.

V: What is the best way to remove all my burdens? Is it stillness or counterbalance, or is stillness the counterbalance?

A: A sudden action that can overturn a burden, is hyperbole: an exaggeration or overstatement of the disturbance; for if tended to within—without being taken literally—it produces an effect, a counterbalance, as it projects a burden beyond excess.

V: Like when I was yelling that I must be stupid, right? It woke me up.

A: One's brainwaves: the rhythmical fluctuation of electrical potential in the brain, altered, and thus, the convictions and beliefs of this intensive and coercive indoctrination (I must be stupid) shifted. It was like one struck a gong; the deep resonant tone, reproducing the germ (the source).

V: So, you're saying: become acutely aware of the deeply seeded belief and let it exaggeratedly sound out like a gong, without taking it literally?

A: One's past self-language (self-talk) is the dialect of a low or base interaction; it is a current that flows from former major conflicts that have become a canon: a rule of law and a trigger. Like a pasquinade, it is an abusive or coarse personal satire that is posted in a recognizable place for one to view and move past, but it is stick-to-it-tive, that is to say: persevering. To renew one's spirit or energy, be Noble. Know that the whole universe—including one—is God (Love). And hence, become freed from this menacing error.

V: Put simply: Re-member my sovereignty while being aware of my erroneous indoctrination, right?

A: One fears the influence of communion, of sharing union. Act contrary to this for balance.

V: Communion with God? As in sharing our Consciousness?

A: One is within easy reach of a self-evident, recognized truth. Think oneself worthy.

V: How do I think myself worthy if I don't, though?

A: Religious orders (past programming, dogmatic beliefs, erroneous conditioning) can easily crumble and or be pulverised by airing these with sharp sighted vigilance. Unite both polarities to bear the fruit of triumph. Do not lower oneself. Do not stoop to depression, for it reduces one's power, and thus lowers one's Spirit.

V: Okay. How's this for stating the truth? I am worthy, for I am noble, because the entire universe is encompassed and permeated by God, and therefore so am I.

A: One has taken one's first universal degree in a higher learning that frees from faults and intense suffering.

V: My true self is faultless, so I am worthy.

A: One's source of fuel is to be at peace; hence, remain tranquil. This has two meanings and effects. First, peace is one's royal residence, it is where one resides in one's Sovereignty, and secondly, peace discharges one from penalty; it delivers one from dis-ease via the craft (ability) of harnessing itself.

12th September 2022

V: I want to learn more about what I really am. Apparently, without all the cargo I've taken on or added, I am faultless, sovereign and noble.

A: The cargo shackles and confines one; it cuts off one's flight feathers.

V: That's what social programming has done to me.

A: It underlies and is the basis of one's support.

V: So, without this cargo/programming, what am I?

A: One, as are all, is possessed of the Spirit of insight, thus prophecy. Knowing one is pure: free from stain or corruption, bears witness via one's innocence to the flow of the copious, the abundant. However, one's *I Am* is still fearful. It is filled with the uneasiness of the unclear, of the doubtful uncertainty that goes around and around, and compounds one's sentence: one's self-stated imprisonment... Recognize and comprehend the selfish and grasping desire for the possession of wealth that assaults and decisively defeats most people.

V: Well, it certainly feels like a prison sentence, how many years must I serve before I am free of this unease and doubt?

A: The constitution of a sound mind is an agreement to be fertilized or enriched by composure, by tranquillity and calmness: effected very quickly by a break in the continuity of drama.

V: And then can I be possessed of the spirit of prophesy again, free to bear pure witness, right?

A: Free to settle by arbitration based on discernment found naturally within, and used in healing.

V: Can you please tell me more about the natural inborn qualities which are concealed by our cargo/burdens?

A: O Lord! We express surprise. One is Spirit in singular presence, capable of effecting transition from one condition to another. For example, a sudden outburst of emotion can raise one to a loftier place of Love.

V: Right. So, you're saying that without my burdens, I am spirit?

A: Spirit walking and moving about in a comedy of manners portraying the customs and foibles of the fashionable world.

V: Sometimes I feel like I am in a play.

A: A wheel designed to keep one on a fixed track that aids attachment.

V: The Karmic wheel? So, I am spirit having a human experience, as they say, in a play of my choosing.

A: The imaginary spherical surface on which heavenly bodies (Spirits) seem to be enclosed by the universe, is a small quantity of Consciousness which has a harsh, disagreeable vibration for all to Turn (transform) into the Divine. All have accustomed themselves to this condition by repetition.

V: So, we are here to make this playing field Divine?

A: It is a place to lodge in, to reside in on authority of the highest quarter. A place holding and professing belief in the Trinity: God the Farther, Son and

Holy Spirit, which is used in warfare. It is a place or base for measuring the explosive power of nuclear bombs.

V: Yep, that certainly describes the harsh, disagreeable cacophony of this place. So, you are saying we are here to raise its vibration, right?

A: The art of drawing such pictures can be immediate when one's currency (frequency) is imprinted with assuring, trustworthy, restorative values.

V: Will our *"At the Chameleon, Turn"* posts help fix those values? Is that why you wanted me to broadcast them?

A: Yes. We broadcast these in order to surround and encompass so that others may comprehend. Together We have devised and accomplished these steps of compassion, with the desire to help and spare.

18th September 2022

V: Does reciting mantras help to raise my vibration?

A: Mantras are Sovereign plants (implants) of inner communication; they are a basic teaching for one effected with seizures or attacks of unconsciousness.

V: So, reciting mantras helps me stay conscious, as in, aware?

A: Correct. Employ them to give forth harmonious vibrations, and to oppose one's earthly games of contest. Use them to settle one down and show one the way.

V: Is there anything else you would like to add?

A: Raising one's pitch is basic. It is essential and fundamental for producing discipline in degrees. Pitch navigates and guides one's little trees (neurons and dendrites). An elevated pitch removes temper and regulates disorders of the mind.

V: Mantras uplift low spirits, right?

A: One's Badlands (programs, conditioned carnal mind) are faulty, they frighten one with empty threats, they deceive and mislead; they consume one, and impair one's character and strength etc. We need to dissolve these gradually by alchemical action with all one's heart, with great willingness and great sincerity, or one will suffer mental anguish and grief.

When destitute of light, which is unpleasant to the senses, use a mantra as a counterpoise, as a counterbalancing force, to create a state of equilibrium.

Equilibrium embeds reproductive cells that act as a unit for transmitting harmonizing characteristics from parent to offspring, from Source to one. This is Spirit gathering one up without pain.

V: Can I use, *"Om mani padme hum"*?

A: Om mani padme hum, is a measure of sound intensity, and, the specialized vocabulary of a group, but yes, one can rely on it and be sure about it. Use it to hold fast or captive the attention of the encephalon (the brain), thus enchant it completely with delight; hence it is not affected by the drunkenness of the whine.

V: Is there anything else you would like to add concerning mantras?

A: Mantras can stimulate and renew one in Spirit; they are an easy and pleasant experience that oversee mental or moral subjection to habits or vices. Speak them to appeal for help or security and for sowing seeds that cast one beyond the gloomy and melancholy. Value them highly for a change in attitude; they are an endowment to the mind, a natural gift.

21st September 2022

V: I've noticed that stressful situations don't trigger me as much, but I still feel this sadness come over me now and then, and I know I should be grateful because I have so much to be grateful for, so then I feel guilty. Can you please shed some light on what this melancholy is? If I am gradually unburdening myself through my practices, shouldn't I be feeling more joy within myself?

A: One's Am is bi; it is both sadness and joy. This is duality. Turn to one side, to the sadness, alertly and inquiringly, this brings one to a position of readiness as it emits an intense light, a penetrating Awareness that breaks the continuity of the drama of sadness. Attribute the sadness to a cause or source, for example: the world's insanity.

To discipline the outer covering (the body), employ trading the merchandise stored, for thus one empowers and enables oneself—as a woman who rules her empire, her kingdom—to empty, unburden or clear it. This pertains to the highest Heaven: the abode of God.

V: So, this sadness is part of the illusion. It's a sign that I need to do more clearing.

A: It is perplexity. It is the state or condition of being full of doubt, confused, full of complexities.

V: Then it's a matter of discipline. I need to continue repeating the invocations and keep reminding myself that I am not alone, right?

A: Be rational, lucid, balanced, and wise. Have full possession of one's mental faculties. Be sane. One learns via trial and error. One proves, verifies, and establishes, via use and experience.

V: I know, I just want to be done with all this limiting programming.

A: One protests.

V: Yes.

A: One brings forth to testify, to state, to attest, to confirm. Hence, make a solemn affirmation as a sooth-sayer able to foretell events. This has calming and relieving effects.

V: At the Chameleon, Turn: Follow your advice.

A: Our Self' advice. Ourselves considered collectively: Our advice helped Ourselves.

V: Are you saying, We: you guys and me, are a collective?

A: Collective is a word that may be used instead of guides for one to deliver officially or solemnly; hence, proclaim it, assert it, declare it.

V: Can you tell me more about our collective?

A: We are nearby for the reunion of broken parts, transmitting to a restricted number of receivers, requesting that they forsake and abandon the coarse and desolate that is without Awareness; for example, any anxiousness which troubles the mind.

V: Right, so, I'm not making any of this up. You are here, communicating with me, correct?

A: One is able to receive or perceive as a radio station and hence recover one's Spirit, thus health. To improve, become skilled in taming one's inharmonious manners.

V: Will I eventually be able to fully sense your presence?

A: When one complies, We will be observable. One is being tutored to take responsibility, thus stand-up with a balanced point of view.

22nd September 2022

V: Please comment on the following: *"When thine eye becomes one, your whole body will be filled with light."*

A: Anxiety—any fear, emotional tension, or apprehension—is born of the same source as ruin: a condition of destruction, of degradation, of loss of honour. Being: existing as one's essential nature, as opposed to not Being, which in truth is nonexistence, keeps: retains possession or charge of one as a daughter of Nobility, of Goodness, Graciousness and Decency. Being assists one to rise rapidly. Being abets one to leap to a state effecting one's agency of service or relation to self and other; Being, advances development.

V: Right. So, Being is being one pointed. Focussed.

A: Being is a premise that is premium, it is of the highest value.

V: A principle, a basis to abide by.

A: Being is adjacent to Consciousness; Being is near or toward the See of Awareness. It is Collateral, it is Security, Surety; it is being together, side by side with one's scope or range of icons: the parts of one that tell-a-vision. Which, due to the id: the unconscious part of the psyche actuated by fundamental impulses toward fulfilling instinctual needs, may be icy: forbiddingly aloof.

V: Holy wow! That is a lot to focus on.

A: Use Being to accelerate one's Sovereign power, practice Being to generate an avalanche of avant-garde, ingenious ideas. Being is the fundamental element of Knowledge.

V: In other words: "Know Thyself." Know what is going on within me in relation to what is going on in my environment, seemingly outside of me.

A: Being above See level (Conscious level) is an applicable appliance that acts as a reflector of evident frequencies.

V: So, I, or rather, we humans, are very much like aerials. Most of us are just not tuned in. Our receivers are scrambled by the bombardment of all the crap we are constantly exposed to, right?

A: Like money, which takes on special characteristics and usages, to mention one specifically.

V: Yes, money is a massive distraction and scrambler.

A: As is the political organization of income tax used for the ownership of minds via spiels like the noisy, high-pressure sales talk asserting *yellow peril*—the alleged power, both political and numerical of the Oriental people, conceived of as threatening to white, Western supremacy.

V: I see. You are warning me to stay calm and not buy into the spiels of our media's fear-laced propaganda.

A: Owning one's own mind is optimum; it gives one the right, the power, and the liberty of choice. It allows superficial deposits that are stored up, to pass through one and fall, decrease, plummet, collapse.

24th September 2022

V: While meditating today, I felt you very strongly advising me to know, not just believe, but *know*, that you are with me.

A: Turn to the God of the See, the God of Understanding—Conscious Awareness.

V: What do you mean by that?

A: To rise sharply above a usual level, Turn to Awareness, and attain a lofty or exalted state.

Pan all. See all, every, the whole, for a large gain. Panning serves a useful purpose; it fastens one firmly by engrossing or attracting the attention, causing one to Turn.

V: Is that why you stressed that I need to *know* you are with me?

A: One is reading (understanding) the indications of our Hierarchy of tones, so that one may rise by degrees. We notify one of this to enable one to view the authentic in advance via Our watchful supervision—Our superintendence.

We relate in short narratives, that We are wholly Spirit, one's helpers, and comforters.

One's central nervous system has come to a centre; it has detached from one's fanciful collection of stories: one's catalogues.

V: Are you saying I am ready for more?

A: One's beliefs have proved themselves false; they have failed to fulfill one, they have misrepresented and disguised the Truth.

V: Does that mean I will be able to see and know the truth, rather than rely on mind lies—past beliefs?

A: It means these pathways will correspond to being corrected. We will straighten them together.

V: Because I will be able to receive your guidance more clearly?

A: It is because one remembers that the first, the Alpha response comes from one's heart, from Love, and that the cardinal virtues—justice, prudence, temperance and fortitude—will follow. One recalls that anything that depresses or disheartens one is in accordance with the nature, wishes customs or habits that are in conformity with the catalogue (memories) one has selected from upon seizure of this field of force.

25th September 2022

V: I feel quite calm today, in fact when an argument began to ensue between David and me concerning work, I was able to rein in the emotions and let go of the need to be right.

A: To vilify: assail someone with abusive or contemptuous language, is to act in a base or vile way, and sets the pace for another in a race. Our radar scope is intertwined; one has used it as a warning signal when this earthly existence treats one to one's old ways of life.

V: Yes, I've become more aware of your presence and of your warnings to pull back from any former ways of dealing with things.

A: We are dependable, honest, loyal, good, and comprehensive in capacity.

V: Therefore, I need to pay heed when you sound the siren.

A: Turn to Us for small nourishing fruits (results).

V: And on each occasion that I Turn or transcend, I will engage in at-one-ment (reparation), which will only strengthen me over time, yes?

A: Being of One Mind (At-One-Ment), offsets a reaction via the light of Awareness in one's nucleus, one's core central structure. Conscious Awareness initiates biofeedback: voluntary control of involuntary functions, such as those that depress and deprive one of receiving Us and enjoying Am. Thus, listen to We who are not drunk with whine.

V: Us, as in a unified state of mind, as in At-One-Mind, right?

A: This is the subject of discussion.

V: Yes exactly. We are a collective, we are of One Mind.

A: This is an established principle approved by agreement.

V: Yes, please let me receive your input clearly.

A: The choice is between being an unconscious body or knowing the state of Being Divine. It is between representing oneself as a mere shadow who functions as an interrupter of Our interaction, or of Being a dispenser of healing.

27th September 2022

V: *"Just an old fashioned love song, coming down in three part harmony..."* This song came out-of-the-blue into my mind this morning. I assume it was a message from you to remind me that God's harmonizing love is always around, and always available.

A: Amen. And so, it is... Love ameliorates, it enriches, perfects, revolutionizes. Hence, hold, adhere to Love as a principle, for Love supports the vines of one's machinery (nerves and dendrites of the body structure).

V: I was feeling a bit crappy this morning, so thank you for the reminder.

A: One alters Love's signal, mixing it haphazardly; hence, one struggles in a disorderly manner.

V: In other words: Don't stray from love's course or frequency.

A: The frequency of Love is a teacher; it precedes time, encircling all with quality, excellence and worth. And a capacity for being skilful in seeking ownership of Self.

29th September 2022

V: Is Knowledge the simple state of recalling, as in knowing and being conscious or aware that *I Am Love*, and therefore everything presented to me other than Love, is part of the illusion called Maya in this world?

A: Everything else is pretence, a false assumption. Posturing is a hook wanting in civility, graciousness, respect, and consideration. To end said dis-ease in one, bethink one is the house of God, thus Love. This intercedes as a prayer re-minding all souls—that have departed from this Knowing and become episodic, disjointed, and lost in their serialized story—of the Truth.

V: So, I am correct. Knowledge is to know what and who all my earthbound siblings and I truly are—Love.

A: Amalgamate, merge, form a union, an alliance that is *not* open to the corrupt, dishonest, immoral or perverted. Determine and establish the highest. Depression, or low spirits is a membranous, cloudy structure that shrouds part of the body and captains it without resting on the Wholeness of the Soul's foundation. Do *not* dignify depression. Dignify Love.

V: How can I know, as in really allow this knowing that *I Am Love*, be fully felt?

A: To begin developing this Knowing, follow the example of the Galilean, Jesus. His teachings support the body; use them like fertile stimulants, for they will cause one to be fruitful against the lower voice. Like Hercules, the son of Zeus in classical mythology, Jesus, too, is renowned for his great strength.

V: Are you implying that like Hercules, Jesus is a myth?

A: Jesus reassures, encourages, comforts, inspires, emboldens, and heartens the grey matter covering the brain, relaying that alternation between two things is a foreordained and eternal purpose.

V: Between Spirit and matter?

A: Between one's superficial covering and one's Higher Attendance. Interchange and wavering between these two is a natural consequence.

Use the Galilean as a crutch to prop and support one; hence, the world's hocus-pocus, its trickery and deception, can be treated via Jesus' shining example.

V: Should I be reading the New Testament? I know it reasonably well, but should I read it from beginning to end?

A: Together We will seek the state of being competent, accomplished. We will propose a plan.

30th September 2022

V: I looked up some of Jesus' teachings today, and Mark 12:30-31 stood out for me: *"Love the Lord your God with all your heart and with all your soul and with all your mind and with all your strength. This is the greatest commandment. The second is this: You shall love your neighbour as yourself."*

When I read this, I exchanged the word God with Consciousness, meaning to thoroughly know, which understood this way, the verse translates to: "Love Consciousness, *love thoroughly knowing*, with all your heart, soul, mind, and strength." And, through loving Consciousness, by way of attending to being present or utterly aware or as mindful as one can possibly be, we come closer to the truth of knowing God—Consciousness—our true self as love, which is also why we need to love, as in be conscious of our neighbours (siblings), for we are all children of Consciousness ... Am I making any sense?

A: God may be viewed as a hypothetical entity admitting of no division, exhibiting mass energy characteristics.

V: Admitting no division because as Consciousness, we are all One?

A: Consciousness is that which originates and emits. Censure of this currency and exchange causes fear and dis-ease, which is not pleasing to the senses; it is bemoaned as a loss. Walk through life together with Consciousness. Together We suffer and have compassion for the discontented, grumbling being that is the lower voice: an advocate for Darwinism.

V: So, like the prayer you gave me states at its very beginning: God is our illuminating Consciousness, right?

A: God is the science that teaches one how to lessen one's tension while one is in time.

1st October 2022

V: In time . . . hm?

A: Suffering dis-ease, uneasiness.

V: God does not want us to suffer, but while we live in time we suffer because we feel separate from God, but that is an illusion, right?

A: It is a state of being uncertain. A state of not having clear, definite Knowledge or assured conviction.

V: Yes, that's part of the problem, or perhaps all of it. I was perusing the gnostic gospel of Thomas today, and he, through what Jesus taught him, states that knowledge is understood to be the knowledge of one's divine origin: knowledge of the fact that one has come from the Kingdom. He states that we are on this earth only in a sojourn, and we get to have this knowledge by way of knowing ourselves through becoming conscious of this fact. I *believe* this, but I do not *know* it. I do not have assured conviction. And I am trying to be as conscious of myself as I can.

A: The studies one has taken to advance one's expansion are still causing fear or alarm in one's structure, for they are beyond in degree. It is lack of harmony causing this shallow status in one's stream. For the most part, with good grace and via remaining good natured, one's essential role is to participate, share and cooperate, to progress towards fuller development. This has a particular pace.

V: What am I afraid of?

A: One's origin. Engagement with Our Revolution. Replacement of ones govern-ment: the rules of one's mind. Engagement with an exchange of prominent importance.

V: In other words, I am afraid that you, my collective, may take over my mind, and Vicki, my personal individuality, will be gone, and Vicki is afraid of being bigger than she thinks she is. Is that correct?

A: Anything that persuades or entices the one who steers or has charge of this small vessel, which relates to Us and Our department of justice, if seen to compel belief that one is a cog of great size and capability, is regarded by one's ego as a downgrade.

V: So, you are advising me to just keep the pace as it is, slow and steady, because if you compel my belief, it will be worse for me regarding my ego.

A: The expanding of a small channel's field of knowing and scope of imagery, requires togetherness. Our closeness, via a Unified state, directs one to be limitless and free of these rogue, base thoughts; hence, We encircle one as mediators that help prevent premature reactions.

2nd October 2022

V: So, you are helping me to awaken and recall my origin, so I can know and not just believe?

A: We re-educate and rehabilitate, to rouse and summon one's courage, Spirit, and confidence in the face of difficulties.

V: Well, I appreciate your help very much.

A: We serve as escorts that attend, accompany, protect, guide, teach and repatriate: send one back to one's home of origin.

V: You are my spiritual companions.

A: We are brotherly, affectionate and sympathetic. We use kind, caring discourse to discourage the hodge podge of dis-eases causing one damage via disorders that bewitch one as if by a spell. We defend and shield one from danger. We protect one.

V: Are you my guardian angels?

A: We have established that We unite and function in close association with one, for one to consider the value of *Being Fully Aware* of the benefit, importance, and magnitude of de-escalating conflict.

3rd October 2022

V: What will humans be like when we are no longer fearful?

A: Effective. Humans will have adequate power to produce their intended effect.

V: Intended?

A: One's intention to subdue and conquer the offensive, overbearing, incongruous disagreeableness that surfaces on earth.

V: That is massive.

A: We specialize in healing the dis-eases of children.

V: As in God's children? We, who have become dis-eased or troubled and poorly programmed from infancy?

A: Children in whom their Kingdom's currency, their Sovereign frequency is weak, thus vacillates, making them hesitant in manner. Therefore, consider one's thoughts and words carefully before one speaks. Resign, relinquish the feeble, give mind over to the Light of Consciousness together with Us, the Heavenly bodies that revolve around one.

4th October 2022

V: I feel like I am making progress.

A: Sterling or genuine progress is to be cherished and esteemed, for sterling qualities are the approved standard of the Kingdom's unifying currency. Be wise then and prudent, concern oneself with self-kindled, self-initiated instruction. Govern, preside over one's sails to navigate one's vessel.

V: Sails?

A: Putting an absolute end to any dispute, confusion or disagreement concerning one's everlasting core, one's innermost principal, one's golden currency, formed for mutual support.

5th October 2022

V: I seem to be hearing your messages through songs that pop into my head, am I?

A: We converse, chat this way for organic equilibrium (spontaneous, unforced balance) for one, the player, to return home.

V: Yes, returning home seems to be the conversation of late.

A: Liberty is guaranteed to all individuals by God's (Consciousness') law via communication of thought to man and to woman daily, sung by the Divine as prophesy and revelation.

V: As in, we are God's radio, so to speak. I think I am getting better at receiving.

A: One is provided with the capacity for overturning unison or agreement with dual time (duality).

V: So, though as humans we are living in duality, we have been provided with the capacity to nullify it through *Knowing* and *Presence*, or vice versa.

A: To detect or to recover the signal from a carrier wave is a flying start, as it is to deal in Truths tending to produce change.

V: Is my receiving capacity improving?

A: Any disturbance of one's composure, discourages and obstructs discourse.

6th October 2022

V: I had some visions last night. I have no idea what they were, they just got my attention.

A: Biofeedback of biogenesis—of one's life evolving.

V: That's the impression I got, that it was some sort of innate feedback.

A: An arch imparting a chief principal flowed through one presenting a choice between two things.

V: Yes, come to think of it, there were two visions side by side; one was very colourful and vibrant, and the other dull; not worth looking at in contrast.

A: A cog plays a minor but necessary part in the large and complex process of compelling belief, assent and action.

V: Let me guess, I am the cog, and I have a choice between the colourful or the dull image?

A: One carries into effect whether to devote oneself to good or evil while in human form.

V: Well, you already know that I choose good over evil. If I have ever chosen evil, it was through lack of knowledge, so I must have been confused or full of fear.

A: One makes reparations via cutting one's support of the rebellious and fractious, via dismounting and disassembling waywardness, lack of discipline, and insubordination.

V: Okay, so did the vision mean I have passed a certain degree of capacity?

A: An arc of 60 degrees towards knowledge that treats of wise forms of life—Us, one's collective, joined together at birth, prepared to be of service after adding Consciousness as one's ready currency or frequency.

V: Are you saying I now have better access to you?

A: One can distinguish one tone from another, revealing the degree of exposure one has had to the loss of a conditioned mind's testament. One has become a witness against any state of corruption in one.

V: With your ready help, right?

A: With one's inborn tree, now having clusters of bright refreshing fruit (outcomes).

V: My neurology, which flashed brightly last night.

A: Which provides a path for more via quelling the opposition, a result of one Turning to Us, which when valued for Our beneficial qualities, transmit frequency waves to one's sacred receptacle, one's tabernacle: the human body; the dwelling place of the Soul.

7th October 2022

V: I had another vision: A large hand appeared, handing me a little gift box that was white and blue, like a blue sky with white clouds.

A: The gift is a peep as though from out of the blue, just becoming visible, of a salutary condition, appearing via correcting error and promoting good. This is arising intrinsically from one's True essence. Annoyance or suffering can be seen as semi-necessary when viewed as transcendent. One's unease and apprehensiveness wane as one understands these to be superficial aspects, outward appearances; sparks or triggers that may be used to connect one to reverent feelings of profound respect mingled with awe and affectation.

V: So, you are saying that I am *beginning* to see the truth?

A: Accurate, an answer of high resonance. Together We use this tone as a safety lamp, a protective illuminator that prevents the ignition of explosives such as anger, agitation, frustration, stress, depression, etc.

V: Thank you. I assume this gift (insight) will grow the more I use, and gain trust in it?

A: We work together; hence, cooperate, pitch in. When one has an outburst, greet it, welcome it with respect for a healthy outcome.

Later that day

V: Work was really, really, stressful today, people kept coming in one after the other not allowing me to finish replacing the watch batteries I already had on the go. I got irritated and blew up at my son Chris, who was engrossed in his own work, as I felt it was all too much for me. He then began to help.

I was able to reign in my agitation and not push the matter. What I am trying to say is that I know it could have been so much worse if I wasn't conscious of my stress, as in, if I hadn't shone that safety lamp on it.

A: One engaged in unifying one's state via observance, uniting one's Kingdom via Our guidance; thus, tending to concentrate one's fidelity to one's duties, obligations, and Truth via receiving and transmitting input signals without distortion.

V: Yes, exactly! I was very aware of what was going on within me, and as a result, able to turn away from the distorted emotions that were ignited.

A: The small glitters of froth and foam.

V: Yes, I see! Emotions dazzle my attention with their glitter, as you say, but it is just small-mindedness and all froth and foam which, when seen, dissipates.

A: Emotions range from the harmless and beneficial, to those that cause disorder and dis-ease: the corrupt and immoral, defective, and incorrect.

V: So, my little gift is in play now?

A: When agitated or stirred by rage or passion, when suffering from the delirium of mental disturbance, when addle-brained, confused and mixed up, treat with one's purifying Consciousness. Be the drafter, the skilled artist: the creator that prepares and designs one's structure.

8th October 2022

V: What would you like to discuss today?

A: The elaborate, the overstated, the wildly fanciful or exaggerated, the capricious and impulsive; the grotesque. These are imaginings to be frowned on, as they are thoroughly hollow.

One will benefit as—Together—We compose and deepen an analogous identification with the ancient dialect of wisdom: the archaic word (language or octave) of the Archangels. Together, We compound and intensify this expression via one's Turning to the Light of Awareness: A field of inclusion containing structure conducive to feeling reverence—respect and awe.

V: Simply put: frown on all complex imaginings and I will continuously profit, which will compound into me learning the language of wisdom.

A: One concludes successfully.

The currency of the ancient language dwells within one's tabernacle: one's body. Said of a wave possessing rhythm, it converts high voltage into low voltage, as a transformer renewing one, measuring or comparing one's intensity of Light—one's Awareness. Hold Love and benevolence toward humanity. Be of a cheerful and hopeful disposition to become skilful and wise concerning Self-government; thus, one will Increase in Sovereignty, capacity, and excellence: the sterling currency of fineness in a Unified Kingdom (optimal state of coherence).

9th October 2022

V: What more can you tell me about the ancient language of wisdom, which comes from the Kingdom—our true home and frequency?

A: It can be worthily compared with homeostasis, for it maintains a uniform and beneficial physiological stability within and between one's parts. It yields an organic equilibrium that pleases and gratifies via harmony, excellence, grace, and Truth. And, it communicates Knowledge to students seeking Higher Learning.

V: Yes please. I am all for that.

A: Extrasensory perception and related psychic phenomena can spike as one receives guidance.

V: Will this spike in me?

A: To be directed, remain with one's eyes on Us (on a Unified state). We give one rest, which refreshes one.

V: Remain focussed, this produces the connection?

A: To advance, recall that thinking one is alone is incorrect. Cherish careful examination of all, everything, the whole, to override and overrule any established practice or custom.

10th October 2022

V: What can you tell me about All that is, was, has been, and ever will be? In other words—God.

A: All that *is* continues and lasts forever, it is incessant, perpetual, constant, eternal. It is an interminable flow of energy supplied through its own operation. To dare to say: "I believe," is to engage in its crusade, its cause, its re-form movement.

V: Is love simply the absence of fear?

A: Love is a Consciousness used for purifying and enlightening. One who receives regular meals (nourishment) from this cleansing Awareness is a devotee of Us, a Unified state. We walk together with humanity planning a campaign with the children of the All, to which All belongs, for together We bear Witness.

13th October 2022

V: I have been feeling a bit disconnected lately.

A: Own it. Relating to that which belongs to oneself is *Being* in the closest degree. Reintroduce one's feeling, ask it earnestly what its part may be as far as one is concerned.

V: I'll do that. Thank you.

15th October 2022

V: Regarding what happened with that customer this week—the one who insisted that we replaced the battery in her watch 2 months ago, when in fact we replaced it 14 months ago. And, who refused to acknowledge our documentation—I really struggled to let go of my exasperation, as she was totally in the wrong. Not to mention she snatched the watch from the counter, exclaimed I was trying to rip her off, so refused to pay for the new battery I had fitted, and then threatened she was going to give us a bad review when I'd had enough and waved her off, sharply saying, "Just go."

What I struggled with was that I don't think any of us should be allowed to simply get away with that arrogant type of behaviour; we need to be made aware of the error, don't we? I mean how else can we learn from our mistakes? I was willing to forgive her, but in turn I strongly felt she needed to be made accountable. Just letting it go on my part didn't feel right.

A: Any conflict or opposition requires clarity, clear and resounding. A human being—as opposed to the Spirit's cognizance, understanding or perception of the facts—expects, presumes or supposes; human's look for what is right, proper or necessary, particularly as judged by time past, which dampens and depresses the Spirit.

One's husband, David, explained and charted an agreement with said customer; he cleansed as one would a wound, discouraging and preventing the woman from acting out her threat via arousing uncertainty in her; thus, removing her hysteria, resulting in a song of gladness and praise.

V: Yes, that's exactly what happened. David phoned her the next day; he was on his day off when she came in. David kept a cool head, unlike the customer and me. He explained her error and how she was liable, which deterred her from giving us a negative review and made her think twice, resulting in her sending us an email of apology. This sudden turn of attitude gave us all reason to be glad, and because she apologised and offered to promptly pay what was due, we waived the payment.

I think your answer relays, that clarity—when one finds oneself in a clash—comes with forgiveness (letting go), which comes with keeping a cool head, which consequently offers the correct solution to these matters. I needed to let my anger and compulsion to be right, go. Instead, I held on to the fact that the customer behaved poorly and had made a mistake. But, how do I let go when every fibre of my being is screaming that my feelings are justified?

A: One sharpens one thing against another.

V: I don't understand. What do you mean?

A: One refines, one polishes and perfects via placing a model of excellence beside the error, hence one imprints falsehood with a new unified testimony of a particular point.

V: That is not easy when all the frantic emotion is igniting the body into fight mode.

A: Use Self-government or Self-control to Self-heal and cure the dis-eases that come with selfhood: the state of being a separate, individual personality; the state of selfishness, of self-centeredness, self-importance and of pompous self-conceit. For Self-improvement, which is Self-induced, use the frantic energy of disquiet to Self-Initiate a change; thus, resist not the degree of current flowing in one's circuitry that gratifies the desire towards these self-involved weaknesses, all self-inflicted due to self-interest.

16th October 2022

V: Continuing from yesterday. So, the anger I feel is a gripping current of energy, that's why my body shakes sometimes, the flow is too intense.

A: The condition of the flow becoming worse, is a deterioration due to one giving it a derogatory or disparaging meaning or sense, dividing one in three.

V: Right, so I am basically divided against myself.

A: It throws a shadow over one which dominates and obscures all, thus causing one to fall with the upset.

V: Then what meaningful sense can I give it so that I don't fall into this trap?

A: Be Absolutely certain and Self-confident, as one who steers one's vessel, that when a flareup of sudden or violent emotion breaks out, one can be tutored and coached by Us (a Unified state), one's most reliable source, thus one will prosper and thrive.

V: Trust in your guidance?

A: When We (Our Unified state) last longer than the outlaw that habitually defies the law of harmony, We disburse the currency, establishing an outlet or channel of expression and escape for creative energy.

V: So, you are saying the longer I hold your tutoring in mind, the easier it becomes for Us to channel this agitated energy into the most creative means.

A: This means is weakened through neglect, through lack of practice; hence is in a rut—a settled habit or course of procedure or routine.

V: Do you think I am making progress?

A: Yes. Stately, honourable, lofty.

V: Really? It didn't feel like it when I was in the thick of that anger. I felt like a proper failure.

A: Because one was playing two decks at once. Ask for directions to access Us, and ascribe to Our course without reason, logic, judgement, thought, motive, or goal; thus, one completely prunes the details dealing with particulars.

V: Again, you are asking me to simply just trust you, yes?

A: Either deliberate mentally, scheme, conjecture and forecast, or Turn your vessel towards Us for evidence that sculptures one, and helps one see clearly.

V: Become still?

A: For details of one's bibliography, of one's authorship and antiquity.

V: Why am I still so doubtful of myself, and of this experience?

A: The foam produced by conscious agitation is a frothy mass of manufactured armaments and invented barricades.

V: Defences that are insubstantial, like foam.

A: Defences through which data is processed, that operate and are involved in handling and storing information of a particular point in time.

V: I see. So, it is this machine-like body and computer-like brain that my true self is up against?

A: It is cybernetics: the science that treats of the principle of control and communication as they apply both to the operation of complex machines and the functions of organisms.

V: Oh. So, this body is pretty much a cyborg?

A: Of the Roman Catholic church.

V: Hah! As in, that is what this organic cyborg body I am currently using was programmed with: the indoctrination of Catholicism.

A: Tending to pervert the meaning or sense of things: a forceful construction via compelling or vigorous warnings and reprimands.

V: So, it is our job to reprogram this cyborg?

A: Via Sovereign exchange as one's unit of currency. Via harmony, thus, one may flow in rhythm with vantage: a condition that improves and benefits all.

20th October 2022

V: What is my role or purpose in the world?

A: It is to be a counterpoise. One is to bring about balance by opposing fear with an equal power or force, via being a conscientious objector, which is achieved in accordance with integrity, ethics, and knowledge of the right or just.

V: And is this why you are tutoring me?

A: Hence, one will be able to neutralize the bitter, the harsh, hostile, acrimonious; the unpleasant, via Turning base human survival traits to harmonious Sovereign qualities.

V: And I will be successful in doing this, will I?

A: One's framework or structure is to be of service; it is to provide honest currency: direct, authentic exchange. Via one's aerial receiving and transmitting Us (a Unified state), that which is formed—one's composition—progressively expands; hence, via implementing weeding, We can form a Whole.

V: Are we, as humans, in for a spiritual war, so to speak?

A: The double-dealing duplicity and treachery are vigorous and aggressive here; it affects all disagreeably, unkindly, vexingly.

V: Did I choose to come to earth, at this time, to help bring in some balance?

A: Affirmative, yes. One is positioned in the appropriate location.

V: How has the situation with my son, Robert, prepared me for any of this?

A: It has replenished and refined one via subtle and precise alterations.

V: Because I counterpoise with forgiveness?

A: Like violet scented water used after cleansing and grooming.

V: That reminds me of that metaphor: "Forgiveness is the fragrance that the violet sheds on the heel that has crushed it."

A: An essential piece, intended to advance human welfare.

V: It hurts to be rejected by your own son.

A: Like a pool of muddy water, one's thoughts concerning this circumstance are unclear; thus, they are confusing and dividing one. Plumb: test the depth of these thoughts, for this will lead one to the semi-divine.

One's currency (flow of energy) in regard to the afore mentioned, is imprinted with evident fixed values, issued via various governing rules of the insignificant. In other words: issued by one's ego. These have become a shrine made sacred via past association. Before one feeds on this simple minded, mentally defective foolishness, be sensitive to the Light. Be Consciously Aware of what is being presented in one's motion picture that is shiftless, that is unable or unwilling to Turn, and that tenders itself for acceptance. Offer this currency up for exchange to discharge and free one of any obligation to it. Observe this offering strictly for respite when struck by a heavy blow. Drink in and absorb one's undiluted Spirit: **S**upreme **P**resence **I**nspiring **R**eal **I**nner **T**uition and be born to the purple—One's Royal Sovereign Power.

V: Is there anything else you can tell me about my role or our function as humans?

A: (1) Affected via the influence of Heavenly bodies, are one's channels of Consciousness.
(2) Know, that the simple minded or foolish destroys its creator.
(3) Comprehend that lack of courage—cowardice—is unworthy of acting as one's deputy.

V: Courage, yes, I could do with a ton of that.

A: Courage is like Boreas: God of the North wind, storms and winter, for courage blows and vents with the highest force. It discomposes and makes one feel uneasy. Employ courage to reunite one's broken parts, for courage is a treatment that cures dis-ease. Practice Being Aware. Air. Vent. Make Known. Be Conscious.

22nd October 2022

V: What would you like to discuss today?

A: The Source-bearing organ of bloom, of growth and its evergreen tree: the neurology and plasticity of this pine organ's relatives.

V: You are referring to the pineal gland, right?

A: To pierce its mystery, to enter or penetrate the pineal, one must raise in pitch, for, the ability to mentally realize the seat of the intellect—with acuteness and discernment—develops various psychological faculties.

V: How do I raise in pitch?

A: One puts forth branches via comprehension, via mental grasping of ideas and facts, via Truths, via work, via effort. This is reckoned by time, by moments, by the year. One's early stage of development is almost complete, causing one merriment. Egotism's rule or government, like a lamp emitting a light of high intensity between two adjacent energy paths, now reveals two choices.

V: Are you saying I have reached a higher stage in my development?

A: One is touching the edge, one is close.

V: What do I need to do to complete this early stage?

A: Interconnect, intercommunicate with the Cosmos and write down its cosmology: the Universe's general philosophy. Earth is a place for running a motion picture, and one's small power vessel: one's pineal, is an aerial which delivers resources and facilities that reveal and regulate hypocrisy—the deceitful assumption of virtue.

23rd October 2022

V: Continuing on from yesterday, I'm a bit confused. I think what you are saying is that my pineal gland (third eye) or as you say, aerial, runs a motion picture. In other words, by seeing something internally, by visualizing it, I can see if I am deceiving myself. Can you please explain this further?

A: The Supreme Being, God, is Existence. It is Being, as opposed to not Being: nonexistence. Being is one's essential nature. That which has reality in time and space or idea—in fact, anything that exists actually or potentially is an individuated unit expressing the logos's rhythm in relation to set values of power: measures of vibrational intensity, which can be used for healing.

Utilise feelings causing sorrow, distress or regret to recuperate; employ sensitivities, impulses and sentiments that are habitually unstated or reserved as well. To change their course and navigate with one's purest most essential component requires treatment via an operative, precise procedure: a mental attitude adopted for remedial effect. Hence, re-present oneself without worry, without disquiet or fear, for thus, one will receive recompense. The small, but selfless contribution of forfeiting the history of one's race, one's origin, or past, etc., exerts an opposite and equal force on one via an alternating current, causing inductance and capacitance.

V: So, whenever I feel upset, I contribute to my healing by letting go of my past, my stories, this is what will help me complete my—pardon the pun—current level, yes?

A: Properly understood, in a strict literal sense.

V: In other words, you are talking about Turning: At the Chameleon (my past conditioning), Turn, transcend it.

A: Turn toward one's Sovereignty. Work at this persistently to receive a cascade of Awareness; thus, matters are capable of being dissolved or de-composed.

24th October 2022

V: What was last night about? I couldn't sleep. The dark was lit with flowing waves and pinpoints of colour, and then came a parade of visions which made no sense, just symbols and strange writings in another language, like Hindu, and blue and red signs with numbers etc.

A: We applied a fertilizing agent, a stimulant of the highest standard via one's Holy Mind. These practices, formed by gradual deposits of Awareness, teach one things to be accomplished; they help clear and cleanse.

V: Did anything change? I felt like I was being recalibrated.

A: It was a communication and testimony of Love. It provided one with channels that break up and plow through the territory of one's mind. It was an act of God (Consciousness), for one as the player in the motion picture, to overwhelm one with proof and disproof, to confuse and disarray.

V: I gather that confusing the mind, in this case, is a good thing. It proves that there is more to reality than my mind knows, and disproves much of what my mind thinks it understands, correct?

A: Yes, pertaining to one's typical functional characteristics and the representations that tend to repress one's reprieve: one's relief of suffering.

V: So, I don't need to understand what is being shown to me, just accept that these visions are part of my progress, that they are creating new channels, or pathways, and in a sense, yes, recalibrating my mind.

A: We consolidate, smooth, calm, strengthen and refine. Like metal, one's mind is malleable: capable of being moulded, sculpted.

V: So, at the Chameleon, just keep Turning?

A: Turn from the backlash of faulty casts; maintain and concentrate the energy to dismantle the dismal, the cheerless and bleak, the devoid of joy.

V: You said I am close to passing on to a new stage which will bring me joy, yes?

A: Add the measure—Turn—administer it. One has the charge and the direction to provide the healing. Earth's measure or judgement system, characterised by degeneration, insolvency, contention, controversy, argument and rivalry, stops the flow of Life. It is chronic.

V: In other words, I have the answer to the problem, which is to Turn to Love, to Consciousness, to Awareness. Allow the fear, dread, or panic to come up, and accept it. Don't try to escape from it, just Turn it over to God: Love, Divine Intelligence.

A: To reverse the pest that is advocating anarchy, disorder, lawless confusion; the pest that crouches in fear, that trembles and quails, tend to one's stock of the galling, the annoying or exasperating, and audit it. Hear the daily transactions recorded that interfere with, and retard one's progress, for the pest that remains unknown needs to be published—made known—and edified, informed, enlightened; hence one will benefit morally and spiritually.

V: Right, so, *At the Chameleon, Turn* doesn't mean to turn away from the fear or illusion, or to avoid, resist, or not think of the disturbance, but rather, it means to Turn head on to face it, make it known, become totally aware of it, accept its presence within me, regardless of whether I like it or not.

A: One defined it precisely. Awareness of the semi-intoxicated and the semi-invalid, or the unsound, is essential to the prevention of blindness. Use Awareness as a counterirritant to the dominant sightlessness in oneself.

V: Turning is not what I had thought. I thought it meant to oppose the disturbance with happier thoughts or affirmations, but it actually means to acknowledge and embrace whatever comes up. Opposing any fear, concern or difficulty with resistance only causes it to persist, it only strengthens it. Turning, or opposing any stress with acceptance, allows it to be heard, which therefore dissipates it.

Why has that taken me so long to get? Ariel's prayer has been telling me this since I received it: *Allowance be thy way.* Oh my God! Seriously?

A: One's animal nature, along with its ego, is pith-less, it lacks force, it is weak-willed, it is fearful, Spiritless. One summed-up its defiance (resistance) well. Giving disturbances the substance of the Highest: the essence of Awareness, initiates a Victory; thus, rejoice over the Law; consider it as an influence that preserves and purifies cognizance in humans. The utmost precept or guideline is to recognize and allow the first form of anything which causes separation; hence, anguish.

25th October 2022

V: Good morning. So, today, whenever I feel any kind of discomfort, I need to observe it, not push it away or ignore it, right?

A: To remove the bones or the structure from fear, study it intensely and quickly. Be all ears, be eagerly attentive to the viewpoint of the incident, connect and strengthen the light beams—the firings synapses—to a point in time, to a Now marked by the beginning of a new development, a new state of things.

V: What happens when I do this correctly?

A: When one acts in this manner, one assimilates, one integrates, adapts, understands. One takes up and incorporates energy; fear becomes absorbed; one counters the irritant via this counterintelligence, one changes from one condition to another, one intercepts the defective intercellular measure of capacity that is firmly established, the calculator that haggles about terms and uses chagrin, distress or vexation caused by disappointment, failure, or mortification to come to its analysis.

Being extraordinary, being beyond the common as a system of measure or evaluation, is a teacher of the Highest rank for the mentally defective. It is a conscious stabilizer used in cleansing castings (paradigms, templates, archetypes). Being extraordinary—beyond the ordinary—has a protective function, as it is from Our Original Source.

V: Wow! That is quite a list of benefits. I will do my best to employ this today.

A: This has little or no resemblance to the apple.

V: Apple, as in the fruit of the knowledge of good and evil?

A: Yes, this is a handicap, a hindrance, a disadvantage, a sub-relation of communication, a mask for the eyes, and a large structural constitution for exhibitions that inflame one's currency (flow of energy). Thus, let Us collaborate, cooperate with one another.

Later

V: I tried today, but I'm not sure if I succeeded. I am used to supressing and opposing uncomfortable emotions. I am uncertain of how to embrace them. Can you please help me understand?

A: Treat with a sudden flash of Love, a communicative glimmer of affection.

V: A flash of love?

A: Aired briefly and to the point, Love closely and firmly bonds to an idea or system of belief.

V: And that bond transforms the idea?

A: Love weakens the structure of data from which false conclusions may be drawn, it eliminates waste: burdening matters, via natural discharge; hence, pursue the acknowledgment of disturbances with intent, to establish Love firmly in the mind.

V: I keep forgetting that Love is the highest form of Consciousness; so, when I make something conscious without judging it, I am essentially showing it love.

A: Allowing the passage of Consciousness into a split mind has adhesive properties; it connects one to an intuitive appreciation of what is fit, proper or right.

V: And this will begin to happen organically?

A: Consciousness transmits a currency of forgiveness via light quantum, or radiant energy, to the coarse or improper, the unrefined or unbecoming, making an impression on the plastic like substance that is one's brain.

27th October 2022

V: Love God—Consciousness—with all my heart, soul, and mind. This is what you are basically affirming, right? You are advising me not to let myself slip into unconsciousness, therefore be run by my programming, and so become thoughtlessly automated.

A: To be the Sovereign leader or director of one's state of mind, clear or unclutter it via making known that which has been ignited, set on fire or triggered. This state, or condition of disquiet, discontent or agitation, provides one with a passage to the sub-conscious, the choker that supresses one's progress.

V: Are you saying that by simply becoming conscious of my agitated states, I can be free of them, or is there something else I need to do?

A: Do not be a slave to one's past learnings, one's established forms of being, or rules. Do not push these pedals. To bring oneself under the Sovereign government of one's Higher Mind, which is clear and understandable, stress-free, straightforward, and guileless, sever, disjoin, undo the past by applying Us—Spirit—one's Unified state.

V: As in disjoin, let go through **S**upreme **P**resence **I**nspiring **R**eal **I**nner **T**uition.

A: SPIRIT is an ancient Conscious measure that is effective against these snake bites; thus, one will celebrate a victory.

V: How does simply being conscious of a program dissolve it?

A: A session of sitting with one's firmly attached programs, verbalizes and communicates their concerns and disputes; however, rather than trusting the ideas they convey under turbulent, difficult, or poor conditions, observe their biographical feedback; choose intentional Conscious control to view and investigate these seemingly involuntary functions, which *are* biodegradable, which *are* capable of being de-composed through biogenesis, through Life, through Consciousness generating evolution. For example, Turning to Life, to Consciousness, to Awareness, to Love or Spirit, cannibalizes, or dismantles programs arising from one's damaged vessels: the past injuries one contains and holds to. Consciousness overhauls, mends, and heals. This is earth's measure of progression; its way of evolving; hence, each adherent or devotee to Consciousness becomes greater than its predecessor.

V: So, Consciousness evolves us?

A: Yes; however, there is a probability of being deceived via a coagulation agent that changes consciousness into an obstruction.

V: Are you referring to freewill?

A: One has the freewill to make mistakes and stumble.

29th October 2022

V: So, I, we, humans, are free, allowed to blunder.

A: Freewill is certified, guaranteed; it is attested via evident information.

V: Please comment on this: Being conscious and honest is being fluid; it makes things flow. Being unconscious deceives and obstructs flow; it coagulates and clots, it misinforms.

A: One either strikes gold or becomes bankrupt.

V: I would prefer to strike gold.

A: Consciousness and unconsciousness are incapable of coexisting harmoniously, they disagree in nature; hence, one must make all things known. Headline the state of bankruptcy, announce the unconscious in one's sacred vessel, propose a marriage between both for a sumptuous feast, for consumption of the heedless, the thoughtless, reckless, and ignorant.

V: Can you please explain how I may be able to feel your presence?

A: Be Present. Know what is going on; not what is past or future. Know what is being actually considered, what is current. Presence of mind gives one command of one's faculties; it is alertness, it is an invisible Spirit or influence felt to be near; it helps one travel through this world safely, free from deception. It is trustworthy and enlightens the pineal.

V: Enlightens the pineal?

A: Unburdens one's aerial and clears reception.

V: So, when I am present, that *is* your presence?

A: One's progression is developing swiftly; it will spread thoroughly through one as one assumes one's greatest responsibility—serving as a guide, an exemplifier of Turning in order to bring about changes in human destiny.

V: I don't feel like I am progressing swiftly.

A: One is an announcer of a way up in the age of Aquarius, a bearer of Consciousness belonging to a Higher level. One is approved as a representative and demonstrator.

V: Me!? I mean I know our conversations and my daily practices must be happening for a reason, but apart from these discourses, I really need more to go on. I guess I need more confidence. I need to sense you are with me. I believe you are; however I don't really know it. How can I overcome my doubt?

A: It is fundamental and relatively simple; and, suggestive of the powerful forces at work in nature and in man: One is a basic part of a Whole. This is an essential principal fact. The Chameleon, dear daughter of nobility and excellence, is troubled in mind, it is dolorous and mournful; it is full of pain. Henceforth, insist, assert firmly and forcefully on building a higher story that commands a loftier view, a higher frame of reference that is not given to escapism: to entertainment of the mind, but sustenance fit for absorption. Fortify one's position in the Now: the Present. Begin to be what is indicated by the Main Element, by God, by Consciousness: a woman chosen as a minister employed for pulverizing the dishonesty that covers the seeds of Truth, who conveys the guidelines of fidelity, and the practices for healing the subconscious; thus, ensuring the flow of Life's fount—Consciousness.

V: Thank you. I will do my best to *insist* on a higher view, as I would like to receive and sense you more clearly.

A: This is an elementary teaching, for the Highest in all of humanity is innate, it is natural, inborn. To soar, purify and enlighten all one's bugaboos—anything that is an object of dread or hate, any nonsense or insincere talk—oversee with a greeting of welcome to render them ineffective.

30th October 2022

V: I've been affirming that the presence of my teachers is with me daily. Once again, I seriously want to feel this.

A: The Celestial, the Kingdom of Heaven, of the Divine, of Consciousness, is indescribable, too ineffable, too overwhelming to be defined in words, too lofty to be uttered; however, it is in a sense arable: capable of being cultivated, able to be ploughed, tilled, uncovered, revealed.

V: So, the only way to truly experience Heaven on earth is through ploughing on and Turning up all the deceptive programs.

A: The world is two faced; it has two meanings and effects.

V: That's duality, right? The true and the false?

A: That is parallelism. The true and the false are parallel, they are beside one another. One retrogrades, it degenerates and moves one backwards; the other is Omniscient; it knows all things.

V: Gosh, when you put it that way, the choice seems easy.

A: Progression is moving forward and proceeding step by step.

V: And you are content with my progress?

A: Beautiful lady, rise-up, connect with Us, relate; harness the power and potential of Wholeness.

V: Thank you for the compliment. I am trying.

31ˢᵗ October 2022

V: Is there anything else you'd like me to know that will help me progress?

A: Be rigidly observant and prohibit entertaining the mind, to receive an old-world dove.

V: By old-world dove, you mean Holy Spirit, right? When I am rigidly observant of not getting lost in imaginings: fancies and stories that entertain my mind, I have better access to the Holy Spirit: to being Wholly Conscious, Supremely Present; therefore, I can feel God's Presence more and more, correct?

A: Irrefutable. That is stellar.

1ˢᵗ November 2022

V: It is Remembrance Day today. May I please remember that Consciousness (God) is with me every day?

A: Remembering, initiates a rhythmical fluctuation of energy potential in one's brain which creates a furrow, a channel, as if by a plough.

V: In other words: practice, repeat, repeat, repeat, practice.

A: Apply and devote oneself habitually to these teachings.

V: Why am I receiving this? I mean, did I choose this, or did you choose me?

A: One's beliefs have caused one to seem small or less than.

V: Yes, I agree, but the light of Consciousness will shine away these belittling beliefs, correct?

A: The unexposed and unexpressed are hence, not explained, causing deprivation: the state of lacking something necessary and desirable. This alters thought so that it expresses negatively instead of positively, producing sickness, melancholy, jealousy, sensational offensiveness, cowardness, meanness, dishonourableness, etc.

V: Wow. All that dis-ease from not being conscious.

A: The farthest one is from the Light of Consciousness, the less power one has to accurately communicate due to mind's pathology.

V: I am not a great speaker, or so I believe, yet you have mentioned that I am supposed to be some kind of minister of this work. Will applying myself to being constantly present and conscious make me a better communicator?

A: Frequent frequency modulation—in which the carrier wave or thought: the carrier of information, is varied more in frequency rather than amplitude, like the loudness of the Chameleon: the program—cultivates large golden bloom (peak development). Each frequent episode of Knowing, or of being Conscious of the carrier thought's altered benchmark brought into Court (Mind), directs and Turns one's course.

V: Okay, let me see if I understood you correctly. Each time I bring my attention back to the present and away from the louder, amassed, malformed programs of the Chameleon, such as my unchallenged attitudes, beliefs or judgements, or my self-criticism, or unquestioned fears etc., I am changing the frequency modulation, and each episode of this, which is an altered, elevated tone or state of being, is evolving my brain to become a more capable receiver and transmitter of Consciousness, therefore a better communicator. How did I do?

A: Support or assistance for moving along Our specified course, depends on one's close attention to the counterclaim. Discrepancy, lack of agreement, contradiction and incredulity are key.

V: So, don't believe my programs, but be aware of them. Allow them to express, expose and explain themselves; however, remember I am not them. I am the one who observes them.

A: They are like a back-seat driver: a passenger in one's vehicle who persist in directing and advising one on how to commute. And, they always backslide, returning one to wrong ways.

V: Don't resist them, but also don't believe them?

A: To Hear a defect clearly or be Wholly or Divinely Conscious of something aberrant or malformed, impels one forward; it raises one higher, permitting the passage of Light, thus all is transparently clear and simple.

V: It seems simple.

A: Unlike the Chameleon's Voodoo, which cast spells that murmur seductively.

3rd November 2022

V: *Love thy neighbour as yourself.* Can you please help me understand this?

A: Love is the yoke which binds and connects. Love is a bond. The bond of Love creates and reproduces itself via the Light of Consciousness; thus, the seemingly separate self, the individually different, the various and diverse, can go beyond this realm. Surrendering to Love: giving oneself over to Love's influence, rectifies, refines, and purifies. It changes an alternating current into a direct current that allows the amendment of errors.

V: So, in regard to loving my neighbours—the other seemingly separate, individually different aspects of Consciousness—as myself, the undertaking seems to rely on a matter of perspective.

If I consciously accept that Consciousness *is* the Source of all, and that through its connective quality of Love, it bonds us, I am, in a sense, surrendering or yielding to Love's or Consciousness' influence, which purifies and corrects illusions, and so, I would understand on a grander scale, that in essence my neighbour *is* myself.

A: But, being low in Spirit: low in Supreme Presence (Consciousness), impresses a mark on self via low emotions. See the other as an innocent, as an angelic, beautiful being in an interval of time ... The critic that announces the other as foolish or weak minded, impairs and devalues one. To strengthen oneself and have sharp sightedness, fasten to a clear narrative, not a counterfeit sham.

V: Because when I see others as weak minded, foolish, or through a negative lens, I am seeing myself this way, because in actual reality we are all One Consciousness.

A: This serves to instruct and impart knowledge. Allow this to serve as a driver for one.

V: That's why I shouldn't judge, because it impairs me.

A: Judgement is frequently happening, time after time; it is occurring again, and again, and again.

V: So, if I was able to stop judging today, what would happen?

A: One would have autonomy: the power of Self-government and Self-determination; hence, one would be able to express the hodge podge, the jumbled collection inside one, with depth and profundity of thought or feeling. Thus, one would find favour within and come to look upon oneself and others with approval, love, and acceptance.

V: I gather the hodge podge is my current way of thinking and judging?

A: Which can be biting, sharp, stinging and sarcastic, causing self and others painful sensations. One attempts soothing beyond one's capabilities, for self is—as are all selves—wounded, aggrieved.

V: But loving our neighbour, so to speak, will heal this?

A: Love gives one direction, it puts oneself in order; thus, greet all with welcome for wellbeing and healing.

4th November 2022

V: Good morning. What would you like to teach me today?

A: A mental attitude adopted for effect. Belief in or practice in this attitude constitutes one's relationship with the powers and principles of the Universe. This requires conscientious devotion or scrupulous care in employing a series of steps that aid in surmounting the wall of separation between Us. The attitude or mind-set is as follows: Regard as cherished, and treat *all* one's smears, smudges, and stains, lovingly.

V: As in—Love all my imperfections and others' shortcomings, too? As in, accept them, allow them; don't make our inadequacies wrong, or right?

A: This is a good thing, a blessing; it is a Boon.

V: So, by Love, we are talking awareness and allowance and acceptance of what unfolds, correct?

A: Allow the illusion: the crocodilian's false weeping and below-conscious hypocritical deceit.

V: As in—the Chameleon's two-faced duality, its judgemental, cautioning analysis that causes grief with its false narrative?

A: The Chameleon's evaluation is glaring; it looks fixedly on things with hostility. However, it emits an excessively brilliant light that is plainly conspicuous.

V: Yes, I guess it is very conspicuous due to the emotions it ignites.

A: To mourn or lament with it stupefies, bemuses, and preoccupies one. This belongs to an earlier stage in one's development.

Later

V: I had several examples at work of the Chameleon's glaring hostility, today. I was trying to finish a book review and kept getting interruptions from *innocent* customers whom I became *internally* furious at for breaking my flow of thought. It was intensely conspicuous to me, and I knew it was unreasonable for me to feel this way. But, due to the desire and preference to work on my review, rather than have to get up and serve, the feelings were there.

A: To *alter* these hyper-sensitive feelings, experience and investigate them, learn with certainty from them; thus, one will ascent, one will rise in state, and advance.

V: Well, due to me being aware of this glaring annoyance, I was able to settle myself. Is this what you mean—Notice, allow, acknowledge, accept, and move on?

A: And Praise with a song of Thanksgiving.

V: So, notice, allow, acknowledge, accept, and thank?

A: Showing Conscious courtesy to inferior thoughts that cause hyperacidity in the body, has a protective influence against the act of condemning and the state of being condemned.

V: Thanking protects?

A: One's archives: the internal place where all one's known and past records, or collection of stories are kept, requires an interim of tuition and training. Practice giving Thanks to heal and clear this cloud chamber of the projectiles that disturb one's calm; that disorder, confuse and produce chaos and dis-ease.

V: Thank you.

5th Novermber 2022

V: What say you?

A: Consume the counterfeit gradually via alchemical action. This strengthens and confirms Our togetherness. Look aside to the Higher Mind for amity, for peaceful relations and friendship.

V: In other words, being conscious, as in being constantly aware of matters, burns away, or gradually consumes my old programming, which strengthens and confirms our inseparability, yes?

A: For, Our polycentrism, Our plurality, Our multiplicity of independent centres of Self-determining power, is of mutual, shared importance.

V: Because we all share the same Ultimate Consciousness.

A: A Unified state (Us) follows and serves as a continuation, or a development from the state of separation or disconnection.

V: So, in a sense, I am working toward being reconnected?

A: As one's thoughts percolate and pass through the fine filter of Consciousness, charged under the world's pressure, Our companionship and perspective prepare one for the saddle; hence, for harnessing control when in contact with the Author's (Consciousness', God's) assumed identity—the Consciousness that has fallen.

V: Me? I mean Vicki, the character that Consciousness or God has assumed in this realm? In other words, I think you are saying: Know thy Self.

A: Knowing One Self is an opening that gives access to spaces beneath the identity covering such an opening.

6th November 2022

V: This passage is from Steps to Knowledge: *As I realize that alone I can do nothing, I am reclaimed, rejuvenated and am being prepared to receive the power that abides in me, the power that is my Source and True Self.*

It sounds like what we've been discussing. Please comment.

A: Surrender the exchange of energy that burns with great heat, that ignites intense emotion, and which elucidates the rudimentary, the undeveloped, immature or unripe; thus, We nip it in the bud, and hence begin to grow or develop another type of tree.

V: So, instead of *the tree of the knowledge of good and evil*, I can begin to grow *the tree of life*.

A: With no or little resemblance to the apple tree.

V: Hah! Exactly. So, the tree of life—the new neurology—helps me realize that I am not alone.

A: It discloses, makes known, exposes the Truth; hence, regard this exchange with wonder, with pleasure and approval. Have respect and esteem for Us.

V: Alone I can do nothing, right?

A: Including the beneficial and pathogenic: the valuable and advantageous, and the capable of producing disease; the good and the bad.

V: Really? So, even when I am dis-eased, or infected by deception, I am still not alone? Even when I am unconscious, as in on autopilot?

A: Our Energy (Consciousness) is in Abundant supply, even when one is infected with the contagious malady characterized by the false idea of being separate from Us.

V: I see... Okay... Let me run this by you to see if I've understood it, correctly.

Becoming Conscious or Aware of a disturbance, which is easy due to the fact that it disturbs and produces a strong charge of emotion, is step one. Allowing it then to show me its message of pain, grief, guilt, self-righteous anger, bias, unworthiness, or fear etc., without being swept away by the current of energy it is producing, is step two. Realizing that it is simply a program, and therefore, treating it lovingly or kindly because it is a re-action and doesn't know any better, is step three. And thanking it for revealing itself, and for trying to be of help—though it is far from it—is step four.

Applying these four steps repeatedly, changes the program, therefore the habit, and consequently the neuropathways. This protects me and others through harmonization, through creating peace, and this neutral calm currency consumes the old tree: the tree (neurology) of the knowledge of good and evil, making way for the new and more evolved tree: the tree of life, or the neurology that Consciousness expands. How did I do?

A: The act of applying these steps, clips, curtails, and cuts short disorder; it unites one with All.

V: So, following this attitude, or steps, unifies us?

A: Against separation.

V: As in, the illusion of separation, which arises through falling for the deception produced by the program. It's like Ariel's prayer declares: *And let us not be deceived into credulousness, but let us depart from the re-actor.* The attitude you gave me allows me to depart or Turn from the re-actor: the program that acts again and again in the same manner it always has which, if I apply the steps to, reveals the delusion. But, which I unthinkingly and recklessly keep on falling for. It seems so simple until the concurring emotions sweep me away and deceive me into believing them.

A: Do not believe the nonsense, but chime in with it, summon and welcome it to join one Consciously; thus, one interrupts it harmoniously.

V: Harmony is key, right?

A: Harmony is incorruptible; hence, increase it. The greater the harmony the greater the cannibalism.

V: Cannibalism, as in consuming the parts of myself: programs, conditioning, road maps, neuropathways that do not serve me.

A: Maps that tend to split, that spawn separateness.

V: What will I become when harmony has consumed all these dividing parts of myself?

A: Sound, healthy, whole. One will give off a specified impression that signals order. One will celebrate and express sensible, honest views and processes of thought that are complete and effectual; that are thorough, stable, trustworthy, and based on good judgement founded in Truth, which are unified and beneficial.

V: I would love that, bring it on.

A: Remember, Spiritual Sovereignty: the shared, common wealth of All, serves as a guide through difficult circumstances.

7th November 2022

V: I had several visions last night. The first was a book with an army green jacket that had pictographs on it; then I saw a sequence of unreadable scripts, followed by images of newspapers, followed by a flash appearance of a soldier in military greens wearing a helmet. And, as I tried to connect the imagery, the thought: *We are combating a decline in communication,* announced itself. Was the proclaimed interpretation, correct?

A: It was perfect.

V: Well, I obviously had help. But why did you want me to know this specifically?

A: One's visions are outriggers; they project beyond the natural limitations of one's vessel to free one outrightly from its reserve of restraints.

V: Okay, are you saying my visions are . . . what? A supportive framework?

A: That changes a non-comprehensible frequency into a coherent, meaningful, understandable frequency via assimilation.

V: As in, changing a non-intelligible frequency or vibration into an intelligible one?

A: Thus, one accumulates a vast structure tending to Be what is indicated in the Main Element (Consciousness, God, Love). Hence, Life Is, One Is—God IS . . . For care and maintenance of normal physiological functions, one needs to frequently plug in and instantly make known. Work toward this cause, fasten and secure it with an authoritative seal of assurance.

V: Work toward reconnecting myself and others?

A: Keep reconnection before the public as a controversial issue to excite or stir-up interest and action. Keep Our connection before the eyes.

V: Me?

A: Via discipline, via instruction, via training of one's mental, moral, and physical powers, one can heal the feeble mind. Thus, believe in the genuineness of

Truth. Have Faith. Trust one's Source of Honor. One *is* approved for action. Have confidence in one's ability to fulfill.

V: So, all this tuition is about disciplining my feeble mind, which is still riddled with fear and lack of confidence. Is that what you are saying?

A: Thus, it causes one to circulate Turning; thus, one initiates free motion via a reversal of direction away from the sharp and bitter.

V: Is there any way I can speed this up?

A: Avoid small talk or gossip as it is disjointing, divisive.

V: Small talk?

A: Devote oneself habitually to dismembering the addiction that is the adder's tongue, for it only fills with consternation, disheartens, and depresses.

V: I spoke unfavourably about a friend to my son Chris today. That's what you are referring to, isn't it? These critical assertions are keeping me from progressing quicker, right?

A: One who wields an axe procures a demerit. This territory is held in one's own power.

V: But what I told my son actually happened, it was true, I didn't make it up, and it was annoying.

A: Thus, one perpetuates the annoyance, one makes it endure; one feels the resentment of the real or fancied wrong again and again.

V: So, I am continuing in the same rut, or frequency?

A: One maintains and prolongs the state of what is indicated in the root thought.

V: Right, so, stopping this and any other kind of complaining or judgement, whether real or imagined, will quicken my development?

A: One owes oneself this, cherish it. One's success is owed to one's efforts; thus, harmonize at any given opportunity to be of service to oneself, and shed the scales.

V: What do I say when others judge, complain, talk small, or gossip?

A: Do not initiate blame or criticism. Do not begin to make exaggerated, distorted caricatures or poor imitations of people. Do not add to the other's projection. Coexist. Exist together with an-other in the same place and time by design: via purposeful intelligence, as opposed to chaos. Be adamant, unyielding, immovable, concerning this.

V: Thank you. I will do my best.

9th November 2022

V: Greetings my dear teachers and companions.

A: We commence to commemorate—to remember together.

V: Yes, I wish to remember. Today I was very aware of my equilibrium.

A: The ground level.

V: Yes, it's a good starting point. I was able to notice every time I felt off balance, as in stress-wise, and I was also able to calm down by way of simply noticing the irritation and just observing it without getting involved, which then made it dissipate.

A: Canis Major and Canis Minor: The Greater Light and the lesser light are an essential principal fact.

V: The Major Light of my Awareness extinguishes the lesser light of my irritation, correct?

A: That which benefits and gives one advantage—The Major Light of one's Awareness—is befitting and required. And, rests upon one as a Noble obligation.

V: Well, I got the distinct feeling today that when I became calm, I was actually helping the frequency of the planet a little by not adding more stress or chaos to the morphic field.

A: We fasten, connect together by this means. We make certain of Our state and settle—calm down. This is high born, this is of Noble origin; it is a Unifying State, and a way of navigating for the recently recruited to regain their lost reserves of well-being and potency.

V: So, I am remembering?

A: Piece (peace) by piece (peace), gradually.

V: It felt good to have that mastery over myself. Like Ariel's prayer says: *Thy guidance and Mastership come.*

A: The distress was cut with a saw: a saying condensing the wisdom of experience.

V: Yes, my Self talk was wise. No doubt you were guiding me.

A: One received Our transmission.

V: I sensed you.

A: Above the cacophony of the disagreeable and discordant.

V: Yes, I guess so. Does that mean I've gone up a slight degree?

A: We, Us, Our Unified State, puts one in order. It adjusts and restores one; hence, influences the outcome.

V: So, by continuing this attentiveness, I can only improve and regain more of my Spiritual Memory?

A: We accompany one to accomplish, thus bring to pass one's completion.

V: Thank you, I love that you are here with me.

A: One's treasury: one's accepted customs, foundation or established principal rules, Be; they exist. Compound, put Us together to compute and multiply one's interest toward changing the nature of these. Make them known, direct one's attention to what is around one, to what is borne, exposed, carried, withstood. And hence, Our tutoring and guidance will build by degrees, giving one advantage over error, with amenity, agreeableness and civility.

V: Good! That is why I am practicing, right?

A: One practices to become larger, to expand one's Consciousness, to express in All's way.

10th November 2022

V: I had two visions last night, the first was of a group of people standing before a large billboard which depicted a clear blue sky; they appeared to be endorsing it. I felt that blue sky represented calmness.

The second vision portrayed a male and female positioned between a sky-blue square above them, and a white square with black prison bars below them. The image seemed to signify a choice: up for the tranquil blue or down for the worrying prison bars. I gather the message is that choosing serenity or calmness, is optimal to keeping me out of the self-made prison my conditioning constructs.

A: Precipitate, hasten the occurrence of calm, of peace, of stillness and composure. Do not become weakened or impaired through its lack of use, as does a quick-tempered person. Use a song of praise to soothe and harmonize; thus, one leaps lightly over the superficial.

V: Calmness harmonizes, and harmony is key and incorruptible, and allows me to give and receive.

A: Via bluing.

V: What do you mean? As in literally imagining a blue sky, or are you referring to the act of calming myself, or both?

A: As said. Test to ascertain that it is thus and is not the carrying out of an assault.

V: Hah! Of course not, an assault would be its opposite. Hm . . . so, does envisioning a clear blue-sky help? As in, is it some kind of mind hack?

A: It accumulates accuracy, correctness—Truth.

V: Wow! Well then, I will give it a go, test it as you say. Thank you for the tip. Serenity now, so to speak. I guess blue is a reminder of Heaven, and in meditation, a clear blue-sky represents a clear mind.

A: Imagining blue, causes one to discontinue a habit; it helps one surpass current tendencies, and thus excel, for one dissolves and disperses the clouds.

V: I feel like I'm receiving you more clearly, which is especially pleasing.

A: Our Unified state restores one while in earth's logical, linear time scale, via any means; hence one can obtain the signal imparted. One is bound as though by ice, and We are icebreakers and "Be" keepers of a goddess of Love, and daughter of God.

V: Wow, goddess of Love, and daughter of God, now that's a tittle! I just need to believe it to be true.

A: Truth is a hidden condition here, an unseen state of Being; an unknown quality of splendour realized when one's uncertainty leaves.

V: Really? So, if I become certain that *I am* a goddess of Love and daughter of God, what then?

A: Ambassadorship. One becomes a representative of the Highest degree against the lowest voice.

11th November 2022

V: I had another two visions. The first was a bright red *stop* icon, alongside a switch with the arrow symbols *rewind and forward*. The message immediately became obvious: Stop letting my mind wonder into the past or the future. Stop thinking back to what I thought happened and stop imagining what I think might happen. Stay Present.

A: Being Supremely Present: Being Conscious of Consciousness (God), is a measure of sound, healthy intensity. It is a frequency or vibration that can be depended on; that is worthy of trust.

V: Thank you. The second vision was hazy; it appeared to be a large, especially soft blue, velvety rose.

A: We announce a pathway with access to Awareness, with an approach to seeing and making corrections together after an admission of error, and an assertion of Trust. Immersion into Consciousness is a return to Life. It is a resuscitation.

V: Are you saying, the rose indicated a rise in Consciousness, as in a blossoming, so to speak, provided I admit my faults and trust the process?

A: One reads Our significance, which reveals that balancing the Light of Awareness at any given time, *is a rise;* thus, one can glide and soar.

V: Therefore, the more aware and balanced I become, the better I'll be able to receive and see, right?

A: One will receive more of Our signals, and understand further means of communication agreed upon to convey information.

V: Do you mean like the visions I've been seeing?

A: These are like the pangs of childbirth. We summon or usher an image, or an appearance in a manner such as can be specified via an octave. We proceed with such a frequency towards conveying: *Omnis Vinci Amor*. The all-powerful message from the Omni, the All, that Love conquers all.

V: So, my antenna or aerial, in a sense, is being tweaked to better grasp from the All that is, was, and ever will be, that love conquers all, yes?

A: When showing signs of anger, co-operation with Our fellowship or companionship sets one on a course resolved to Turn (transcend) via personal inclination. The compensation for the delaying of one's anger has the design and purpose of a direction finder, which may be described as an antenna that radiates and receives more effectively.

V: Okay, so when I delay my anger by harmonizing: by way of remaining calm, I am able to receive higher directions and use them more productively, correct?

A: One positions oneself into a receptive frame of mind that can check, regulate, and influence the course of events, thus can transmit or communicate the gift given in the Present.

12th November 2022

V: Please comment on the following: "I am a spiritual being, a light being, a child of God, the offspring of Consciousness."

A: Use this for enlightening and purifying.

V: As in for removing burdens, smears and stains: my imperfections?

A: When something irritates one, it can, if ministered wisely, cleanse and free one from impurities.

V: "Blue skies shinning at me, nothing but blue skies do I see."

A: A thought capable of being digested—understood, incorporated.

V: Yes, it's a change in frequency, and an agreement giving you, my teachers and companions, along with my Higher Self, permission to show me more.

A: It compounds Our progression together. Repeated application of an exchange that is out of the ordinary, that is not typical or habitual, enables one to preside in authority with the morally powerful, the purposeful; courageous, mentally influential, and the especially competent that is abundantly supplied.

V: We are Victorious. Victori4All.

A: Victory is an honorary title especially noteworthy of one who knows the ropes, the connections and relations that the power of speech, expression, or articulation have when nearest the Light of Consciousness.

13th November 2022

V: I had a whole bunch of flash visions last night; the first was of six screens displaying diverse images, followed by a sequence of words with hashtags attached to them, then a long series of pictures zipped by which were too quick to make sense of and remember. It felt like my mind was channel surfing.

A: This is useful, and serves a purpose.

V: Which is?

A: Which is: it puts one in order; it sets right the untruthful and untutored or unrefined; thus, it causes one to Turn and firmly connect. For as it engrosses or attracts the eyes attention to this mutual exchange, it secures an advantage. Flash visions reduce one's scoria, one's dross: that which is not needed.

V: Speaking of flashes, I am still getting hot flushes, particularly at night. Have these got anything to do with my development?

A: They summon and invoke one to solemnly arouse from the sleep of unconsciousness, care of Us.

V: Care of Us? As in, you are deliberately trying to wake me?

A: Awakening is one's birthright.

V: Oh, I see ... flushes are a wakeup call, both physically and metaphorically.

A: Flushes are an intense state of feeling and of being that excite and hold one's curiosity or attention.

V: Well, yes, I guess so. I never looked at them that way. I mean they are impossible to ignore, but what am I supposed to do when I am experiencing a flush?

A: Draw the obstruction of Awareness, the stopper of Consciousness out from one's vessel. Make known, circularize, expose to view, uncover the false and hypocritical.

V: How does a hot flush help to do that?

A: Flushes are purposeful for making right, good or excellent, that which is out of order, harmful, inferior, and, formed from a past moment of tension concerning one's regular or habitual voice.

V: And so, by focussing on, and drawing out these, as you say, awareness stoppers, does the heat of the flush then consume them, or is the heat simply an attention grabber that I can use?

A: The heat colours in higher valence; it influences and strengthens reactiveness.

V: So, the heat amplifies awareness, so to speak?

A: The heat intensifies the impression from an engraving.

V: Right, from an engraving inscribed on my frame of reference; therefore, I should utilize these hot flushes to do some house cleaning.

A: Of pent up, repressed emotions, yes; thus, one's Sovereignty and Source of Being can disclose, view, and drive these engravings out.

V: Can you give me an example of the impressions I am holding?

A: Be a recipient, allow these callers entrance, welcome them. They lie below and are the basis of one's support; hence, underline and emphasize them, for they prepare a way for dimensional healing, a way via one being Supremely and Wholly Conscious of them.

14th November 2022

V: Are you my Spiritual family as well as my teachers?

A: We are of the contemplative order; thus, counsel one to look at Life attentively. We guide one to consider Life thoughtfully, and to meditate and muse via Us—a Unified state—while one perceives through this Temple's template: one's body and mind. We represent Conscious Awareness and recommend one employ insight—intuition.

V: I am taking that as a yes; we are a kind of family or team, so I'm guessing if I progress, you do too?

A: We are like firewood, like fuel or kindling for igniting a fire (Light, Spirit Awareness) for a realm of victory.

V: Can you please be more specific?

A: We carry one to completion, thoroughly, while indicating careful attention throughout.

V: So, you are the force teaching, guiding, and accompanying me to our overall triumph?

A: Entitling one, the holder, to admission via confession.

V: As in entry by way of admission during the *now*, right? Like Ariel's prayer says: *For having the nature of animal and the sensitivity of Consciousness to correct incorrectness, are self-confessing, for to step into now reveals eternity put into place.*

A: Employ self-confessing when affected with anything that causes corruption, dis-ease, evil, or weakness. Or, that charges others with faults. Hear, receive the transmission—the admission, the divulgence of the inferior—to dis-integrate it.

V: Thank you for the reminder. Oh, while in bed last night, the darkness became an ocean of waves, and I received the term: morphogenic field. Then, I had a vision of a brown billboard with writing on it, which once again I couldn't read. Can you tell me more about it?

A: The brown billboard symbolized entombed ego programs marked with the impurities of learnings that need to collapse, that require removal in any way.

V: Right. So, the colour brown signified soil, denoting both being buried within me; therefore unconscious, and being soiled, impure, as in, incorrect. And so, what will these tainted programs be replaced with when removed?

A: Mental deliberation. Careful consideration that weaves patterns which do not conform to one's current accepted standards of conduct.

V: Will I be able to communicate what I am learning? At present, I feel like I can't explain these new ways of being properly, so I keep them to myself.

A: One's anthology of choice literary extracts will gather and bloom. Together We will limit Frankenstein, who is given to contention, controversy, argument, competition, and rivalry.

V: Frankenstein?

A: Anything that destroys its Creator, or Us, throughout Our journey together in this enclosed vehicle. We are appointed to derail the deranged.

V: So, the mud-coloured billboard represented the scoria, the dross, the inferior that needs to be derailed.

A: It illustrates the absence of Light, which makes one suffer a temporary loss of vision.

V: What can you tell me about the morphogenic field?

A: It is immediate. Nothing stands between it and one. There is no separation, no appreciable interval of time or space.

V: So, it is here now, and everywhere?

A: As much as a vessel can hold, yes. Its silent exchange achieves, secures... triumphs.

17th November 2022

V: Will the knowledge I have gained be made known to everyone?

A: Knowledge is complimentary, it is given freely; thus, take one's fill of Our recommended observances. Be vigorously active and assertive concerning this.

V: Is this world a simulation?

A: This world adjusts readily to fit the circumstances attributed to a cause or source; hence, merge with Consciousness, the God of unification, adaption, and assimilation.

V: Can we please converse audibly? I'd like to hear you as I did the first time.

A: Sound, as with a drum, requires rhythmic tapping. Tap into one's instrument perdiem: day by day.

V: So, you're saying, keep practicing and I'll eventually hear?

A: Ultimately, one will cultivate the language of Light, which is in slumber; thus, inactive, for it is obscured by clouds.

V: Still?! I would really like to hear you.

A: One is progressing; hence, adhere to Us for a nostrum: a healing via one's own preparation, affording one sensible ground for belief, which one will taste and savour.

V: And will I remember all, too?

A: Employ counterbalance via a counterclaim: a neutralizing thought and Turn in direction. Foreknow, anticipate, foretell one's fall in Consciousness, and receive one's inheritance—Realization.

20th November 2022

V: I've had a few rough days; I think my pain body was activated regarding my estranged son. He didn't reply to any of my messages, yet again. It felt awful and I couldn't talk myself out of feeling the torment which, well perhaps I was supposed to feel. In any case, it was extremely confusing and disheartening.

A: Upon seizure of the horned projections from the catalogue of difficulties one chooses from, in this case betrayal, allow Us to correspond, and measure the commentary together.

V: Correspond? But I felt so alone.

A: A lonesomeness characterised via an extravagantly contorted, discontented, restless, and uneasy mind due to one's frustration and dissatisfaction.

V: Yes. Absolutely! But why am I still experiencing this? I thought I had progressed from this stage.

A: A composition or program of one or another form that is covered with a hood; hence, not redeemed or set free, or not compensated, will not be beside Our safeguard, which protects one's perception, and thus, the direction in which one's vessel sails. To easily handle or manage the repugnant: the offensive to the feelings that excites aversion, expose the hidden.

V: So, you are saying this horrible feeling of betrayal and worthlessness that reared its head, needs to be uncovered to be set free.

A: One who hears the confessions of a commanding, official composition, can use it to rectify incoming signals. It is like gazing into a clear crystal ball. Confess, and advance via the Eternal Source—Consciousness.

V: Cleansing is painful.

A: It is a photograph taken through a microscope.

V: Yes, the past and present looked at closely and intensely.

A: It is giving right of way to the subdivided, the partitioned, split and segmented.

V: So, viewing and acknowledging the pain will rectify it and give me clearer vision? It will dissolve the pain.

A: The natural tendency to proclaim or make known, exercises authority over a state. To defer or postpone making known, begets ruthless or vehement conformity.

V: Make known, but don't buy into, right?

A: Do not be one who is easily deceived, foolish, or gullible.

V: Really!? So, you're saying those feelings are all lies?

A: Falsehoods are pungent, penetrating; they are sharp and acrid to the senses, affecting the mind and mood. They cause pain; they are poignant.

V: But trickery. None of it is real, yes?

A: Semi real, not fully—partially.

V: Well, it seems and feels totally real.

A: It appears real due to pigmentation: the colouring of the carnal mind, the influence of its corporeal shadings, its sensory tones, its mortal dyeing.

V: At the Chameleon, Turn. At the carnal mind, Turn. Tanscend.

A: Turn to a Unified state. One is a daughter of Us and Gaia.

V: Us and Gaia, duality?

A: Duality is to play in Consciousness via being independent.

V: Speaking of play, I had more visions last night, mainly screens displaying writing and symbols I couldn't understand.

A: We place visions forward via a stream of Consciousness, via a wave, a signal, to transport one over the firm and serious, above the unyielding and sombre, to guide one's vessel to petition visions and approve of them as a matter of routine.

V: Is that because visions help me reconcile that there is more to reality than I currently know?

A: Absence of visions is a disease caused by lack of Awareness.

21st November 2022

V: Any tips for me today?

A: Personalize Us and meditate; reflect upon the turbulent to effectively put it down, and to finally and precisely establish Us—Our Unified communication exchange, thus one can live in Consciousness and not in bondage, which is subject to involuntary servitude and domination.

V: Thank you.

22nd November 2022

V: Am I serving my greater purpose?

A: Thither. One is moving toward that direction; hence, to reinforce the return to one's greater purpose, reevaluate, and consider all anew.

V: Behold, I see all things new.

A: Thus, one travels in a Light vehicle amid the quality of being a skilful operator.

V: So, I'll have better control of this body because it'll be full of light, so to speak—Consciousness.

A: Acknowledgement, via gratitude, of the goods one has received, is a declaration of one's fundamental principles and rights. This attests to the transmission of equity, honesty, integrity, and of fairness etc., yielding a great wave or surge of Consciousness.

V: When might this surge be?

A: When one enters upon one's contract, the agreement denoting the action expressed by one's original word: one's Logos. A period which is characterised by certain events, conditions, and influences.

V: So, practice gratitude, and observe being present—remain conscious.

A: Like Boreas, God of the North wind, air all, give vent to everything: become aware of the flow, the stream; the gust—the storm. We praise aerating highly. Discrepancies and inconsistencies between people and their customs, evidently separate into distinct parts; however, based in fair-mindedness, integrity and neutrality, airing enlightens one.

23rd November 2022

V: I feel like you want me to ask you about boredom, what is it?

A: Very grim or unpleasant; it is all-around, widespread in action and effect. Boredom occupies the attention of the mind with a disquiet that grandstands, that impresses upon one and others.

V: Okay, boredom sucks and seizes our attention, but why are you bringing my attention to it?

A: For protection.

V: Protection from boredom?

A: One has a degree of proficiency, for one is part of a team with a panoramic, complete view of every direction. We aim one toward rectitude: uprightness in principle and conduct. And, correctness of judgement.

V: Are you saying, your guidance protects me from boredom?

A: We suggest ideas for one's consideration, approval and action, which treat and restore soundness.

V: Thank you, I am extremely grateful for all the suggestions and help you can provide.

A: We share via suggestions; Our promptings assist in communicating a message. Consider in advance that these overtures are noteworthy, significant; hence, deserve immediate action. Employ this agency of exchange to Turn. Utilize it as a stepping stone.

24th November 2022

V: Regarding my purpose again. Your very first message and suggestion to me, which wasn't so subtle, was: "We Exist, Our Own Hierarchy. At the Chameleon, Turn."

A: Perform: carry it out in action; execute it. Turn, to fulfill it.

V: Turn, so I can wake up or tune in; be home, though I am here?

A: Turning is a practice in which personality characteristics are made capable of analysis via one's interpretations of the standards and patterns of the collective social structure.

V: This life on earth seems like a game and test, is it?

A: It is like a game played to test one's general character and tendency; one's nature and course of thought. And, manner of progress via exchange with one's overseer: one's chief administrator.

V: Am I passing the test?

A: Like pinball, this is a game in which the contacts or connections made, determine the players score.

V: Contacts, as in connecting with you and my fellow earth game players, so to speak?

A: Yes, with those having human form, and not.

V: Okay, so how am I doing?

A: Our initial teaching was an introduction; it instructed one, the initiate, in fundamentals.

V: And so, I became a student of Self-realization, seeking to recall that our true home is in God—Consciousness.

A: Like a blow hole in the ice, God, Source, Consciousness, is an opening in the frozen, the rigid, the concrete, where one can come to breathe and feel relief.

V: Right, and this earth game is about how many people we touch, as in connect with and move: affect positively, right?

A: Yes, via the brief news dispatch We audibly sent one.

V: What? "At the Chameleon, Turn." Are you saying I can connect to people through applying it?

A: Employ it as a benchmark of intention that elevates one from the detached ignorance and dividing thoughts of the carnal mind, and that forms an arch of support via Us, one's highest principle: a Unified state.

V: Why Me? Why did I receive this message?

A: One has moral force and integrity of character; hence, Turning is one's vocation.

V: That's a lot to think about.

A: We are in the boat with one, thus are equally involved. We have emerged to bring Light and make apparent the language of Christ—Love.

26th November 2022

V: I am realizing that I can raise my frequency by aligning myself through agreement or acceptance, as in not resisting what is. Can you please expound on this?

A: Expressing approval has no resemblance to the understanding of good and bad.

V: What am I approving?

A: Composure, tranquillity of mind; calmness—serenity.

V: So, remain calm with an attitude of ... what?

A: Being open, free from impressions. Just be present.

V: Okay. Be calm. Be free from old programs and be open to receiving.

A: Allow the descriptive to come into being or evidence; discover by observation, and thus, secure an ascent in understanding, initiate renewal.

V: As in: comprehending by way of a higher frequency?

A: Insight, wisdom, keen discernment, appreciation for all, keeps one safe. May these gods of ardent Awareness preserve one. Composed of one's root Source—Consciousness—one grows, one develops, one arises out of this.

V: Is there anything else you wish to communicate today?

A: Reside in present time: that time being, *Now*. Do not dwell in phantasmagoria: the changing, incoherent apparitions of mental imagery and fancy, which divide and separate one from operating in one's proper mode of action; a manner of acting conducive to health, that brings about sound conditions via correcting error and promoting good.

V: In other words, *Be*, remain as present as I possibly can; don't operate from a state of unconsciousness, which appears to separate me from Consciousness.

A: Being, has access to Sovereign octaves possessing unparalleled excellence and efficacy. Be, to unite with one's Sovereign state.

27th November 2022

V: Is being present and devoid of past impressions and phantasmagoria, a way of aligning and agreeing to participate in God's song, as in, Consciousness' higher octaves, so to speak?

A: One enters God's melodies via being in harmony, unity or concurrence; via applying cooperation, via being in agreement or accordance with Life.

V: It sounds easy, but is it?

A: One's ancestral or inherited language imparts a particular bias or interpretation as the point of view from which something is regarded. This grows out of convention or custom, established via the collective social structure. And, the collective's general agreement that one is separate from Source.

Our principal language is not coercive; thus, does not compel direction via force. It conveys Our togetherness, Our coexistence with one in space and time, and coextends through this dimension simultaneously communicating that there is enough for all; hence, be in accord, agree with Life, breathe.

Nervous agitation indicates a backward contraction, which lowers one's frequency or octave, and thus, like the solidity of ice, freezes one within a rigid tension that seems to separate one from Source—Consciousness. Hence, discharge the monkey mind's narrative or story with a protective exchange from one's higher-ranking administrator, which distils and purifies via the act of allowing one's Spirit—indicative of one's origin and Source—audio frequency.

V: Allow my Spirit—Supreme Presence—to be heard. Got it. Thank you.

28th November 2022

V: My son Antonni, wishes me to ask: what the difference is between ownership and control?

A: Enforcing control of Self, overdraws or strains one excessively; it drives one hard or too far; thus, decreases one's power output. Control produces a state of futility, of despair; it lacks intelligence.

Ownership of Self is observant; it has the power of discernment and understanding, rapidly and keenly perceiving that, traditions such as one's doctrines, customs, and practices are transmitted from generation to generation; thus, ownership introduces an alternative. Ownership heralds a means of communication agreed upon, realized and used to convey acknowledgement.

V: So, with ownership we have choice and with control we have stress and apparently no choice?

A: One is able to communicate via both methods; however, control is affected by an excess of ill-temper, and ownership creates probability.

V: Sounds to me like control incarcerates the Soul and ownership frees it. Am I right?

A: Being without Awareness or Consciousness, is being under the control of the unconscious, which is generally reversable.

V: Right, without ownership of our Self-awareness, we are then controlled by autopilot, or the wavering will power of our ego.

A: Instead of the contemplative order that instructs one in fundamentals and effective manipulation of the body. And, which also gives one access to one's book of tales: the controlling programs that demonstrate the corrupt or the depraved, which thus demoralizes and throws one into disorder.

29th November 2022

V: What is this sadness I keep feeling?

A: A pattern within the fabric of one's social structure or framework that is unreported; hence, unreplenished: not brought back to Wholeness.

V: How do I report it and bring it back to wholeness?

A: One advances via clemency, mercy, leniency, compassion in temperament toward it.

V: Are you saying I'm being too hard on myself?

A: For being slow, and for bragging regarding one's abilities.

V: Yes, well I guess I am upset that I don't seem to have progressed as fast as I'd like. To this day, I still haven't felt that all-encompassing joy I've read that others experience when they make a breakthrough. And regarding the bragging, well I wasn't aware that it may be deemed as bragging until my son Antonni told me I sounded self-righteous the other day, which did trouble me.

A: Bearing and exposing that which is around or throughout one, is a flying start, for this effectively influences corporeal structures that gnaw at one with persistent sensations of discomfort or distress.

V: But now what? I've endured and bared it; I've made it known. Now what do I do to get past it?

A: Clemency. Be merciful to the clench: the tight grip of dis-ease that forms a false membrane of separation between one and Spirit's ways of Am and Be. Attend to the discomfort like a wet nurse would to a child. Thus, one softens, amalgamates, and unites with Spirit. Utilize Spirit—Supreme Presence—to illuminate and warm to Spirit's alliance, for together We grow and fuse into Oneness.

V: Can you please talk me through it while I meditate?

A: We care for one and heed with watchful regard, via Our guardianship, the darkened or discoloured meal (concepts) served by the small self.

After meditating

V: "I am in union with my Source."

A: This is the natural, intuitive, highest expression of a Unified state. This acknowledgement is potent in Spirit content.

V: Thank you. I feel better, but I would still like to feel and know my True Self.

A: One is reluctant to remit: to transmit exchange.

V: Me? What do you mean?

A: One is reluctant to submit the necessary exchange: the definite article bounding one to agreement; hence, alignment.

V: What is the definite article I need to exchange?

A: The linguistics dealing with the analysis, description, classification, and thus, the vibrational frequency of communication with Us—one's Unified state, Our Spiritual connection.

V: So, I need to dig deep into what beliefs I am carrying that are holding me back, correct?

A: Beliefs, attitudes, ideas, dogmas, etc., that bluff, that deceive and frighten one with empty threats. Register these, reveal them, transmit this exchange.

Later

V: Well, as you know, I just completed an hour of intensive introspection, and I realized, I am not only sad, but frustrated, angry, and confused. I have done all these years of work, and still no experience of truly knowing myself. All I came up with, was: "I don't understand anything."

A: One has raised a heap of stones, a load of difficulties set up as monuments. Use these reminders to elevate the sunken ships, the buried, unconscious despatches of the muted and silenced via the temporary withholding of Consciousness.

V: But why am I seemingly not allowed to have the experience of self-realization and really *"knowing"* my unity with Source? Are all these books I've read just lies?

A: One is seemingly separate for a purpose. The course or progress of a person's life unfolds an active agency, it develops a means or force to triumph via dint of effort.

V: But I have used so much effort. I simply want to feel the bliss people speak of, the unity. Why am I excluded from this? What is the obstacle?

A: One is converting Our reciprocation, Our mutual interchange into the reverse of Love; hence, its opposite: fear.

V: I don't understand, what do you mean?

A: Similar to simians—apes.

V: Oh... Are you saying that my animal nature is the cause of the obstruction?

A: The organism: the entity or individual, is the one who fears and has aversion.

V: So, you're saying that the "I", I think of as Vicki, the persona, the ego and the body construct etc., she's the one afraid of Self-realization?

A: Vicki feels vulnerable; she fears being hurt.

V: So, how do we convince her that it is for the best?

A: Vicki is secular, she is of this world and present life; thus, she is temporal, mortal, distinguished from Spiritual. She fears the pernicious, and her ultimate death.

V: As in death of the body and personality?

A: Death of agreement with the manifest world; hence, the end of the Chameleon's treacherous distortions.

V: But that's a good thing, isn't it?

A: Vicki is clothed with, furnished and adorned with this general, universal level; she is surrounded by this moulding.

V: Okay, so how do we proceed?

A: Retain, keep in mind, remember the agreement one made to serve via employing *Turning to Spirit* while in this costume.

V: Am I getting any closer to Self-realization?

A: Together We will make straight. We will correct the alterable, the changeable—the Chameleon, via Being Present, and via participating in one's essential True Nature according with the principles of counterpoint, of contrast, of being opposite to this world's leading intelligence.

5th December 2022

V: Hi. I keep waking up still feeling that sadness.

A: In order to improve, refine; perfect oneself through it.

V: Right. By remembering to stay present within the sadness instead of resisting it, which essentially is Turning to Source, to Consciousness, rather than being led by my unconscious programs.

A: Unconscious programs which overdraw and strain one excessively, decreasing one's power output; thus productivity.

V: Please tell me more about Source.

A: Unlike the carnal mind, which colours, influences and affects Vicki: the persona, Source is like a current or flow of Awareness, an energy used to regulate the stream and potential in the circuits of one's organism.

V: So, Source is the energy, not the influence?

A: Source shares and imparts a panoramic view in every direction, with the idea of uniting all the enslaved.

V: Enslaved by the Chameleon, the illusions of the carnal mind?

A: Correct. There is a blackout, a partial or complete loss of vision, and sometimes loss of Consciousness on earth, the abode of mortal man as opposed to the higher realms; thus, Life may be played adlib tum: as the performer wishes.

V: Free will?

A: Earth has the power to allure, delight and fascinate. To advance in one's crusade, in this world that astonishes, overwhelms, confounds and astounds with wonder, requires shared sovereignty or ownership; hence, together We rule, and aim accurately at being authentic with Source as Our wealth. We urge one's expansion via the application of pressure which, due to the resistance encountered, one slowly permits. It is one's choice to resist stubbornly or leap upward suddenly.

V: I would like to leap upward suddenly, please.

A: One tends to change gradually due to a force set up to protect one's ego and its properties. A powerful influence that enforces ego's customs, directives and its laws or principles. A propelling drive that operates under that which one treasures.

V: So, I think you're saying that Vicki treasures her customs etc., more than what Source has to offer, due to fear of the unknown?

A: The amount of energy required to raise one's degree of Consciousness, is attentive consideration; hence, heed, pay attention to ego's fascinating spells and charms, to disperse and dismiss them.

Be circumspect: attentive to everything, be watchful, cautious of the felt. Do not censor anything, for together We are Sovereign and can govern; thus, succeed in any undertaking when in accordance with the established standard—Awareness.

6th December 2022

V: Together we are sovereign. Please clarify, together?

A: We are together when one makes up one's mind to follow Our definite course of action, when one seizes and beholds firmly what is operating beneath the surface of one's Awareness via employing the Holy Spirit: The Wholly and Supremely Present, as a helper or comforter.

V: So, do I need to ask for help?

A: Asking for help is like a spoke that serves to support and connect one to the centre of activity or interest.

V: I see ... Well, please help, as I am somewhat confused. What do I do when something upsets me: pay close attention to the distress and all the internal dialogue or try to let it go?

A: Review the spell, let it circulate, allow it to be free in motion. This is Our initial teaching; thus, begin with this, for the fruit is enclosed in a hard shell of disorder marked by attacks of unconsciousness.

V: Spell?

A: A painful up-rising of one's foundation.

V: Yes, like the stress and rejection I felt yesterday with that customer who turned nasty for no reason.

A: A frivolous person using a blunt edge to cut.

V: Exactly. But why did I feel so cut up by it?

A: The cut brews as a storm, manifesting anger easily, causing one to be confused or feel helpless.

V: So, how do I deal with these situations?

A: Surround the wound with Awareness, and call upon Us, a Unified state, in humble and earnest entreaty, to create and build by degree, to renew and strengthen one via accuracy, via conforming to the Truth, exclusive of incredulity or scepticism.

V: So, remain present, pray for help, so to speak, and believe that relief is coming?

A: According to the proportion of one's Logos.

V: My proportion of belief?

A: One's Logos compels belief; it convinces one to shine its reflected light.

V: I'm going to meditate and quiet my mind now.

A: Meditation has the power to consume the one who elects the adverse, the disagreeable, the ugly, and hateful.

V: Good. That's what I want. Thank you.

8th December 2022

V: Right, well I think my slight meltdown the other day was my ego having a childish temper tantrum which, I guess needed to happen, though sadly I did get caught up in its spell. And regarding that customer that upset me, I realize now that I need to allow the grievance to play out; however, what I was doing was getting even more wound-up because the disturbance was actually there to begin with. Somehow, due to all the years of practice I've put in to working on myself, I've come to believe, or expect, that I should not be feeling anything but joy, because that's what being spiritual is: Not getting upset. But, from what you have explained, I need to become more aware of the distress and simply observe it, not resist it; plus ask for help from a higher force, because while I'm stuck in the lower frequency of hurt, I cannot see the truth; therefore, I definitely can't help myself.

A: One's mind is unorganized in structure; it is not unionized.

V: Exactly. So, calling on the higher force of Us will obviously assist in unifying me, yes?

A: We inscribe or influence one via Light to beget Our Sovereign counsel; hence, receive from above. Thus, one can examine oneself carefully for needed reparations. This enlivens and delights greatly.

V: Can I simply say: "I need your help,"?

A: Yes; however, ask, without one's intellect smearing and naming the hindrance. Invite Us without the anarchist who encourages lawless disorder and confusion; inquire without one's imperfect vision.

V: So, call for help without identifying the problem as I erroneously see it?

A: Request relief, thoroughly untainted and wholly clear of one's conjectures, for when unwilling to commit oneself one way or the other, one erects a barrier to Us, giving leeway to the ill-informed.

13th December 2022

V: Thank you for that song on the radio yesterday, I really, really enjoyed it. As you know, due to all the annoying commercials etc., I very rarely have the radio on while driving. But I suddenly had this intense urge to turn it on, and this song I'd never heard before had just begun. The tune was catchy and bright, and the words were exactly what I needed to hear, and so upliftingly true: "Love *is* everything we need."

A: We desired to make this chorus known and impart happiness. We sought to share, to commune, to converse intimately with Our field agent.

V: Well, I thoroughly appreciate it.

14th December 2022

V: I was reading our past conversations, which you are obviously aware of, and on the 4th of November you suggested I adopt a mental attitude which would be of enormous benefit. The attitude was: *to love my, as well as other people's imperfections.* You also explained that these flaws or failings emit an excess of brilliant light that is plainly conspicuous when firing. So, the notion came to me today: When these shortcomings are triggering my emotions, noticing, allowing, and acknowledging them, and then *thanking* them—instead of resisting or hating them and subsequently being taken over by them—rewires them with that intended awareness of love and appreciation. And, as they say in neurolinguistics—neurons that fire together, wire together.

Oh, and I know you placed this understanding into my mind while I was driving to work today because the insight came out of the blue.

A: Grace rewires; thus, this Love of God toward man, this Conscious recognition, acceptance, and appreciation toward oneself and others, renews and restores. This divine influence operates in man, adding beauty and refinement to the dross—the tainted; hence, raises the base born in honour. Meeting or touching it lightly with unrestricted authority, grants one freedom to impress one's own conditions. Like a fernery, where spores give rise to new individuals, the disconnected come together; they touch and interchange. Accordingly, one gives and receives in return from the bedazzled, from the confused, from the blinded by the blazing.

V: Blinded by the ignited.

A: These gems of flesh are like trumpets that sound warnings.

15th December 2022

V: *"I am one with the Source of all things."* I need to comprehend this, don't I? I mean, as in *really* know it, correct?

A: It is one's duty to know this via agreement. It is a requirement with binding power for one to recoup and recover loss. Thus, trade in the excessively fervid or marked by guilt, exchange the treacherous, amend the act of violating faith, trust or allegiance, replace all the unsound with Our perfect pitch and unquestionable harmonizing frequency. Evoke: *I am one with the Source of all,* to work and cooperate with Us.

V: Okay. So, by pitching this pitch to myself, so to speak, I can tune-in to a higher frequency or harmonic, and we can communicate better?

A: Hence one progresses to fuller development. One advances toward completion. Via this interweave, one wears the raiment of the Higher realm.

V: I "AM" one with the Source of all, aren't I?

A: One is the progeny, the offspring of the progenitor: God, Source, Consciousness, the parent who set forth to beget a female who is feeling isolated due to her discordant sense.

V: And this pitch will help me remove the discord?

A: This pitch increases hilarity, cheerfulness; it moves one in leaps and bounds, involving housekeeping.

V: So, I still need to do more housework (clearing)?

A: Elicit this pitch to bring one to Our Light; thus, one elicits the Truth.

V: Thank you.

16th December 2022

V: Thank you for the prompt today, you know, the customer named Grace. I knew you were reminding me that simply saying the word Grace, will bring to mind my unity with God.

A: Via the authentic nature of Grace, We combine together in refusing to associate with one's current housekeeper, in favour of mutual protection, and trade advantages.

V: The housekeeper being?

A: Governing programs. Hence, refuse to support party policy.

V: As in house rules that no longer serve, right?

A: Figuratively or metaphorically speaking.

V: So, recalling the word Grace will serve in connecting to a higher state?

A: When feeling shame, Grace aids cognition, the understanding that We are together to know; hence, shame is capable of being examined.

V: Shame?

A: Like Jacob's ladder, rising from earth to heaven, engage earthly shame, connect with it, see it via one's Superior, more advantageous heavenly qualities, and rise upward to excellence.

V: Is shame at the base of all our problems?

A: Shame is transmitted via genes, via ancestry; however, as said, it can be used for going aloft, or for descending. Grant permission to it shyly, cautiously.

18th December 2022

V: Someone in my extended family seems to be deviously and deliberately trying to upset me. I could be wrong, but this person's disappointing actions have made me feel distrustful of them. What steps do I take to heal this within me?

A: Firstly, for the time being, one must acknowledge one's protest; see the former supposition—which appears unmistakable, and that shows no mercy—undiluted, at its full-strength.

V: So, first allow the feelings I am experiencing to announce their remonstration without granting this person mercy, without making excuses for them?

A: Thus, one gains information by reading one's sentiments and emotions. One registers one's climate or weather station: one's internal mood and environment.

V: Oh, so I can see the storm that's brewing.

A: Hence, one can advance by carefully selecting one's course.

V: Right, and then?

A: Then, one can be freed from impression via the Christ Mind, via profound Awareness. This is the central gateway. Life is to be investigated, one needs to thoroughly examine what is causing the sirens, the warning signals; thus, one can peel off the coverings. Hence, keep watch, be alert to the roust-about rousing this excitement.

V: Thank you.

21ˢᵗ December 2022

V: So, my function, in a sense, is to witness all that is going on within me without criticism or judgement, or Vicki trying to change it. Simply observe, be aware, shine a light on it?

A: Witness the peacock who struts, vainly making displays pertaining to, and affecting the mind. Witnessing deals with diagnosis and treatment of mental disorders.

V: I don't need to try and change anything?

A: Like a story in an apartment building, one's narrative is the division in the structure between levels or frequencies. The art of playing a vessel's channel or instrument, requires a nervous system yielding a will able to endure hardship.

V: Allowance be thy way. Allow feelings to be felt and seen.

A: Allowance favours clarity of Consciousness in one's vessel; it governs via mental observances that influence and facilitate Our communion.

V: Communion by way of a higher octave, therefore perspective, right?

A: Thus, one speaks by Divine influence as a medium, uttering Truth via inspiration.

V: And this can happen simply by observing the peacock's narrative?

A: Correct. Thus, do not delay or put this pathway off for a future time; this route is encouraged for conveying interactive exchange—communication.

V: Thank you, I will try to follow this path.

22ⁿᵈ December 2022

V: "We Exist, Our Own Hierarchy." Would it be accurate to say that *our own hierarchy* refers to our own level of frequency, or our alignment with a certain vibration?

A: To ascend in frequency within earth's measures or criterions is a boon, a blessing that surrounds one with remedies which reduce disease, emotional excitement, restless eagerness and delirium.

V: So, attaining a higher level of frequency is what helps us while on earth.

A: Like Aurora, Goddess of the dawn, renewing herself every morning, an elevated frequency encloses one in a framework of emergent, promising, regeneration.

V: So, I have my own frequency that surrounds me like the dawn, but which I can fall short of, which is why I feel like crap sometimes: because I'm off my home frequency. This is what helps to guide me, yes?

A: Frequency extends and expands; it draws forward the wizard, the skilful and clever being from the shallow vessel that has been Westernised.

V: Westernised? Well, I guess most of us have been Westernized, and yes, the West can be pretty shallow, not to mention fear based. So, I suppose fear distances me from my home frequency, and love aligns me with it.

A: It is a hunting game; hence, search for, pursue, repeatedly seek alignment with higher frequencies.

V: A game?

A: A game to master, a game to surpass and hence, become superior to the Chameleon's cries that belittle and disparage. It is Our revolution; thus, let the buyer be Aware.

V: The buyer, as in the player, right? The game being: At the Chameleon, Turn.

A: *At the Chameleon, Turn,* is a capacitator. Use it to increase the capacitance to receive, contain and absorb maximum output of one's mental power, to a desired value.

V: This is why you gave me this statement all those years ago: to help me in the game named: Life on earth, so I could learn to align with my frequency—our own hierarchy.

A: To align with Alpha particles of benevolence, which collapse and absorb the shock of the bemoaned, bemused and bemired, via commanding a higher view.

V: Alpha particles?

A: : : : : : : : : : : : : : : : In alignment. Work at this persistently.

V: Work at being in alignment. Please explain.

A: Being in alignment makes circumstances less hurtful here in one's present life; thus, one circumnavigates one's fall in Consciousness in a way that causes enlightenment to happen earlier; hence, one is free of the irritation and frenzy: the state of extreme excitement or agitation conveyed by the frequency of earth's battlefield; a density that is supported when one engages in negligeable or useless activities.

V: Well, I am grateful that you are helping me.

A: We are dependent on each other.

23rd December 2022

V: I had a terribly restless night last night: lots of hot flushes, acute trouble swallowing, more visions of text I couldn't read; and to top it off, due to the conversation I had with my hairdresser about her thyroid operation, I started worrying that I might have a problem with my thyroid. What was going on?

A: Vicki drew together—within the court of one's grey matter (brain)—a cortege of inferior attendants, proposing the infernal state of one being lower than the Source of one's Conscious supply.

V: Inferior because I was fretting about my thyroid? Which, the fact I was finding it difficult to swallow, only added to.

A: Behead, decapitate this behemoth, this beast's beheld behaviour that is acting independently. Behead via using an authoritative, convincing command to the outer garment: the body, and burgeon, put forth buds that flip or Turn any careless remark into the benign, into the kind, gentle and favourable for recovery.

V: So, you are saying decapitate this beastly thought about having a thyroid problem, with a confident request for kindness, correct?

A: A harmonious exchange via nobility.

V: Oh, like Ariel's prayer: *Our illuminating Consciousness, which art to the same degree as our nobility and excellence* . . .

A: Thus, one makes a vibrant sound, one raises one's pitch—one's frequency.

3rd January 2023

V: I am back from our Port Vincent holiday. It was great to get away, but it didn't start out too well, seeing as my son Chris's car broke down about two hours in, and an hour away from our destination, and so, we were stuck on the side of the road in the summer heat while being attacked by a million bush flies until the RAA road service came to help. Heh-heh! We all took it rather cheerily though, with me singing: *"Holiday Road,"* when an hour later, we travelled to Port Wakefield, the nearest town, creeping at a slow 5 kilometres per hour with the RAA van following us.

I ate way too much, but we went on a lot of hikes and beach walks with our boys and beautiful grandkids, as well as swam most days, so that helped, and I also got a chance to relax and read *"Act of Faith, Conversations with P'taah"* channelled by Jani King, again. P'taah speaks of transmutation by way of feeling and allowing, and says that pain is not feeling, it is resistance to feeling, and that pain is created by judgement. Can you please talk me through the process of transmutation?

A: To transmute, simply be peaceful; thus, not in a state of conflict or commotion. Being undisturbed transmutes to the power of a sextillion: that is a six followed by twenty zeros. Conform to this calm peacefulness as one's profession or vocation, for henceforth—as one perceives that it frees one from disease—it becomes one's inclination. Peace, stillness, harmony, amity, etc. are Our endorsed standard for attaining a Unified state and means of exchange, or transmutation. Thus, reflect on peace and Turn, transmute the waves of Light, the currents of Energy, the influences of Frequency which give back an image of the cause and result of one's action or character. Think carefully, for transmutation voluntarily proceeds from the will of one's own free choice.

V: Right, so, I need to desire transmutation, or what you call Turning, and I must be at peace to begin the process.

A: The place of exchange is within the Heart; the Heart gives one the core essence or the summation, as it relates to the vegetation: the undergrowth, the implanted programs of one's zoomorphism: the representation of God in the form of an animal; hence—human. Thus, notice and pay attention to the Heart's feelings. Become Aware of its transmissions. Treat the Heart courteously and with favour. Receive the Heart's announcements; sense its information and warnings.

V: Vegetation, as in the firing neurons which my heart perceives and is trying to inform and warn me about?

A: The Heart is like an accurately calibrated thermometer, use it to determine the body's temperature: its climate, its mood, its everchanging temperament.

V: Connect to my heart and feel, as I allow whatever is presenting itself to just be, without trying to judge it or change it.

A: Allowing oneself to become bruised or discoloured as from a blow via hurt feelings, permits one to leap over the illusory obstacle or deceptive difficulty that—due to one engaging the possessive: my, mine, or I—surrounds, and contracts one.

V: Okay. So, peacefully allowing the vegetation—as you say—that has grown wild over this lifetime, the light of day—transmutes or Turns it. As does calmly seeing and acknowledging the apparent problem as belonging to the *me* or *I* that manifest through Vicki's programming. All I need to do is not fall for the Chameleon's discolouration: its flawed take on things, but thank it for showing me, and of course, desire the transmutation, correct?

A: Thus, one comes to an agreement or understanding. One puts the self who is easily tricked in definite and proper order.

V: Will I be put in proper order this year?

A: One is one's own Sovereignty; one's own commanding Supervisor... able to agree or be in accordance with Us in an instant.

V: Good! Well, I am aiming to make progress.

A: Hence, Turn away from that which *resembles* the genuine, however is otherwise; transmute the counterfeit, the deceitful.

V: Through remaining calm and peacefully allowing.

A: Via allowing the holograph its Wholeness. Via knowing that that which observes this three-dimensional realm is Complete, All-embracing, and Absolute. Via regarding the Whole picture or representation with reverence because one is associated with God, with one's Sacred Origin and Source—Consciousness. This is Holy Communion.

V: Because I, along with all people, are expressions of the divine?

A: However, all humans possess a richly loaded, *reversible*, elaborately patterned structure, tending to excite similar reactions that are ordinarily conclusive. Hence, put an end to questioning the hex: the evaluations causing the spell.

V: And allowing breaks the spell, right?

A: Allowance is a teaching of prime importance; it is a cardinal principle on which matters Turn and depend.

V: Like Ariel's prayer says: *Our illuminating Consciousness, which art to the same degree as our nobility and excellence,* **allowance be thy way.**

And so, at the Chameleon's hex, turn to allowance.

A: And thus, one brings oneself into a state of equilibrium; hence, criticism can be purified over an open fire of authentic radiant energy.

V: Is there anything else you would like to add that will allow me to see the light in this?

A: Meditate deeply on the brood that is one's immature, juvenile creations (manifestations). Sit, and incubate, nurture, develop Spirit—one's Supreme Presence, for meditation involves Spiritual effort; thus, one can pierce and penetrate, and inquire into, illuminating that which is wounded.

8th January 2023

V: Good morning my dear companions/teachers, what would you like to discuss with me today?

A: The human structural capacity for Mind, and one's anthropomorphism: the ascription of human form or characteristics to one's Divinity.

V: Okay, that sounds interesting.

A: That which is attached, appended or added to one's human form, can either be *afflatus*: Divine communication or knowledge, engendering genius, encouragement, motivation, insight, inspiration and revelation, etc., or it can be *afflictive*, which generates distress; thus, dooms one to an unhappy fate of continual suffering. However, stress, grief, anguish or any affliction, can be used as a reference point, instructing one to bring the offender into the Supreme Court of one's Awareness; hence, one can Turn one's course in a certain, assured direction, which will subdue or cause the miscreant to yield.

V: I see. Awareness and allowance of the offender—the troubling affliction or thought that miscreates—permits it to be seen and heard, which I guess gives it some sort of relief rather than it being suppressed, unseen, and therefore able to continue doing harm.

A: To keep something hidden or in the dark, is like slander or defamation; it is an insult to one's being, and it sells one's Soul to the error. It is a faux pas: a false and hence, misleading step.

Appreciation and gratitude of the clouds producing the thunder and showers, is the most advanced, head-on teaching in favour of a truce or armistice: the temporary cessation of hostilities via mutual agreement. Thus, like an artesian well brings groundwater to the surface without needing to be pumped, Awareness, Consciousness, Source, aptly compels a flow or stream of thought up from the subconscious.

V: Makes sense. I would really, really like to be able to employ this faculty.

A: The reckoning of one's points of contention, require one not to use a sledgehammer to break down conflicting difficulties, but to soothe and mollify them via a refined Mind.

V: Can you please remind me of this constantly?

A: Be strictly scrupulous and exacting in the attitude of observance.

V: As in, be faithfully aware and present.

A: Correct; thus, one polishes and refines the grey matter.

V: So, each time I am successful in employing this ability, I refine and recalibrate my brain, enabling me to receive a higher octave or frequency?

A: Yes. The Higher Mind requires a malleable, ductile brain that is infusible: that is capable of being poured into, and that opposes or is resistant to the acidic: the sharp, bitter and biting, the sour, and hence, misleading.

V: Okay. Just to be clear. Presence makes my brain conducive to receiving more. Is that correct?

A: Presence makes one conducive to Turning (transcending), it admits or allows of being Turned willingly; thus, one is favourably inclined or disposed to reverse any transgression via a manner of transfusion, a pouring in of Consciousness, of Awareness, of Source, which transforms the devoid of order—the confusion produced via one's shallow vessel—into a state akin to that of yachtsmanship; thus, one exhibits the art and skill of sailing and navigating one's cruiser (body).

V: Thank you.

9th January 2023

V: I think I am beginning to realize that we humans *are* expressions of the divine. As in, actually!

A: See man as a Divine vessel to have seamanship and thus obtain skilfulness in operating one's cruiser. The entire body of human beings are in the same boat (state), under the same administration and using the same mariner's compass: a compass or scope that separates beings via rules.

V: So, we, the whole of humanity, are so much more than we have been led to believe.

A: Humans are homogeneous, the same in composition and structure, thus uniform in nature; however, humans need to homogenize—combine as one race.

V: We are all one Consciousness, too, right? We are all from the same Source, all divine expression. All energetically connected.

A: Via attendance, yes. Via being present—being Conscious. Via Awareness. Via close and earnest attention. Via witnessing. Via the power of a mental concentration that is not influenced or distorted, biased or tainted by the Chameleon—the false and misleading.

V: To truly know this is to . . . what?

A: To truly know this in the realm of time, one must examine in detail, one must scrutinize closely, one must analyse and describe the accepted standard or level used in comparison, and thus, be able to deliver a summons to all, that the Whole Universe is God—Consciousness.

10th January 2023

V: I feel like I've become more balanced.

A: This is due to the series of regularly spaced support structures that demonstrate how to be homologous with Consciousness: how to be of the same logos; thus, correspond to the Divine—the balancer.

V: You're referring to my regular meditation practice and daily affirmations etc., which have helped tremendously, so, yes, I believe I am beginning to realize who and what we really are.

A: Practice prepares; it puts one in a state or condition of becoming a specialist in discerning earthly or worldly measures; hence, one progresses. One can shift from an unaware state to a Unified state; thus, measure the volume of unconsciousness via the ideas bought and sold.

V: So, in a sense, you are teaching me how the "earth game" works, and how unconsciousness, or lack of awareness—due to the many distractions and the Godlessness being sold to and bought by the world, including me—are rife.

A: Lack of Awareness causes a downward slump into an empty hollowness, aptly labelled depression.

V: And my role as an expression of the divine who is learning about who and what we truly are, is to . . . what?

A: To interfere, to get in the way of this unconscious lack of Awareness, to impede or intervene via exciting interest, attention or curiosity in it. Make Divine expression attractive to others. Garnish the Mind Consciously. Highlight its beauty to all.

V: And you are saying I will be able to highlight the beauty of knowing our true expression and connection with Source, because . . . ?

A: Because one has treated dis-eased conditions in one's own neurology via using Our operative methods.

V: And so, I know that "Turning" works and if I can do it, others can too?

A: Many are completely under the influence or domination of priests and figures of authority who are narrow minded and assume superior virtue and wisdom.

V: I know, so I trust that I will be guided every step of the way as to how I may serve in this capacity in the most excellent way.

A: Excellence is realized via a process of emission and release; a means through which material structures of information: matters, ideas, etc. are separated from one's vessel, and elaborated—thoroughly developed into new substances.

V: I'm not quite certain what you mean?

A: The capacity of one's vessel can emerge in a flash; it can burst forth suddenly and repeatedly, exhibiting a brilliance that spreads outward; thus, brings one to a magnitude of intensity that is decided, definite, free from all uncertainty, and hence, demonstrates determination, commitment, and purpose.

V: And this can happen to me?

A: Like a chrysalis: the capsule enclosed pupa from which the butterfly develops, one is encircled by a cocoon of fellowship, community, mutuality, and support.

V: Can you tell me more about this chrysalis stage we as humans are in?

A: It is a stage for exercising one's command, one's decree, knowledge, power, understanding, and appreciation, etc. It is a phase, or period when ascendancy can be amply impressed upon one, as from a height.

V: As from a higher frequency?

A: As from an octave beheld (observed) to behead behemoth—the beast in one—at one's behest: one's authoritative request, command or promise to put one's animal behaviour behind one.

V: Excellent. How do I behold this?

A: Via a catch word or phrase that is easily remembered and is repeated often. And, via this question-and-answer method of instruction.

V: "At the Chameleon, Turn." The statement you gave me years ago, that's a good catch phrase, right?

A: It is an exchange of Unity, from which something comes on authority of the highest quarter.

V: Well, I trust you know what is best for me.

A: One has an itemized list of investments, and securities.

V: Yes, I do, these recorded teachings. Thank you.

17th January 2023

V: So, I gather that my training here on earth, or in this 3D virtual reality realm, is to try to bypass perception in order to attain knowledge, correct?

A: Correct. One bypasses perception via Being Present, via choosing existence as opposed to nonexistence: Conscious Awareness, as opposed to habitual unconsciousness. One's essential nature is Being; it is existence—Life. Being in duality, one is also *being* an individual: that is to say, a human *being*. Observe the philosophy of Descartes who defended complete dualism between thought or mind and mind's extension—the subject matter of physical science.

V: Descartes coined the phrase: "I think, there for I am." But I think it should actually be: I am, therefore I think, because I, as in my natural Being, have always existed.

A: This is sentient, mindful cause and effect. Like Pragmatism: the philosophy that ideas have value only in terms of their practical consequences, which are derived via practice and experience, and not via speculation, the results of cause and effect are the sole test of the validity or truth of one's beliefs.

V: Makes sense. I experience what I believe, but I also believe what I experience. It's like: what comes first, the chicken or the egg?

A: Amen. We express agreement, verily and truly. And so, it is.

V: And so, *it is* whatever I agree to believing it is, isn't it?

A: It is, or manifests as both the principal belief, and whatever interest it has accrued.

V: In that case, I should be questioning what I am allowing myself to believe every minute of the day, right?

A: Correct. Hence, do not fall asleep. Do not rely on the insentience of one's automatic pilot.

V: In other words: *always, always, always* be awake, remain conscious.

A: Let the buyer of beliefs beware, as the purchase is made at their own risk.

V: Wow! Are we that powerful?

A: Powerful enough to make a complete revolution or Turn.

V: At the Chameleon, Turn: At the false belief, Turn!

A: Turn to Us, to a Unified state. Turn and compare one's own hierarchy, and level of alignment with it.

18th January 2023

V: Regarding where we left off yesterday, do you mean the hierarchy of beliefs we have accrued and the level of alignment or alliance we have with them.

A: Yes, the beliefs accrued while one is in duality, in contrast, division, polarity.

V: In duality, living or expressing as a human animal.

A: Like a ganglion: a collection of cells outside of the central nervous system.

V: Eeww, gross, but I get what you mean: Outside of Source, God, Consciousness... or at least seemingly so.

A: Only a bit, a small portion appears to dwell outside, which is due to the belief one is separate from Source.

V: So, I need to become absolutely aware of my ever-present and constant connection with Source.

A: Permanently, Eternally Aware; thus, one trains for this charge throughout all states of disturbance caused by man-made sources, such as: the partaking of the apple (fruit of the conditioned neurology). Hence, employ simplicity, be free of admixture, ostentation, complexity and difficulty. Be sincere and unaffected.

19th January 2023

V: Good morning. Following on from our last discussion, disturbance is caused by belief in good and bad, right? By partaking of the apple, as you say—the so-called knowledge of good and evil.

A: While in human form, one is coloured or imprinted with difficulties. One is in a material state that repels Conscious Awareness.

V: That's what we agree to align with when we choose to come to this earth game, right?

A: Correct. One chooses foolish, imaginary projections, repeated without cessation.

V: And I can break this incessant foolishness through developing presence and attendance, yes?

A: An unbalanced mentality, like the X mark made by one who cannot write; thus, is known to have limited knowledge, emphasizes a person's limitation or shortcoming. Hence, employ this lack of balance, this mark of instability, this evident disturbance; seek to weaken the falsehoods via piercing them with the lance of Awareness.

V: So, all difficulties, all discomfort, conflict, pain; anything that throws us off balance, presents like an X, as in X marks the spot, and this occurs to weaken false beliefs—untruths—by drawing attention to them, yet we try to avoid seeing them because disharmony doesn't feel good.

A: Disharmony encircles one before teaching one.

V: My job is to allow the disturbance and attend to it without resistance.

A: When pitched to an octave higher than ordinary, via Conscious Awareness, falsehoods lose their lustre; one sees their blemishes and stains: the markings or patterns representing or modelling earth's planetary system.

V: The model, as in what the planet has programmed in me, my frame of reference, which you've been helping me to rewrite.

A: Where upon one electroplates oneself with energy that is malleable and ductile, which is resistant to bitterness, anger, indignation, malice, and animosity, etc.

23rd January 2023

V: I am feeling low again. What is this gnawing, dispirited sensation trying to show me?

A: It reveals the quality of being pugnacious, quarrelsome in disposition, confrontational; combative, etc., thus, join in wedlock with the sensor, the beacon that transmits these frequency waves.

V: How, simply by being present to the feeling?

A: By allowing the feeling to surround one on all sides. Use pain, or discomfort as an illuminator: an illuminator that excises, that erases dissonance.

V: Allow the feeling to be, and thank it, right?

A: Prickly thoughts and ideas have disagreeable, discordant frequencies, allowance harvests, and excises the pungency of these deliberations.

V: Thank you, I will allow this feeling to be.

A: Allowing a feeling to be will yield one a profit: the benefit and reward of revelation. Allowing causes matters to become evident.

Later

V: The feeling dissipated throughout the day as I became busy with customers and the email I had to write to the Spanish Consulate. I feel okay at the moment. I think the feeling is disappointment in myself. It is like a sense of unworthiness or something, which I know deep within is untrue. It's the dross, as you say, the distractions and troubles of this realm; it's so heavy at times, it keeps pulling me back, trying to keep me stuck it seems. What say you?

A: This realm contains many coloured, poisonous compounds, such as chromic acid, and likewise, many influential, noxious mixes and fixations that are sharp and bitting, and wear one down. One must work at solving, at unravelling, at elucidating, at translating Self—Us—to self; thus, one realizes, fulfills and accomplishes.

V: It seems never ending.

A: One stands astride, with one leg on each side of, and on the back of a fabric-like structure, a framework and constitution that is material, that is physical, which has great resistance to stretching; thus, expanding.

V: 3D physical rules and programming that doesn't want to yield, right?

A: Resembling an ill-natured illness that is illogical and of ill-repute, causing time to be ill-spent as though it were ill-stared: under the influence of an evil star that instigates ill-tempered pugnacity.

V: That's a lot of illness! But, I know who I truly am.

A: To know who one truly is—a fundamental part of the Whole and Essential Principal Actuality—is a Turning point; thus, a wellspring of support for one's mechanism.

V: God, Consciousness, Awareness, Source IS. And so, it will BE.

A: God—Consciousness, Awareness, Source—is the One who pilots one's Spirit vessel. Consciousness has a specified voice; it is Aware and concerned with leadership, with speaking of becoming unentangled; hence, unenslaved. It speaks of having the capacity for being shaped or moulded; the capability for growing and developing, for helping and supporting; thus, abide by God, and make Good.

24th January 2023

V: Good morning. What do you wish me to focus on and know today?

A: Unity with the All, for when one thoroughly believes in one's separation from God—The All That Is, Was, And Ever Will Be—one is like an outbuilding separate from the Main-building; one comes apart: one fractures, one becomes not unlike an outcast, a homeless person who, then, may act egregiously, becoming villain like, wicked, malevolent.

V: Such as Bill Gates and Klaus Schwab?

A: One becomes panic stricken: overcome with fear.

V: Why, because they are afraid of death?

A: Due to pomology: the science of the apple—in this case the fruit plucked from the tree of knowledge of good and evil, a well ingrained plant, thus mortality is misunderstood, it is viewed as God's punishment via seeding one with impermanence; hence, some need to pommel and beat death down with the fist, or with the pomp of magnificent and stately displays.

V: But not all people who believe in the separation or split from God become villains.

A: Many believe in cannon law: the ecclesiastical laws of Christian churches, which can heal or cleanse one of grief, sin, or worry.

V: How does one really understand and realize there is no separation?

A: Via cartography: the art of making maps.

V: As in making new mind maps? As in reprograming ourselves by way of remaining Conscious?

A: Precisely.

26th January 2023

V: What does it mean to always choose love?

A: It means to hold Love's company, it means to sustain and keep Love with one as a companion, especially when one is feeling aggressively self-assertive, and or ice-bound: that is, surrounded by frosty, inflexible thoughts that assault one, or others. Love serves to demonstrate and point out. Love slows things down. Love circularizes, spreads, propagates and diffuses, etc. And, in a flash, Love causes one to shine.

V: You know why I am asking this question, right? Because of that self-proclaimed ex-jeweller that challenged me on the price of our fitted watch batteries today for his Tissot. I was self-assertive with him due to how rudely he has treated me in the past when, I have never been anything but polite to him. But today his smug demeanour got to me, hence why I boldly replied: "Do you want a battery fitted or not!?" To which he sarcastically retorted, before abruptly leaving: "Thank you!"

How am I supposed to hold love for someone like that?

A: As progeny of duality, like an iceberg broken and floating away from a glacier, due to one's outward, seeming separation from Source, God, Consciousness—where one receives all that is needed while in this foreign dual state—foolish behaviour is expected.

V: So, you are saying we both acted poorly, however, no matter how foolishly we behave, we are all still expressions of the divine.

A: Hold Love within to have title: to have claim to it. Maintain Love in the mind, observe it. Adhere to Love as a principle and purpose.

V: And thank the other progeny's smears and smudges, their dualistic faults and imperfections, as they show me mine, right?

A: One's smears, and other's smudges, frustrate, confound, daunt, discourage, and at times shame the Agnes Dei—the lambs of God (All God's offspring) who take away the sins (smears, and smudges) of the world when they unwittingly *accept* agnosticism: the theory that man cannot know God, Truth, or anything beyond material phenomena.

Later

V: The Chameleon is similar to the Gnostic's Demiurge: the deity they believed created the material world, and viewed as the originator of evil, isn't it?

A: The Chameleon is thick scaled; thus, covers and camouflages the vile, and contemptible, the despicable. Hence, dismiss it, cease seeking after its promises.

V: Was the Demiurge the vicious, jealous God of the Old Testament?

A: The Old Testament chronicled a blasted blight, a blasphemy, an impious, profane speaking of God.

V: Because the Old Testament's god is not God, right? It's the Demiurge they're speaking of, and so it is blasphemous to relate that as being the Source of All.

A: The Old Testament god is dissonant, harsh in voice; thus, said god's frequency is inharmonious; naturally hostile—incongruous.

V: So, people who believe in the god of the Old Testament, are essentially believing in the Demiurge.

A: People collectively follow this body snatcher, which juxtaposes, that is, places them together side by side with the immature—with those who, like the juvenile delinquent, exhibit anti-social behaviour.

V: So, the Chameleon/Demiurge is the god of this world, which keeps us in ignorance and darkness.

A: Thus, one becomes overwhelmed with grief, one suffers physical or mental collapse.

V: So, the name of the game is to turn away from ignorance. At the Chameleon, Turn.

A: Turn away from the functionally disordered, from dis-eased conditioning, from the rotten, terrible and excessive, via perspicuity, via lucidity, via clearness of expression.

29th January 2023

V: Good morning.

A: One is able to propel forward as one's brilliance ignites, moving one ahead quickly; hence, re-seek reordination: the rite of one's consecration, one's blessing, one's beatifying. Declare this clear, evident portion of Awareness—the Self—following detachment from material or physical elements.

V: In other words, decree the truth of what we really are: Luminous, Splendid Spirits (non-physical energy beings) having a solid material experience, right? Knowing this with certainty inspires, motivates, and advances our evolution here.

A: Matter: the physical, possesses pejorative. It offers one judgemental, derogatory, critical and disparaging meanings to sense; thus, matter downgrades; it enables one to makes matters worse.

V: So, all this time you have been trying to explain that the Chameleon is the "spell" of matter: the ruling force in this world, the Demiurge, which captures our attention through the negative and belittling illusion of fear.

A: Fear that obtains all via deceitful, misleading methods, which engrave, or imprint one's, let Us say, iconoscope: one's imagery scope, with iconoclasts—cynical, denouncing, and dissenting representations; discordantly converted images transmitted into energy impulses that attack esteemed philosophies.

V: And I oppose this by . . . ?

A: By receiving both sides. By being attentive to both articulations, both presentations, both expressions; both formulations. By highlighting reliance on Self, as opposed to self. By good citizenship. By wholesome social responsibility.

V: And this will transmute the iconoclasts, so to speak?

A: This will transmute the heartache, the mental anguish, the grief of one who practises Self-denial, enabling one to ascertain: to find out via experiment and investigation; thus, learn with certainty.

3rd February 2023

V: What can you tell me about mantras?

A: Like the Aegis of Zeus and Athena, mantras resemble a shield of armour, for they offer support, guidance and protection against the unpleasant or the fearful, attracting and emitting bright beams of illumination; hence, one's smile becomes more radiant.

4th February 2023

V: How may I better feel your presence?

A: As one moves through life with the strong and steady force of one's Awareness, one makes progress on this journey to the sacred via reverting to one's Us: one's inherited Unified state. Together We convene with our sister, who while in a body on this grand tour, requests to quicken the expansion of her scope; thus, as We *Turn* together, We gradually move toward one pointedness. We converge within Presence.

V: So, in a sense what you are saying is that Presence is always here now, it's already with me, but it is up to me to turn inward and recall this, yes?

A: One must blend or merge Us with one's customary state until one has Our same energy rating under pressure; hence, one can challenge, weaken, and wear-away any underlying, fundamental inferiorities like doubt, forgetfulness or ignorance.

5th February 2023

V: I went to a wedding yesterday, and unnervingly could still feel shadows of past conditioning affecting me. However, I was curiously aware of them, which I normally wouldn't be. I still find it difficult to approach people that I don't know well; the unease can be quite disabling. Argh...

A: All are greatly Loved, Beloved; however, most feel unworthy of Love. This sense of unworthiness resides in one due to the ruler of Babylon.

V: The ruler of Babylon? As in the rules or dictates of worldliness, secularism and materialism that therefore cause judgement and inequity, etc. The

Demiurge's/Chameleon's frequency is what makes us feel this lower degree or grade of being, right? It is the world's collective voice, so to speak, the earth's frequency/vibration, as distinguished from that of more evolved realms, correct?

A: To make corrections below the conscious line in one's treasury—the subconscious—one requires a current, an electromotive force like anger or anguish. Remember: The Greater Light of one's Awareness, let Us say, Canis Major, balances the lesser light of one's unease—the fear that distorts; thus, causes corruption. Let Us call this: Canis minor.

V: I see, the mighty light or focus of our awareness on a situation, stabilises the fireworks or triggers caused by the lesser, but noticeable light of our qualms. It's all energy work.

A: Always re-present in detail the position, stance, or attitude of a pre-judged, determined, or calculated value.

V: Thank you.

6th February 2023

V: Last night when I was arguing with David over what to watch on TV, it came to me that it was an opportunity to put what you've recently taught me into practice, as Canis minor was being lit, and Canis Major was well aware of it. I feel like I had a small epiphany; it seemed like a game. The realisation made me smile: The Chameleon, or collective frequency of this world, applies the pressure which triggers us. And, becoming aware or conscious of these fireworks—applying the light of my focus, or seeing it for what it is—dissolves or harmonizes the situation. Therefore, I no longer felt any discomfort, in fact our argument seemed kind of funny. I could see through the illusion. I could see how the Chameleon's promised land: it's glaring assurance that it knows what's best, is a house of cards.

A: The appearance or form of something, casts a net, and thus, a trap that sets one adrift, shipwrecked and off course. Apply the current—the electromotive force, the strength or intensity of the magnetic field, the potency of the alluring pitch, theme or matter—to inform, to illuminate and lighten the bulk: the greater or principal part of an issue. This serves to clearly interpret or explain the plainly expressed; thus, one can suddenly expand via the cacophonous, via that which is harsh, disagreeable, and discordant in vibration; that which makes one act recklessly without deliberation, which like jumping headfirst into brambles, plunges one sorely into deeply rooted, problematic programs.

9th February 2023

V: Good morning. As you know, my estranged son and his wife attended the funeral of a dear family member a couple of days ago, which took me by surprise because for the past eight years, he has chosen to disregard every major family event, his grandparent's funeral included. However, a niece convinced me, after the beautiful and emotional service, that I should try to approach him, which unfortunately for me, I did, simply to get yet another heart-wrenching rejection, this time in public.

A: Persevere, persist with one's purpose; strive on despite all difficulties.

V: But what they did was humiliating. I felt like a low life. Like I had crossed a sacred boundary that I should not have. I felt like I had violated them, merely by wanting to talk.

A: Focus on progression, on advancing, on moving toward one's fuller, richer, and deeper development toward wholeness; toward foresight, toward the capacity for inducing altered states of Consciousness that have beneficial, restorative value for all mental turmoil and disorder.

V: Under pressure, right? Like a diamond. Each time I am in a difficult situation, and I allow it to be, as well as become grateful for the opportunity it presents, I transmute it. And so, I progress.

A: Hence, one can advance to being unafraid, unaggressive, and unagitated. One may pool: combine one's efforts and resources in a mutual exchange that spins new threads: new neural networks; thus, one can play the earth game in a fairer manner, for the Soul—the lower part of one's foundation—is now sensitive to Light, to Truth; thus, can reproduce it.

V: I know who I am in actuality, for real, yes?

A: An Overseer of one's sacred body's crooked—that is to say—complex, and deceiving pathways.

10th February 2023

V: I think that I've progressed.

A: This occurs in small quantities.

V: But didn't you say once that my progress can expand suddenly?

A: Dear, beautiful lady, the fact that one cried intensely at the basilica after the act of touching the wife of one's son, is a fact from which conclusions may be drawn.

V: Yes, I lightly clasped my estranged daughter-in-law's forearm to get her attention as she was walking ahead of me amongst the gathered, and she freaked out as though I had violated her, which utterly shocked me and sent me off trembling to sob away from concerned stares. I am not sure what conclusion you are referring to, though?

A: The conclusion is that via this harrowing encounter, one became, if one will, platinized: overlaid with a malleable, amenable, permeating element that is highly resistant to acids—bitterness.

V: Oh, because I didn't let myself become bitter about it, because I allowed the grief to be, but chose not to hold onto it. And so, it's like being electroplated and infused with a protective precious substance. It's like being shielded with gleaming light. Is that what you mean?

A: Correct. Being, possessing, or resembling what is expressed in the root: the origin of one's misery and heartache, removes the pits from the fruit, the difficulties from one becoming ripe—from one developing.

V: So, I have progressed, yes?

A: One has advanced to acknowledging a Sovereign domain, where the frequencies represented are beacons for the guidance of all vessels; thus, like the rhythmical working song of sailors, which unifies them, navigate this world via employing a kindly, pleasant, cordial disposition; impart warmth, comfort, and Life. Be as one's tutelary Spirits.

11th February 2023

V: Hi, just to be clear, my frequency has risen a degree, right?

A: Correct. Via believing in one's Divine Authority and serving as a mediator of it.

12th February 2023

V: I keep hearing the lyrics to Bon Jovi's *"Livin' On A Prayer."* They are constantly repeating in my head. Is this you encouraging me to keep on persevering?

A: We encourage one to move along in a noble and dignified manner. Begin with this song's energy, and proceed bravely and confidently up from a lower feeling to a higher feeling; hence, frequency, to release one from servitude or bondage.

V: So, are we halfway there, as the song infers?

A: One is still affected with small eruptions of dis-ease. The process has a particular pace, for it affects the mind and the senses; thus, be keen of perception and discernment. Expose squirms: one's signs of distress or grief; refine these, give them a clean and a polish, if one will, to soften life's shocks. Become an enthusiast, a devotee of this.

V: Clean and polish, as in allow it all to be seen, felt, and acknowledged, right?

A: Be convivial: welcoming of all. Assemble, come together, meet with all that is felt; this is one's vocation, one's way to validate Self as from evidence, one's way to consume the intrusive via the Light of Awareness. Trust one can discover direct knowledge via invitation.

13th February 2023 3:05am

V: I can't sleep. I feel agitated. I am trying to process what I'm feeling, but kind of feel numb, too, as in unable to identify what I feel.

A: Bring the agitation into definite connection, bring it into assured relationship. Do not hinder or restrict it.

V: Well, although I feel I have forgiven my son and his wife for their rejection at the funeral, I feel cross and hurt by the *seeming* insensitivities of some extended family members who, knowing how extremely difficult the situation was for me, did not ask me at a small gathering that same weekend, how I was coping. I guess I feel disappointed. It *seems* like no one truly cares.

A: Survey, review, examine, comprehend this feeling in its entirety; view it carefully, minutely, draw it forward, map it. Giving the observer—one's Self—a clear vista of one's incoming thoughts, initiates an effective healing treatment; thus, when one holds a bewitchment fast with one's attention—Awareness—one gives off Light; hence, the spell, the fascination, the beguiling influence, dies by fire.

V: So, you are saying to "just look" at what I am thinking and feeling?

A: Observe the structure, look at the composition and formation of all matters. This is an exercise taken for one's health; a practice required for a constitutional amendment of the dream.

V: So, observing what I think and feel validates it, but I shouldn't try to justify or judge it, just witness without buying into it?

A: Observing, or witnessing, has the power of consuming; thus, examine via alert listening, too. Hear, attend to the furtive, the stealthy anger, rage or agitation beneath this swell or undulation of consciousness, for emotion is a general exchange which, without beholding, has a power to enchant one with an undue sense of one's own superiority.

V: Behold, I make all things new!

A: A statement of sound, high sonority, of sublime resonance, of prominent significance; thus, productivity . . . Soon.

V: Soon? How soon?

A: When one has the specified foundation, via our teachings and guidance, to take on this strong opponent.

V: The Chameleon: the strong opposing belief that we are separate from God, which consequently causes us to lose ourselves in our stories . . . ? But I'm halfway there, right?

A: Go back to the grindstone; remove the rocks, boulders and pits: the difficulties and depressions, the rebuffs, denials, rejections and rebukes displayed by the stonewall that is one's defences.

V: Is there anything else you would like me to know?

A: Most people's assessment; hence relationship to the incorporeal: the Spiritual, is incorrect. Spirit is of a Sovereign Substance; hence, employ Spirit: *Supreme Presence Inspiring Real Inner Tuition*, wisely; husband Spirit's forces—formed by gradual deposits—constantly. For, resembling a heterodyne, Spirit can shift signals (thoughts) from one frequency range into another via adding a signal (idea) generated from within one; thus, Spirit is involved in the process of modulation and demodulation. Relating to the highest realms, Spirit is an empyreal amplifier.

16th February 2023

V: Regarding our last conversation, I think what you are trying to make clear is that the incorporeal or spiritual is superior, or as you say, of a sovereign substance to the corporeal: the physical, therefore our origin or nature is of a higher reality, which we can access through our Supreme Presence.

A: This is an elevated stand, a viewpoint to be proclaimed freely or via virtue of necessity, for it declares one's inherent and essential quality, a power achieved via self-discipline. Remember, Goodness is one's innate condition.

V: So, you are saying we were born with this virtuous attribute because essentially, *we are spirit*, which is the ruling substance.

A: Correct. Hence, proclaim it as with a clarion: clear and resounding, for thus such a frequency is formed. Expose the immature and unwise implants (programs) that restrict, impede and lessen one, to the Great Light of this declaration.

V: "I AM VICTORIOUS SPIRIT!!"

A: Awakened from an enchanted sleep via the science of surveying, describing, and mapping one's Awareness of the brute's whines: the complaints arising from one's corporeal nature, from its programming. Thus, be attentive to everything, look around at one's circumstances, the conditions and influences affecting one.

Later

V: What would you like to discuss now?

A: The bitter.

V: Yes, well I have certainly felt and experienced some bitterness lately.

A: Bitterness is a sideshow connected with a more important show par excellence, beyond comparison. Bitterness can steer one to change direction, and thus, to express obvious Truth.

V: Are you saying I should be grateful to the bitter?

A: Be in favour of it, and thus be unaffected; this is artless simplicity, it lacks any craft, or deceit.

V: I see, bitterness is part of the spell that captures our attention, like a side show diverting us from the main attraction: the truth.

A: Bitterness has the power to penetrate one physically and mentally, splitting one into either a brainless, foolish person, or a Being duly authorised to exercise the powers of Spirit.

V: So, bitterness can turn me either way; I can use it to become more ignorant, or to practice employing my Supreme Presence.

A: Which serves as an agency of balance: as a voice that awakens one from the entranced sleep of the foolish, sensual brute.

V: This is all a dream, and bitterness can suck us deeper into it.

A: Contemplate order: consider calmness, envision harmony, intend peace expect direction. To act as a delegate of these is to do one's bit, for it derails the small role bitterness plays within the dream show; hence, one is strongly supported, and comforted.

17th February 2023

V: Every day in every way I am getting better and better!

A: A core remedy or stimulant for improvement is to be grateful. Be thankful for one's benefits and the kindness of others, be appreciative via giving welcome to all. Delight in one's agreeableness.

V: Right, so I need to work on my gratitude.

A: The offering of gratitude is a complementary, harmonizing gift, bringing a current of a higher order: the sensation of appreciation into one's present notice.

V: Are you saying that if I practice gratitude, I will speed things along?

A: Employ gratitude for the undertaking of one's internal cleansing, and hence, the utterance of Truth, for thus, one is practiced and skilful when affected with anguish or distress.

V: I have a lot to be grateful for, but my mind tends to direct me towards the negative.

A: Employ the negative: the discouraging, harmful, disapproving or unhelpful, etc. for winding the mainspring.

V: For winding the mainspring? As in use negative thoughts as a driving force to recall being thankful? Use the adverse as an impetus?

A: Pick-up: detect the circumstance where a negative broadcast originates, or notice any period of increased glum activity, and renew with thankfulness.

V: As in be grateful for it coming up? Accept instead of reject, right? This is what renews. It is a new path.

A: A new path produced via the action of seeing the old path. And, via evoking familiar maxims: principal truths which condense the wisdom of experience.

19th February 2023

V: My body is an instrument of communication and contribution, right?

A: Correct; however, having the nature of animal, it can be beastlike: cruel, rude, or filthy. Granted as a privilege, allow one's body to be a vessel of Light, clearly and expertly playing the harmonious tune of Awareness. Allow one's body to be a chalice of communion with the Whole of one's Spirit, where in, the whine of the beast is consecrated.

V: I want to allow this, you know that, right?

A: Hence, allow Spirit to permeate, to spread thoroughly through one, allow it to pervade one's polarization: one's contrasting natures; allow Awareness to fit and equip one's vessel when it is fraudulently controlled and manipulated.

V: As Ariel's prayer says: Allowance be thy way. I need to trust more in the process.

A: Trust is one of the principal members of connection, especially between high and low tides when stranded in straits or difficulties.

V: How do I allow?

A: Via a refill: via replenishing one's choice and support for such a procedure again and again; thus, one refines the practice of allowance, which frees one from impurities—misrepresentations, distortions, falsehoods.

V: So, keep choosing to be present and aware, keep allowing what "is" to "be" without rejecting it; keep observing my inner and outer world without judging it.

A: V is for Victory not vacancy.

V: "I AM VICTORIOUS!" Thank you for the reminder.

A: Make this a solemn affirmation. Assert it earnestly and positively.

28th February 2023

V: Good evening. Why do I feel compelled to read the Anunnaki bible?

A: To console oneself via combining with archaic and ancient frequency modulations, for one is uncertain of one's origins.

V: So, by becoming aware of my origin, I am consoled. Does that consolidate or confirm my union with you?

A: It confirms one's unity with the multitude, with the host of composite everyday avatars: with the diverse incarnations of God. Thus, one can be in accord—via being keenly watchful and ready for action—with the intelligent and bright.

V: Are we connected to the Anunnaki, and by we, I mean you as well?

A: All are connected via psyche: the Mind, the Soul, which is often regarded as an entity functioning independently of the body, for psyche moves backward to the past, and forward to the future, regularly.

Having the power of perception to stamp or impress one's body, psyche evidences body's authenticity via informing one of body's imprinted responsibilities, and how to meet these obligations.

V: Okay, but who are you?

A: Radiant energy on a light sensitive surface…

Be still… Be silent… Be peaceful and tranquil to employ and pluck out the splotches: the discoloured imperfections that murmur to one seductively. Throughout the splotches' (Chameleon's) period of instruction, be sensitive to the light of all colours of the spectrum; have a Spirited interest in all one's network of communication, use one's periscope to look around.

V: Be sensitive to all the hues of thoughts and their effects to all the shades of influence presented to, and through me; to all the inclinations occurring, yes?

A: Correct.

2nd March 2023

V: Good morning, dear friends, what do you wish to discuss today?

A: One's Dignity and Nobility: one's Self-respect and Sovereignty, for these have great power in the field of communication. Most beings are like rough, imperfect pearls; thus, employ disagreement, utilize discord with one's bedfellow or companions, engage all that harasses, torments, worries and confuses; spoils or corrupts, and moisten these, soften, permeate them with due Consciousness—with appointed Awareness—to spontaneously regain one's True Nature, to enable one to readily adjust; hence recover quickly from emotional and physical distress.

V: So, to become pearls, we need to remain consciously aware during times of conflict. Awareness makes us better communicators; it's where we draw our power from.

A: All are jewels of importance; however, most are still in day school, most are still in a state of bewilderment, charmed by the dazzling display of their old testament teachings: their old programming—a communication that is ill-advised.

V: Right, so most of us are still wading in or trying to navigate through our old testimonials and past indoctrinations.

A: Hence, secure one's sea legs via following a definite course previously unknown; thus, not according to ordinary ways, and bear Light for Us.

Although one is still inexperienced and unsophisticated, one has the right of selection. One has choice.

V: I am trying to bear light.

A: As teachers, We introduce such transmissions of knowledge, and instruct one in practice, an honour to be striven for as a reward highly esteemed.

3rd March 2023

V: Thank you for the song yesterday, I had an impulse to turn on the radio and received the lyrics: "Together we are stronger," and "Stay on course."

A: We, the counsel that shares, refine one's language of polarities: one's opposing past testimonies and new revelations, for one to taste, know, and savour.

V: Therefore, I must remember that I am never alone, that I am in union with Source, with Consciousness, and that together We are stronger.

A: Consider entrusting or committing oneself to the care of another—to a Unified state: Us, Source, Consciousness, God. Contemplate giving up or turning over, with one's seal of approval, the reptilian brain in one's sacred basilica (skull temple), which like the fabled Basilisk, who's breath and look are said to be fatal, can envision and snort out ruinous destruction.

V: Turn the Chameleon over to you by being aware that we are together, that we are an Us, a Unified state. Is that what you mean?

A: This makes one's hair stand on end, it frightens one.

V: No, I am not frightened, maybe a little apprehensive as Vicki (my ego/chameleon/persona) is used to taking the reins, but I will try.

A: The thunder lizard (Chameleon) will show contempt and derision.

V: I am certain it will, but you will help me.

A: The Chameleon is an obstacle and difficulty to be surmounted; it exists via its bank vault of judgements. One needs to stop judging to cease the inquietude, the restlessness and unease, the anxiety and distracting thoughts. Seek information via Self inquiry.

4th March 2023

V: I sense that you are also speaking to me through the books I feel guided to read. Is that correct?

A: One's discernment is correct. These books contain revelations, they unveil the counterfeit and deceitful; thus, read them in reciprocation, as an exchange with Us. Hence, We correspond.

V: I knew it. So, these books are the real deal?

A: They contain fundamental principles which are the bedrock between High Light, and deep shadow—Supreme Presence, and profound ignorance.

V: Therefore, reading them will help me see clearer, as in understand, right?

A: Understanding helps one leap up to capital correspondence, a most penetrating stage, for one becomes Unified in state via Spirit's techniques, exchange and discourse, etc. A means for discovering, following, and recording the force and disposition of the Heart.

V: That's good, I'm looking forward to reading more of what my intuition points me toward.

A: This forms a framework via interlacing one's earthenware vessel (body) with the language spoken by Christ, a guiding course to repeat from when first established: thus, rejoice as it treats of the origin and development of Being, removing contention, controversy and competition, etc., which gives agency, support and desired structure to one.

7th March 2023

V: Well, I have begun reading this new book you have led me to, and it appears I need to realize—as in fully grasp—that God is present in everything: this pen, this book, this hand, this room, the floor, the air, these clothes, my dog Sharli, her bed. Please help me understand this.

A: This Realization is overpowering and intense; however, this Awareness is also a refuge that shelters and protects, it is one's recourse, one's haven; it recognizes the brook, the stream, the river, sea and ocean as Source. All is Consciousness—God.

V: I guess so. Wow! I am surrounded by God. Yes, that is overpowering and intense, but also comforting. How do I come to know this experientially instead of simply as an idea?

A: Via being Argus-eyed: sharp-sighted, vigilantly observant, attentive and alert to God's Aria—the airy melody of One Voice.

V: In other words, just keep reminding myself that Consciousness: God, only plays one song: the song of unity, the unified verse, the universes' melody: "God is."

A: Or, be easily cheated and fooled.

V: No thank you. Wow! That means I am already what I have been searching for, as is everyone and everything.

A: Reclaim this to experience an easier more pleasant time. Or, be unawakened.

V: Stop denying God or I will be fooled by the dream of separation, yes?

A: And misled by the rules and programs put forward by religious, political and other regulating or influential bodies projecting their ideologies on the world's stage.

9th March 2023

V: "I am surrounded and protected by the love and the grace of God." I need to know this, right?

A: Hence, one attunes to a Nobler state ruled by Higher teachings.

V: Yes, like our, that is, Ariel's prayer declares: "*Our illuminating Consciousness, which art to the same degree as our nobility and excellence...*" We, as Spirit in a human body, need to reclaim our sovereign heredity.

A: One needs to reclaim Our Father's: Our illuminating Consciousnesses' interchange, and undertake Being Creative and Communicative against previous collective ways of being.

V: I envision a school of fish swimming in one direction, with a few of them turning and swimming the opposite way.

A: To swim with the many, is to act in a way that impresses others and wins applause.

V: That is the collective's stratagem, leading to one-upmanship, as in: impress, get recognition and grandstand. Our nobler tendencies, or God given dispositions, turn us away from this.

A: Daughter of God, people feel persecuted and oppressed due to their race, religion, status, and persistently harassing, lower frequency subconscious beliefs; thus, one needs to persevere in Turning, (transmuting and transcending).

V: Stay on course. Together we are stronger. Together—as in remaining in a unified state of consciousness—we are whole. At the Chameleon, Turn.

A: Turn one's major conflicts of the past over to Us.

V: All I need do is remember that Source, God, Consciousness, Love, is All in all.

A: *God is All in All*. This recognition, this knowing is a prophetic sign of an imminent and significant happening, which causes extraordinary marvel and rejoicing over this Law. For, *God is All in All*, is the call of the free and natural Life; it issues a Sublime Unified state of healing. The acknowledgement that *God is All in All*, ceases one's association with Pandora's box: the unconscious, ill-informed constraints containing all human suffering.

V: Sounds great to me!

A: Like one's energy work: one's short writings, which will progress quickly and explode.

V: You are referring to what you have dubbed our Testaments: the short writings I've put up on X and the even shorter—At the Chameleon, Turn—Instagram posts, yes?

A: Yes. These Testaments comprise of an organized system of direction and management; they unite, fasten and support parched, thirsty minds.

V: But I hardly have any followers?

A: Under inquiry, that which forms their foundation will be understood, assumed, and agreed upon by all.

11th March 2023

V: Thank you for the vision of the beautiful flowers the other day.

A: The flowers were a declaration and reassertion; a temporary compensation from one's unemployed Higher, Unified communication system.

V: But how do I employ this higher system, the visions come and go as they please.

A: To help one's visions flourish, utilize the strength and intensity of the magnetic field; think of it as a protective escort, for this force accompanies one on this journey.

V: So, constantly remind myself that this force, which is obviously God too, because God is All in All, is always with me.

A: And always illuminating the way. Behold the constellation Boötes, the celestial kite, seen as a symbol of connection between the earth and Heaven, conveying the human Spirit yearning for liberty. Kites epitomise the desire to achieve great heights while remaining grounded to one's roots. Thus, bear the Light, hold it in the mind; maintain it, accept, acknowledge, and assume it as a guardian and overseer of the prison (programming) that aims to herd one.

V: So, just holding the light, as in Awareness with a capital "A"—as in Source, God, Consciousness—in my mind, and viewing it as my protector and seer of all, will strengthen my realization of our connection; therefore, I am employing the magnetic field: The Force.

A: We poke, push and prod to re-mind and arouse one mentally via the brightest Light: Awareness. For Awareness reveals one's treachery to Self, it exposes one's violation of allegiance, confidence or faith to Being. Awareness (Source) engenders prophecy, it generates foresight: prediction made under Divine influence and direction. Awareness shears away harmful, repetitive thoughts that demonstrate their authoritative toxicity. Thus, commit to Awareness, and Consciously reproduce and repeat only that which illustrates Ascendancy and Sovereignty.

V: Right, keep repeating my affirmations. "I am one with the Source of All." "I am an expression of love." "I see clearly, I think clearly, I trust my decisions." And so on...

A: And for acceleration in development, pick-up on all one's energetic impulses. Notice the place or state where the broadcasts originate. Observe any unspecified or vaguely defined element or activity such as the effect of worthless ideas that have been woven into one's material: one's neuro network; thus, one's vessel.

V: In other words, employ the field, engage my escort.

A: Seek to weaken the lies: the illusions, via piercing them with the penetrating lance of Awareness.

V: So, the vision of the flowers I received was a prod and reassertion to employ the magnetic field (the law and force of attraction) by recalling my unity with All, and therefore burgeon, as in flourish.

A: Behold Boötes and acknowledge, recognize, accept Our Togetherness. Employ this connectedness for amendments made in the subconscious.

V: Is there anything else you'd like to add?

A: Do not usurp what is entrusted to one's care. Do not appropriate the Force fraudulently. Do not misuse.

V: As in, don't use the magnetic field (the law of attraction) as the collective have broadcast: for ego aggrandizement.

A: Believe that the magnetic field is real, that it is true. Think, assume, accept its existence and worth. Have confidence and trust in its everlastingness, in its Godliness, for, and at all times to come—Always.

V: Thank you, your answer is very clear.

A: Hence, face it, cara a cara, bear, exhibit, allow, convey, manifest: Turn towards one's expression.

V: I am an expression of God.

A: A correct analysis, thus statement; a logical synopsis of the separation of the *Whole* into its parts.

12th March 2023

V: Last night I felt an impulse to look up information on frequency, and I discovered that listening to 40 hertz tones apparently has a healing effect on the mind and body, therefore David and I played this frequency while we slept.

A: One has the power, and the right to make such decisions.

V: Yes, but I feel that I was guided to know that.

A: We exchanged a gift with one, a tip that transfers and nurtures wholesome, beneficial outcomes. We announced, in one's temple, a proposed union with said sumptuous feast.

V: Said sumptuous feast being the 40 hertz tone, right?

A: Correct. This tone is well-appointed and equipped for prolific development conducive to comfort and gratification, it assures and affirms; thus, brings results to a critical pass.

V: Therefore, I should be listening to it more frequently.

A: Do not be shy with it, or draw back as from doubt or caution.

V: Well, I just tuned into it on my phone, so am listening to it now.

A: Frequency can reveal knowledge, for it is a type of manipulation for debris. The pyramid at Giza is in the vicinity of this association.

V: Are you saying that the great pyramid was used to remove debris from the mind, so to speak, and attune it?

A: Tone prepares one, it lights one up, heals, and equips vessels.

V: I see, then I should continue listening to it, yes?

A: For a more graphic and vivid pictorial, yes.

V: Is that why I felt more connected and had visions last night?

A: Tones benefit one to an extreme degree; thus, God: Consciousness, Awareness, Source, may help one via utilising the precedence of one's Unified state, precisely, and without delay. A move toward the right.

V: So, tones, such as the 40 hertz tone, can attune me?

A: They can attune one to grasp and hold the force of Source: God—Consciousness.

14th March 2023

V: As you know, a family member visited yesterday and some troubling subjects came up, which triggered all our past hurts and victim mentalities; therefore, I had a very restless sleep and felt quite low this morning... Then! You gave me that Van Morrison song: *"Bright side of the road,"* which I began humming, realizing, when the compulsion to look up the lyrics took me over, how very appropriate and cheering it was. Thank you.

A: An allowance and leeway of scope, given to one of recognized ability, one who has knowledge of how things are created when one becomes divided through disagreement; hence, We share Brightness.

V: Well, thanks once again, I needed that as I really did feel quite divided.

A: One exists as an individual entity with turpitude: the inherent baseness of one's armoured housing: one's reinforced programs; hence, ready to assault the body. However, recall one is always, always esteemed as a gem, a treasure, a prize—a Precious Light.

V: Well, the song was perfect, simply relaying that I just need to get back to a brighter way of thinking.

A: Back to carrying an appropriate state of Authority, or healing frequency.

V: And help God sing.

A: To help God sing, be still. Be constantly peaceful, tranquil—Calm.

V: And listening to 40 hertz tones, as I am currently doing, will accelerate my progress.

A: Tones give one charge of navigation; hence, regard them with wonder and high esteem, for they grant the possessors the freedom to write their own conditions.

V: Is the 40 hertz tone I've selected the best one? I read that the pyramids emit a tone of 33 hertz inside, is that better?

A: Neither is distorted, or incongruous.

V: But which is better?

A: Both circumnavigate and feminize with an illuminating meal of receptiveness to wisdom, creativity, intuition, forgiveness, reflection, acceptance, gentleness, sensuality, and collaboration.

V: Can the tones be overused?

A: The tones can cause agitation, but like froth, unsubstantial.

V: So, perhaps an hour a day is sufficient.

A: Sufficient to prohibit trickery and deception, employ tones as an implement for weeding out untruths, and for improving self-restraint.

V: Can I change from 40 to 33hertz tones, or stick to one?

A: Proceed with either tone as they are processions of the Holy Spirit, and hence, from Source. One who listens and learns from these combining forms of the feminine, becomes receptive, calm, and balanced.

16th March 2023

V: Good morning. I've been listening to the 40 hertz tone.

A: What We proposed one do, which was to merge with said tone, is settled, the mind is made up; hence, dis-eases of implants that pollute and defame the foundational print of one's animal-avatar, are better able to be reached in range or extent of thought via this influence.

V: So, just trust the tone or frequency is removing debris.

A: Tones generate rhythmic division points that cut off or remove debris, allowing for a mutual exchange that admits Us—a Unified state—as a reality, via interweaving a system of imprinting for the blind.

V: So, tones help to change my neuro-network which enables me to receive, see and understand better.

A: Tones enable one to see one's projections honestly. Tones allow one to witness one's defences, when stricken with the strongest feelings or affectations, with frankness, intimacy, and sincerity.

V: Thank you. Moving on. What are my antagonists teaching me?

A: They are demonstrating what it looks like to be broken, fractured, disturbed, incomplete, in disorder, crushed, weakened, infirmed, spiritually bankrupt etc.

V: Wow! I never thought of it that way. So, you're saying the lesson is to turn away from this as it is not what we are.

A: Disorder, disarray, confusion, makes one incommunicable: incapable of being reached.

V: So, what can I do to help them and myself?

A: Exchange what one produces via imaginings deposited in many forms and influences within oneself, for these inventions form a structure that lacks training and skill, thus is immature. We have taken one on as an apprentice; hence, one can understand.

V: And how do I exchange these products, or imaginative creations, so to speak?

A: Exchange these in one's chamber of commerce: one's mind. Dredge, search for, and clear the dregs, remove the debris, dismiss the worthless residue of anything hateful, vindictive or malignant that is absent of Light.

V: How?

A: One removes the fanciful via believing, without proof or conviction, that doing thus will unveil bliss, harmony, blessedness, delight, which hence becomes a luminous signal recorded on one's radarscope (Brain).

V: So, what you are saying is: When I believe in my true nature, which is bliss, delight and happiness, which can only come from my unity with God, as in my Awareness of what I actually am—Consciousness—this will register in mind, and therefore on my brain, which can only evolve the more I embrace God as All, in All.

A: This is black and white; it is Obvious. And, it is offered as a means of atonement, of reparation for all, for all are in the same boat; all are equally involved; thus, give special prominence to this belief in bliss, imagine, and do: act harmoniously, ensure delight, achieve blessedness, bend toward one's godliness, incline toward the worship of Brahma: The Supreme Soul of the Universe—God, the Absolute Creator—Consciousness.

V: Love God with all my heart by remembering that we, all of us, including my seeming adversaries, are also the Supreme Soul of the Universe. We are all expressions of God.

A: Like clay worked with water, matter works with, and within Consciousness. Clay, or matter carries transferable dis-eases: anger, anxiety, sadness, agitation, worry, etc., while the water, or Consciousness is the vital force, the life acting independently of all material and chemical drivers.

17th March 2023

V: Regarding your last statement, I think I understand... Though I seem, or appear to be the clay, I am actually the water: Consciousness, the vital force, life, God acting freely of all discomforting matters that fuel and drive the physical.

A: Hence, head toward the coast: the territory next to the sea, the Mind adjacent to Consciousness. Direct one's course toward Seeing.

V: See the Sea. See, understand the Ocean of Consciousness we are.

A: We are within Consciousness: Source—God. Thus, coexist together. We coextend alongside one through space and time. Together We exchange, for We are all bonded, married one may say, with the Whole range of All, such as the gamut of emotions, or simply the first note of the harmonic scale.

18th March 2023

V: I felt an urge to listen to Barbarra Marciniak today, the channel who wrote *"Bringers of the Dawn,"* and wow, her messages absolutely spoke to me, and so, I wrote down an intention the Pleiadeans, through Barbarra, suggested we say to ourselves.

"I want to accelerate my personal evolution. I want Spirit to assist me in a greater capacity. I want my body to regenerate itself. I want to emanate health. I am willing to give up difficulty so that I can be a living example of what humanity can be."

A: A clarion call from the Heart of the Celestial for Divine Beings.

V: As in, a loving frequency of thought given by the Celestial to help us evolve. Is that what you mean?

A: An expression, or communication of thought for manifesting beneficial feelings, conditions, and qualities.

V: Things are beginning to make more sense.

A: This is apt: likely, fitting, pertinent; hence, one is quick to learn from Us.

V: Does that mean my personal evolution will be accelerating?

A: To hasten progress, use the Super Highway in exchange for one's trails.

V: When can I better receive you telepathically?

A: When one relinquishes one's old claims and declares oneself free to the fullest extent in the presence of one's Sovereign Spirit: an invisible influence felt to be near.

V: Is Spirit a frequency, too?

A: As a force that effects the physical, frequency has been improperly exercised, for it is perverted or distorted in meaning and intent, causing the violation of one's state of being.

V: Which is why I need to turn the dial, so to speak, and relinquish my claim to old patterns of behaviour; therefore, I can be free of the past, and I will be better able to feel my sovereignty: my true self.

A: With assurance and self-confidence according to one's prophecies and revelations, which are near in space and time, any, and every choice to know Self beforehand becomes comprehensive for one's complete understanding. This is akin to the Galilean—Jesus.

V: Really!? I mean, yes, of course Jesus would have known himself.

A: Knowing oneself is akin to employing an ultra-microscopic filter: a passing agent that has the power of extinguishing dis-eases, dilemmas, and difficulties, etc. in one.

V: Therefore, know my frequency, my spirit, my Supreme Presence.

A: Reserve *knowing* for a specific purpose, such as recognizing or realizing the fundamental cause, reason, motive or intent for an action or belief; thus, one bears fruit.

V: Are you Pleiadeans? Sorry, had to ask.

A: We are one's star-board, one's right-side-steering-hand, one's guiding light council.

V: Is that a yes?

A: We smile broadly.

V: Okay . . . That's not a yes or no, but I guess it is safe to say you come from the family of light, right?

A: And Light is chivalrous, gracious, magnanimous, generous, noble, excellent, benevolent, etc.

20th March 2023

V: Hi guys, I had a lot of quick visions last night, the first took up my entire visual field; it was a network of lines like a telecommunication system of sorts on an eggshell background. Then, there was a series of condensed writings which were too quick to read. I got the impression they were transmissions. What say you?

A: To dial Us, think and expect Us; thus, one can compute and rely on Us to plan and design.

V: The eggshell background appeared to be a living form, which is perhaps why it strongly presented as an egg in a sense. I feel drawn to calling it the inner-net.

A: An inner-net that is frugal: that exercises providence, foresight and guidance; hence, consume its fruits, utilize its economical results and produce a joyous yield.

V: This is the light network, right?

A: This is a commencement in Higher learning during which degrees are conferred; thus, commend: commit to it with confidence.

V: So, there is more to come?

A: One has eager desire for possession.

V: Yes of course. This is what I have been working towards, isn't it?

A: The harsh and unpleasing to the mind aids the creative sense, dear one, it is the hearts blaring clarion; hence, look, see behind the theatre of the brazen and gaudy displays paraded that freely wave to one.

V: The bigger the parade, the bigger the charade, as they say.

A: Cognition, Awareness, Understanding of this charade, is to Know that independent, autonomous ideas constitute a bounding: a constraining and attachment. For to feel or be of an opinion, is the determination that passes sentence on one.

V: Thank you. I love you.

A: "I love you," is the absolute, perfect pitch, employ it to sooth and to relieve one from unconsciousness.

V: Oh! That reminds me, I woke up to the song: *"Love is all around me,"* playing in my head this morning. Thank you.

A: Accredit it to Brahman, to God the Author, to Consciousness the Creator, and accept it as True; thus, one brings Love into acknowledgement, acclaim and honour. Believe and Trust in Love.

21st March 2023

V: I was going over an answer you gave me on the 7th of March which said: *"Be Argus-eyed: sharp sighted, vigilantly observant...etc."* And an out of the blue thought came to me: *"Listen with your eyes and see with your ears."* Can you explain this, please?

A: One's eyes and ears are bodyguards; thus, responsible for one's physical safety; they escort one, and are expanded by expenditure of a specified thing: effort. Hence, establish one's temple of wisdom via commitment and ardency. Hold one's eyes and ears—one's primary receivers—in high esteem.

V: Oh! Presence! So, seeing with my ears and listening with my eyes is an ardent way of saying: be committed to the effort of being Supremely tuned in—Present, right?

A: And Be Supremely Present to the past in such a manner as to go beyond it in time and degree; thus, one can furnish and support oneself with scaffolding that fills one completely to overflowing, so that one consistently conveys one's powers of observation, enabling one to interpret transmissions or communications, eminently.

V: That reminds me of the section in our prayer: *Thy change and evolution be done as a step of preparation for the mutual interchange of ideas.* Being Supremely Present prepares and evolves us.

A: One will not fail to fulfill one's belief in, or acceptance of the Truth. The ignorant or unenlightened in one will be transcended.

V: It will?

A: The gate that gives one access to success has the ability to speak two languages: the worldly and the Celestial. A sound mind fertilized by composure, tranquillity and calmness, allows the Celestial to come forth convincingly with due excellence characterized by the foresight to direct the attention to one's current records: archives that are frozen, controlled, restricted, held, and concealed.

25th March 2023

V: We exist!

A: With the mark of censure: disapproval, judgement and blame, etc. Where thoughts are exchanged in destructive rations that reject integration due to partial loss of vision—Awareness, Consciousness.

V: Yes, that is the current state of this 3D collective world; therefore, we exist along with these distortions.

A: Hence, one belongs to, adheres to and lives in a comedy of manners dealing with human folly, which portrays the customs and foibles of the fashionable world.

V: The sentences create the sentence, right? The word formulations and stories we tell ourselves pass sentence on us.

A: Correct. In the mind's album where one's records: one's stories and images are stored as fussed residue left by emotional energy.

V: And I agreed to come here to remember all of this and help raise the level of awareness.

A: Correct. To hold the Force. To see Vishnu: God, Source, many came in numbers, so that the Old Testament: the past programming, the economic doctrine or system of protection, the shielded or covered, the shrine made sacred by historic or other associations, contracts and diminishes.

V: We came here and do this in multitudes—as a collective.

A: With the power to advocate. With the power to act conferred and granted. With principles, beliefs and philosophies. With use of a Superior Force. To hold a powwow with the dreamers, to cure the sick (the unaware), and effect success in conflicts as supporters collectively in service.

V: Are we in a spiritual war, so to speak?

A: To announce, to voice, to speak solemnly: sincerely, soberly, is to penetrate and undermine the stability of the mercurial trade within oneself: an exchange of impulsive, volatile, devious intercommunication.

V: In other words, being honest with ourselves destabilizes the frequency of the old testament (past programming) that keeps us all in the prison of self-censure.

A: Engage Us—one's Unified state. Though not in command, We are assigned in an advisory capacity to re-present the tendencies pitched to one with qualities not admitting of doubt or denial. Hence, openly and plainly express Us via affirmations.

26th March 2023

V: You are my star board, my council of light, my team of advisors, my Unified state, right?

A: We are with one for the purpose of guarding and observing; directed from the primary essence—Consciousness (God).

V: You have said there is more to come as far as my learning goes. Can you please elaborate?

A: This relates to the exchange of currency in one's foundation, it pertains to the science: the knowledge and learning or understanding of teachings concerning immortality. Life tantalizes, it teases and torments via repeated frustration of one's hopes and desires. 3D life is designed to frame a view of the outer world; however, it is a semblance, a mere show without true reality. There are signs one will pick up via the study of extrasensory perception and related psychic phenomena that will accelerate learning and seal off the repetitive, parakeet-like frequency of the parasitic Chameleon.

V: So, essentially, you are teaching me to pick up on the signs that point to the falseness of this 3D reality, and therefore speed up my, and other's evolution.

A: One aspires to this. One has an earnest desire: an ambition to use knowledge for the relief of delusion and suffering.

V: Yes, that is my aim.

A: Hence, agree to alternate, assent to exchange or substitute corrupt frequencies (distorted thoughts), and diminish their regular, habitual dishonesty.

V: Agree by being willing to hold a higher thought, and therefore frequency. Is that what you mean?

A: Like a sudden burst of wind or an outpouring of passion, one's frequency of Spirit, one's Conscious Awareness, affects *all* worldwide, for together, via contiguity: relationship and connection, We weave the context that surrounds and influences the environment and circumstances; thus, adhere to the state of being in genuine contact with the fair, gracious, courteous, pleasant and free from distortion.

V: So, some of the ideas I receive are advice and suggestions from you.

A: Ideas which refine one, and which are absorbers of one's distress; thus, accede to them, grant their request, admit them as True and aid the transfer of ownership; hence, the lies and empty talk of the tormenting thoughts that frighten, oppress and harass one, etc., are derailed via the entrusted idea appointed to act for another.

27th March 2023

V: What a night! I hardly got any sleep.

A: We pin-point and define one's pineal.

V: I had a vision of an amber temple *within* an amber heart. Then, upon wondering what the colour amber meant, I got the answer: Am Be R (Are). As in: I Am, I Be, We Are the temple: the sacred vessel of the Source of All, which expresses through Us when We Are willing to align with love and Be loving, which accounts for the heart. I also got the very strong impression that you Are and will Be assisting me further in a telepathic sense. Am I correct?

A: Pray thee for this . . . because the state of being private, separate or in seclusion, is the state of turbulence; it is the condition of being intensely disturbed, restless and confused. Telepathy is a reflector, like a telescope that transmit an image from a reflecting surface to the eyepiece, telepathy reveals the substance with which anything is filled.

V: Was that a yes?

A: When one enlightens, one frees the pineal from stain.

V: The pineal gland is the fruit of the tree of life, as in our neurology and nervous system, right?

A: Where a continuous stream of Consciousness, having a high pitched and penetrating tone quality, is poured; thus, one's pineal, the cone shaped fruit of the tree of life, steers *with* one's steering committee, which arranges and directs one's course to move others in great numbers. This pouring is a gratuitous gift of exchange.

V: So, this is happening?

A: One agrees to pay one's share before the stupor of feasting on Samsara, the merry-go-round of birth, death and rebirth, begins. One decides before one is full of and covered in grime.

V: Grime?

A: Grossness. The apparent tarnished by guilt, shame, imperfection and distortion—the stained.

V: So, you are saying I signed up for this before this incarnation.

A: The mortal in one remains nervous with excited interest.

V: Yes, the mortal me is very nervous, but you will guide me, right?

A: As one prunes the fine threadlike structures of one's tree of life (neurology) in exceeding minute measures, one undergoes modification; hence, via a collage of creative compositions, one airs and forms one's climate condition; hence the atmosphere of the earth.

V: As in we create a more ambient condition within, and therefore without, like when I air and prune a disempowering thought with a replacement such as: "I am one with the Source of All."

A: A wise proclamation of glory and power, and fundamental call to the Supreme Creator: the Conscious Awareness that flows in the veins of the gods.

V: Gods, with a small g, as in human form?

A: Correct.

V: So, last night my pineal gland was being opened or worked on. Is that correct?

A: We spoke at length, which was perceived with the mind as an experience.

V: I thought so, but I wasn't sure if it was me speaking to myself.

A: We speak via a constant bandwidth, via a subtle substance, transmitting power from one cyclic energy system to another.

V: Was that what all those coloured waves and filaments I saw were?

A: Waves produce, waves form, waves are poignant and penetrating; thus, apt to create an exchange with something that stimulates and renews Spirit.

V: Is that why the top of my head felt tingly?

A: One's pineal recorded the intensity of transmission automatically.

V: So, my pineal is what now?

A: Able to examine inquiringly and meticulously.

V: I am trying to understand what I experienced.

A: One experienced an opportunity, as one's cornucopia, one's horn of plenty; one's clarion (pineal), received—via a bandwidth designed to provide support in the Consciousness through which it moves—a blessing.

V: Is there anything I need to do?

A: Allow this allowance. And allow the ideal qualities of one's knighthood, such as kindness, courage, nobility, attentiveness, loyalty, excellence, and graciousness etc., to arise in one. This is of great magnitude. One's experience was an appetizer that will put forth branches.

V: So, if I am One with the Source of All, as you poignantly pointed out last night, then telepathy is quite normal; therefore, I will know myself beyond what I thought was possible, right?

A: *All is God, and All is sacred to God*; hence, quote this. Reproduce these words. Repeat them, cite them with authority, and illustrate.

V: "All is God, and All is sacred to God."

A: To be noncommittal or noncompliant to this, is to be like a believer in the Ptolemaic system, which assumed that the earth was the central body around which the sun, planets and celestial bodies revolved.

V: In other words, failure to believe and state the truth that: God is All in All, is to fall for the illusion of separateness.

A: It is ignorance of Self, self-idolizing, and self-hypnotism.

V: I am an individualized expression of the Source of All, yes?

A: To hasten the occurrence of one's Godly expression, employ the substitute: one's individual subordinate persona, to study, learn, and determine meaning from traditional philosophies; for these save one from loss of knowledge, and aid one in being effective and well throughout one's sentence in time, constructed in this realm so that completion or achievement of both sense and structure is suspended, resulting in conjecture, guesswork or presumption.

28th March 2023

V: Following on from yesterday, you are advising me to read more philosophical works and try not to speculate anymore, but rather, *Know* that God is All in All.

A: Knowing is the art of dispensing healing; it is stellar, outstanding and key to advancing via careful selection of one's course. With knowing, any intensification of dis-ease or outburst of emotion, can propel a vessel from being confused and feeling uncertain, to being undistracted; thus, focussed, and no longer distressed.

V: I slept well last night, I was so tired from the long, strange interaction the night before, that I simply dozed off.

A: To Know on which side one's bread is buttered is to Be Aware of the True Source of one's fortune and security.

V: Is that also why I slept so well: because I know I am one with the Source of All? Is that what you mean?

A: Conscious energy unites Us as though with glue; hence use this energy as one would a dial for telephoning, and thus We communicate.

V: Right. So, are you saying: I *know* we are in connection now?

A: Apartness or separation has taught one certain fundamentals; it has established a foundation of autocratic self-rule. The autoclave: self-key to decontaminating oneself of this dictatorship, is to praise Awareness. Harmonious compositions of acclaim that honour Conscious Awareness, are now a law adopted by one's corporation (body). One will feel awkward and unskilled for a while; however, remain with pure Awareness to correct form. Employ the higher, absolute, untainted clarity of Conscious Awareness as the currency exchange in one's automatic mechanism.

V: So, you are saying that all our work together has paid off, and though I am still not skilful at it, it has become my new way of correcting my past conditioning.

A: Thus, one reunites the pieces of oneself, mending one's components into a Whole.

V: So, I am becoming unbroken, as in I am healing, right?

A: As a result of proceeding gradually, step by step.

V: Slowly, but surely.

A: Where one utterly and absolutely stands, paves the way; it prepares one for interchange, for clearing outdated articles such as old conditions, past commentaries and stipulations, before restocking with higher level qualifications.

V: By way of allowing, and therefore receiving a higher frequency?

A: Correct. Via transmitting and receiving an active element that restores order, that rectifies necessarily perforce, like a sieve that separates the fine from that which is coarse.

V: Will I begin to notice anything within myself?

A: The end of indulging in long-winded, wordy discourse that flows abundantly.

V: Discourse with?

A: Self.

V: Oh, as in that voice that rambles on and on.

A: Visualize a deep pure blue sapphire colour while becoming silent. Make a habit or custom of this practice.

V: Deep pure blue? Why?

A: This colour—when integrated with silence—is an implement for defeating the popular, common or general, which are suited to the intelligence of ordinary people.

30th March 2023

V: Wow! I just looked up some information on sapphires; I didn't know that in Latin the word sapphire means blue, and that sapphires had so many spiritual qualities such as: wisdom, peace, a calm clear mind, renewal of divine connection, sovereignty, improvement of vision, assistance in releasing unwanted patterns, balance of emotions, not to mention a connection to the throat and third eye chakras. So, I gathered from yesterdays' conversation, that you want me to work with the colour sapphire. I feel that you would like me to visualize my pineal as a cone or pear-shaped sapphire, and see my throat chakra encased in blue, too. I also sense that it would be helpful to practice surrounding myself within an ovoid orb of sapphire, consequently forming a forcefield of protection against all the negative frequencies we are exposed to. Did I receive this correctly?

A: Bathe thick in this orb.

V: Thick as in generously? You want me to bathe liberally, substantially in an imagined, ovoid, sapphire-coloured orb?

A: Correct. And apply the pear-shaped sapphire to one's pineal; utilize this for connecting.

V: As in, envisage it, my pineal, as a bright, sparkling, sea-blue jewel, yes?

A: Correct. Employ this small gift and friendly tip to help one journey with speed and hasten one's unexperienced sight, affording one reasonable ground for trust and belief.

V: So, this new practice will accelerate my capacity for insight and ability to connect with you, which will help me express Source more clearly. Did I understand that correctly?

A: The practice helps one censor, prune and amend the secular: this world, the temporal, the material as distinguished from the Spiritual.

V: And it is like a forcefield that protects me, too.

A: Via vigilance and alertness; hence, stay Aware, stay Awake in order to observe, protect and guard against shortcomings.

V: I see; therefore, I need to constantly remind myself to envision my sovereign wisdom shield which, as a consequence, keeps me alert.

A: Envision Ra, a Sovereign entity crowned with a solar disc. Reminding oneself is an essential element of primary education; thus, remember to practice, and one will be resistant to the tumult: the disturbances and agitations of the multitude.

V: Ra, hey, but instead, I crown myself with a sapphire, so to speak, and surround myself in an ovoid orb or disc of blue.

A: Creating or affording oneself reasonable ground for trust and belief; thus, allows it to be logically assumed as True.

V: Thank you for the tip.

A: Clarity of Awareness is an axis: an alliance, an affiliation We promote to ensure mutual interest, cooperation, and solidarity in relations, in order to derail the deranged.

Later

V: I bathed frequently in my sapphire forcefield today.

A: Bask in its royal favour. Bathe often in it. Lay in and enjoy its pleasant warmth as though it were sunlight. Benefit from it.

1st April 2023

V: I am feeling somewhat low today.

A: One has been abducted to the underworld: the subconscious; hence, it will benefit one to prune the foolish or mentally defective, the worthless and trivial.

V: Okay. Well, I am confused. Everything is God, right?

A: Baked food, pastry, fruit, custard, meat, etc. The sixteenth letter of the Greek alphabet—Pi. Also, the ratio of the circumference of a circle to its diameter, etc. The delicate inner membrane that envelops the brain and spinal cord, etc. The Magpie, and what it collects, etc. One's surrounding region, area and country, etc. Grain and Spirit, etc. Whisky distilled from rye, etc. etc. etc.

V: Exactly! Everything! Even what seems vastly insignificant. So, how do I grasp or have the awareness of God in all, when things feel so utterly disconnected or removed from God?

A: To bring the Awareness of: *God in All,* into equilibrium, reconcile it via keeping it in proportion or relation to God (Life, Spirit, Consciousness). Weigh this in the mind wisely. One may also enclose all within a halo, a luminous splendour investing a person or thing with Divinity or Holiness; thus, one can hold entities in reverence. This action is champion.

V: Envision a halo surrounding everything?

A: When one's path is crossed by conflict, employ the halo, use it as an icon of Godliness upon one's visual scope, this converts the image transmitted. Like an iconoclast, the halo is an image breaker, for it is precise, and stimulating. Do it quickly; hence forth, All will be thoroughly complete.

2nd April 2023

V: So, enveloping things and people *speedily* with an imaginary halo, particularly when I'm confronted by conflict, will break into my current view of what I think, and therefore I will eventually see the cup, so to speak, as divine. Behold I make all things new!

A: One's eyes are bleared by tears (traumas), and thus, are dull of perception; they are without moorings, adrift and distracted, adroit and expert in absorbing tumult and confusion. To cause this institution—this principle and customary way of seeing that forms part of society—to collapse, bathe one's erratic mass of difficulties in the Absolute: in Source, in God. And turn away from all previous creations.

V: By bathing all difficulties in the Absolute, you mean within a halo, right? Because the halo reminds me of everything and everyone's holiness.

A: The halo serves as a medium of conveyance; it transmits, supports, and confirms holiness; thus, bear it as an attribute. And, remember, one's words carry conviction.

V: It seems too simple. It is a practice in re-membering, isn't it?

A: It is a practice in harmonizing, in agreeing, in joining, for it interrupts the conversation of one's chimera: the absurd creation of the imagination that is given to fanciful dreams.

V: Last night at my friend's son's wedding, I forgot everything I've learnt from you.

A: The body holds great distress; thus, is torn, split. However, one made great effort toward mutual understanding. Though not direct in one's intending, one inclined toward Turning; hence, changed one's usual direction of flight (escape) toward one's course of study.

V: I'm not sure I understand what you mean?

A: When feeling perplexed or challenged by difficulty, one's neuro-network became still; hence, silent.

V: Oh yes, I know! But I hate that about myself. Why do I clam up that way? Why do I feel less than and fearful of having nothing interesting to say?

A: This is due to one's past major conflicts; they keep one stuck.

V: How do I release these and become free of them?

A: Put forth proponents. Champion, become an advocate, support acceptance of one's warmth; believe in one's kindness. Weave friendliness, openness and easiness within. Do this with ardency, with enthusiasm.

V: "I know I am warn and friendly. I know I am open and easy going. I know I am kind-hearted and thoughtful."

A: Impress these upon one's mind and feelings to produce a marked effect. These statements influence one; hence, establish them firmly.

V: Gosh, there are so many demons (low quality thoughts) to flush out.

A: Demons that dwell and are fixed in their abode, that reside and linger on a matter, that focus on an issue or concern; hence, one continues in a state that leads one astray.

V: I suppose my estranged daughter-in-law would be dealing with such demons, too, right?

A: One's temple contains a litany or inventory of comparative grades and levels of defences, arguments and justifications, guards that bound and constrain one, which are characterized via their similarities and via excessive use of alliteration (resonance) and antithesis: the direct opposite. And, also via rhetoric: affected and exaggerated display in the use of language for the power of pleasing or persuading.

3rd April 2023

V: Good morning. What a night! So many visions and waves of colour.

A: Used in making cordage, connection to chief Consciousness, the architect who creates anything whatsoever, everything, All.

V: I got the impression that I am going to receive something from you on my birthday, two days from now. Is that correct?

A: The standard exchange unit or currency of a Unified Kingdom: that is one's Sovereignty, requires a varying measure of capacity to tune in; thus, the quality of being at proper pitch, or in the befitting key for concord or unison.

V: So, on my 62nd birthday, I will be better able to tune in, and therefore I will receive something?

A: Hence, any irregular, inferior or counterfeit thing will be seen as a horned viper—a clear warning, a clarion foretelling venomous harm or threat to one's ability to prosper.

V: Are you saying, I will know truth from illusion?

A: One's brain waves: the rhythmical fluctuations of electrical potential in one's brain, will become more sensible, tending to affect the senses; hence, they can restore one to soundness as they cleanse one of grief, error and lack while in this lower realm where one exists as an individual unit in a collective motion picture. As a projector—broadcasting gracious, honourable, honest service, protect the young via shielding them as with Angel wings. Look carefully at, and over all, particularly the so-called impossible or contrary to the current reality, which is categorized, branded and portrayed via ceremony or ritual: custom or habit.

V: Will I notice a perceptible change?

A: One originates and produces, for all are possessed of generative power. In order to accelerate one's scope: one's capacity for achievement, effectiveness and range of view, which is characteristic of one's calling, We unite; thus, escape. We break free from the restraint and control of the world's runaround, artful deception.

V: Well, I am quite excited about this.

A: Hence, one will pick-up a measure of capacity as nourishment, as invigoration, as stimulation, as energy from the swirl: the whirling motion within, beside, and beyond one that is Life (Source). Thus, when criticized by self or other, one can shelter via a sprinkling of Spirit (Supreme Presence) in Our Father—Consciousness.

V: So, big night on April 5th, yes?

A: There are several phases to producing alternate currents, each consisting of many frequencies or voices of Source, the holy seer from which anything springs. The perfect pitch is to be ardent, committed, keen. This shapes ideas, for passion develops expression and embodiment.

V: So, am I ready to receive?

A: More gods (signs and symbols) than one. We bring one a school of applied knowledge, teaching the art of manifesting. This is a course taken via the unexpectant, and via a sense of longing for home.

V: I am excited.

6th April 2023

V: Good morning. Apart from that very vivid, very strange dream I had, did anything happen?

In the dream, I was at an overly crowded, dreadfully rowdy party in someone's home, and was married to, or partnered with someone whom I did not recognize. To get away from the hullabaloo, I locked myself in a huge bathroom, but all these people began to gather outside the bathroom, knocking and hollering to let them come in. There were several doors into the bathroom which those assembled outside somehow managed to unlock, but which I frantically kept re-locking, allowing no one entry, and so, although it was exhausting, I was able to escape them.

People I knew and was angry with in the dream, along with some security guards and this husband or partner I didn't know, just kept trying to get into the bathroom wanting me to join them, while all I wanted was to be left alone. And, I also remember dearly wanting to take a soothing warm bath. Other than the strong feeling of frustration at the situation and the fear of being overwhelmed by all these people, which I truly didn't want to face or deal with, I don't recall much more. Interestingly though, at the beginning of the dream I was a woman, but by the end of the dream I was a small child...

I think the people at this party represented my fears, difficulties, judgemental thoughts, disempowering beliefs and unwanted emotions, etc. which I know are there, but don't particularly want to confront, and therefore, I hide away from and try to supress. The husband, or partner I didn't recognize, symbolized supportive, reassuring sides of myself which I often don't acknowledge, that's why I didn't know or appreciate him. The bathroom exemplified a place of refuge, a place where I could go to be cleansed and soothed, so to speak, like when I meditate; however, no amount of relief was coming to me in the dream. In the dream I was trying to escape all the noise and people: all the tumult of my uneasy thoughts, which wasn't working out for me, as the people: my problematic thoughts and feelings, along with the security guards: my defensive and reactive safeguards, wouldn't go away, instead they just kept trying to get my attention.

I believe the message of the dream was not to shut these parts of myself out, but instead let them in, let them be seen, heard, and wholly acknowledged, as in, allow more, and don't push away. And the fact I ended up as a small child, reminded me of the biblical saying in Matthew 18:3 *"Truly I tell you, unless you change and become like little children, you will never enter the kingdom of heaven."* In other words: unless I have a change of heart and mind, and think as an innocent child, who is trusting, simple and honest, I will not have peace of mind. Children trust their parents. I need to trust our Source, our Father, our illuminating Consciousness—Awareness.

What do you think?

A: Breathe...

Life... Existence... Homo Sapiens produce energy; hence, Source may flow in a barrage of overwhelming thoughts and words.

V: Okay. But I don't understand, was the dream the experience or insight I was meant to receive? Was there nothing else?

A: This is an anticlimax to what one thought, which was to receive the qualities of the ideal knight: a champion of the Celestial, the Spiritual, resulting in beneficence.

V: Um... Yeah... I'll say. So, what exactly happened?

A: One who has thorough experience in something, such as a torrent of engulfing thoughts, has this congregation, this gathering under one's charge; thus, can dismiss foolishness, and return home to Heaven: to peace of mind, having become Victorious in the radio-active element of receiving and transmitting.

V: I am not feeling very Victorious, or like my radio is active.

A: One's passion or strong emotion is an honest and authentic part of one's wholeness; thus, influential in one's state of affairs, presenting one with a choice between the prince of darkness, or the prince of peace.

V: You know I try my best to choose peace. But I thought I was going to start receiving you more clearly, as in perhaps audially... I am feeling really, really tired.

A: Salvation: the process of release and recovery, of reinforcement and improvement, of relief, renewal, and liberation, etc., requires one to withdraw to a place of privacy for shelter and rest. Consider this as a restorative influence on one's human beingness.

V: Is that what my dream was about: salvation? Is that why I ended up as an innocent child?

A: Like one's dream, one is pelted with words in this world: assailed with many thoughts; thus, one moves or acts hurriedly as one is struck repeatedly.

V: Yep. That sounds like my dream, and that describes the world perfectly: fast-paced and stressful.

A: The world sidetracks one, it diverts and distracts all from the main subject—Consciousness. *"Pause"* is a frame of support on which to rest.

V: Am I at least progressing?

A: We would have one succeed rather than fail; thus, to seek and manifest clear-sightedness, move or act with bright, quick-witted steps.

7ᵗʰ April 2023

V: Can I say: I am the Absolute?

A: One carries the Absolute via the way one bears One Self.

V: Okay. What about: I carry the Absolute and the Absolute carries me?

A: Recognize that there are two creative powers. And, know that the final triumph is of good over evil.

V: How do you define evil?

A: We define it as a device and foundation for teaching, having various functions in establishing duality, such that, persons make needless display of these learnings (programming), and of the acquiring of material assets: the parade of the arrogantly vain intellect and ethos etc. of those who insist upon the importance of trifling points of scholarship.

V: As in, displays of indoctrination that are ego-centered, however are necessary to create contrast and comparison to have duality.

A: Displays of indoctrination from and for easily trained, tailless apes.

V: I see. Wow! Hmm... Is there anything you would like me to focus on today?

A: Blues: Azure, sky-blue, sapphire, cobalt, indigo, lazuline, cerulean, navy... Cover oneself and others with a glaze of varied blues as though lavishly beautifying and enhancing with precious, excellent jewels.

V: As though adorning all, including myself with the brilliance of varied blue coloured sapphires. In other words, visualize an aura, glow, or atmospheric quality of outstanding excellence over everyone because it reminds me of their divinity and value.

A: The bonus is good, for it teaches one the relationship of All to Our Originator—Source.

V: Yes, it would remind me that we are all from the Absolute, and the colour blue would prompt me to recall each and everyone's sovereignty.

A: Be vigorous: enthusiastic, motivated in the conception and expression of this act, as it is a means for quantifying one's Awareness. Consider visualizing this blue aura as the aerosphere surrounding the earth, for global equilibrium.

8ᵗʰ April 2023

V: Baby steps. I think I have a better understanding, but I am still crawling.

A: Hence, the Son or Sun: the Christ in one, evidently returns to the same position amongst the stars, amongst the light, the stellar, amid excellence in order to proficiently create, to originate and demonstrate the same Logos, the undeviating, corresponding, constant Word or frequency of the: So Powerful that no light can escape.

V: Hence, why we are all one, we actually can't escape the Absolute.

A: The Absolute provides one with a breach: an opening to enable one to violate and defy Oneness. The Absolute provides one with a loin cloth in comparison to the Truth, a material garment: the body.

V: Yes, very true, this body and world have been provided so we can experience individuality and separateness.

A: The body, provided as an endowment, may be furnished with talents or natural gifts, an exchange given for the permanent use of each Son/Sun each Being.

V: Right. So, what I gain or learn here in this world of separateness, I can never lose.

A: Hence, aromatize, make this life fragrant, pleasing, agreeable to the senses via projecting from a clear open view. Build up from this lower level.

V: I am sorry that I'm so impatient.

A: One is excessively eager to acquire the sense of hearing Us auditorily. We console via soothing and sustaining one's fallen Spirits, bringing relief to one's mind while embodied in human form. This impatience is a minor fault in the workings of the machine: the body, for its ailments or dis-eases make one illogical while clothed with breaches: the infractions making separation possible.

V: I am receiving you more clearly though, and this can only improve, right?

A: Keep Turning from one's past-permitted or favoured opinions and conduct, for the distorted spoils; it impairs or destroys the valuable expediency and benefit of the slight stream required through which Source: The Absolute, issues, flows, and separates gold from ore.

13th April 2023

V: Good morning.

A: A specified kind of idea within one's physical structure strengthens its appearance.

V: Specified? Oh! You mean the idea I've been repeating to myself lately: God, the Absolute Consciousness, is All in all.

A: Observance of this overview adjoins the earth: the physical or material, to All via association and relation. Recall this when having little Spirit or courage.

V: So, keep being observant of this, particularly when I'm feeling down.

A: Adherence to the observance of this knowledge seals one's ability to walk aboard earth's vessel, especially when seas (circumstances) are rough, without losing one's balance.

15th April 2023

V: Following on from the other day: observance of myself, others, and physical matter, all being one and therefore in relation to each other, will help me through the storms of life.

A: To ascend, do not quench the parasite.

V: The parasite . . . ? Oh, I see, you are referring to the Chameleon, in this case our para-sight, our subsidiary or inferior sight: the sight that feeds off the illusion that we are separate from God—the Absolute Source of all. You are saying: don't satisfy its unexceptional view of things.

A: The Absolute Source of All—Consciousness—is the conduit for supplying Awareness to the community; hence, allow Consciousness to lead, to inscribe, and to confer authority upon one. Allow Awareness to empower one without selfish grasping and desire for possession of its wealth.

V: That is what I am working towards.

A: Thus, with vitality, and a noble disposition of mind, bring forth a copious flow of the principle of Life—Consciousness. Inculcate this: impress this upon the psyche via frequent repetition, to instil Awareness.

16th April 2023

V: Should I continue to conceptualize and visualize my pineal gland as a pear-shaped, brilliant blue sapphire, significant of clear-minded wisdom, sovereignty, and peace?

A: Frequently employing audio and visual aids, serves to examine, adjust, and certify oneself; thus, attend to this higher learning, enabling one to receive the things to be done for mapmaking.

V: Mapmaking as in making new maps of reality, right, new neuro pathways? Therefore, keep on using the visual (imagination) and audio (affirmation) aids to stay on the right course.

A: Life consists of two co-responding parts. The first to come forth or transmit is one's table of comparative grades, or rather, the frame of reference one's primitive aspect employs as a service of defence or protection. But, let the buyer beware, for this view pertains to the outer world, the world of appearance, while the second, which has heard the first, frees one from troublesome situations and is felt as an intuition, an awareness of the existing, present variation of the current or flow of energy within that induces motivational force.

V: From diversity to unity, or from separation to a unified state.

A: Via benediction: the act of blessing; thus, recognize grace as a standard of excellence.

V: I will do my best.

Now on a slightly different note: Is Jesus an archetype in an allegorical form?

A: An epitome of benevolence, disposed to do good.

V: Yes, absolutely, but a story to help us learn, right? A metaphorical model, so to speak, or an actual historical figure?

A: A narrative that imbues, that pervades, that infuses persons; hence, society and culture with emotions and ideals that saturate humanity with motivation and encouragement, with colour, with influences capable of being imitated or followed as examples.

V: So, Jesus, or Yeshua, is, or represents the physical: the man, the body or avatar, and Christ is the God within and without, the Source, the Absolute—Consciousness. It is the story of Us.

A: The Absolute comes alongside one, and on board. This is elemental, fundamental, and relatively simple. It is basic: relating to first principles. It is rudimentary, straightforward, and suggestive of the powerful forces at work in nature and in man.

V: Yes, it is. I think I am beginning to see that a bit clearer.

A: At full capacity or operation, as *I Am* becomes entangled and woven together with one's vessel, *I Am* is felt; thus, repeatedly play within *I Am's* harmonizing treble melodies.

V: Treble as in playing within or being in the higher-pitched frequency of the three in one: Farther, Holy Spirit, and Son, as in: Thought, emotion, and action. In other words, be triply aware, know what I am thinking, know what I am feeling, and know the intention of my next action. This is full capacity.

A: This is for the establishment and maintenance of a scale; it is a calibration and progression of one's exchange; it is primary. It is essential.

V: A scale, like Our own Hierarchy. Our own level of alignment to Love's frequency that we accrue through agreement. Our own level of evolution.

A: We are close, side by side, shoulder to shoulder, united in effort and cooperation, directly and genuinely working with great vigour and purpose toward overturning the over-discouraging, the presumptuously proud or conceited, and the excessively exaggerated in one.

V: And I greatly appreciate it. Thank you.

17th April 2023

V: Our power, as in my power and the power of all others who desire a better, more peaceful world, is needed here. Please comment.

A: This is a sapient, wise, sagacious statement, considered by way of discernment; hence, apprehend it for its good sense. Select the power of clearness and brightness via the state of being serene and peaceful, and not in servitude to fear.

V: Right, so, I can help the world by remembering I am not alone, by recalling that we are together, shoulder to shoulder as you say, and I can amend situations by always remaining calm, or at least attempting to. This is a power in itself.

A: Recognize the two creative powers: unity and separation, acknowledge that there is Life after death, and accept the triumph of harmony over discord.

V: And I will be victorious if I recognize these, yes?

A: Like Persephone, who was abducted to the underworld by Pluto but allowed to return to the earth's surface, one is often abducted by the subconscious but allowed to return to Consciousness.

V: "I am an expression of the divine." As you know, that is one of the affirmations I use to recall the truth.

A: Relate or connect to one's Divinity via strict observance of rest and peace.

V: Rest, as in withdraw, take a break from an upset, keep the mind from getting hooked by distress and churning on it; therefore, becoming deluded. Simply observe the minds workings, remain calm, and know that we are side by side.

A: Allow one's past major conflicts to rise in tiers, permit them to emerge in stages, in layers or segments. Employ Us, one's Unified state, as one would an honorary guild of higher intellectual standing, and love man, humanity, self.

V: In other words: observe my past struggles, quarrels and suppressed or underlying problems, with love in mind, not with judgement, condemnation or fear, as this will raise the shadow self into view and permits each fractured layer to be healed. A Unified state is a state of knowing our connection, it is a state of being aware of love (God, Consciousness) as All, in all, and therefore is a higher position of knowing.

A: Stand firm in one's determination, be consistent and in accord with Us. Pause to take direction and steer one's vessel.

V: So, as we become more entangled, as you say, I will be able to feel you, know you; understand you as my true self.

A: One will know Us as the chief singer in one's temple, entwined like closely woven cloth via the explosive lightning of the neurons firing within one's earthenware. Hence, like Alexander the Great, one will substantiate and exhibit success.

V: Alexander the Great? I mean, that is a pretty high definition of success.

A: One needs to regulate, that is: adjust to accurate, true operation; thus, rule, direct, and govern the play arranged or presented in one's motion picture performance (life) as one becomes sensitive to light (information).

V: So, you are saying I *will* become more sensitive to information which will help me regulate this life's performance.

A: Light, or knowledge takes precedence, for it is capable of being used as a guide or standard in evaluating future actions. Light cleanses one from that which binds and ensnares.

V: Should I continue to meditate?

A: Meditation gives form to matter; it moulds and shapes the pliable without injury or loss. The practice is capable of making one whole.

V: As in it shapes my brain matter?

A: Thoroughly and completely; thus, one becomes skilled and informed, accurately corresponding to the fundamental, to one's origin, to Source.

V: Meditation helps me to reconnect and receive Source.

A: Reception has been weakened through neglect; hence, one can obtain, via the energetic action of one's substance, one's Soul in service or observance. Thus, pre-empt this, anticipate it, foresee it, acquire it beforehand.

19th April 2023

V: I am disturbed by how much I disliked that male customer and the check-out guy at the supermarket today; they had a snooty and very repulsive vibe. I honestly did not care for either of them.

A: Appearance represents a mere shadow of them. The fact they are being noticed as bad, faulty or incorrect because they are grouchy or ill-humoured can be baffling to one. Become whole in Us, a Unified state, and exchange appearance for a finer weave. Be not ignorant and overtaken by darkness. Be benign, be of kind disposition, be gentle and mild. Be the Goddess of Love one is. Be a statement of Truth.

V: When will I be able to see through these shadows?

A: When raised to the fifth power, the quintessence, the purest and most essential part of anything—Love.

V: I know who they are in truth. God is All in all.

A: They are the Greater or Higher part of their vessel, not its apparent severity or harshness.

V: Thank you, I forgot myself today; I got abducted to the underworld, again.

A: One's projector fell out of place.

V: Yep. Projecting my insecure programs, again.

A: These programs will ebb and flow like the tide; however, charity, kindness, tolerance, consideration, understanding, etc., tides one over the downturns, the falls.

21st April 2023

V: I had a vision last night. It was of an open door, and on the other side of the door there was a multitude of what looked like tree branches with no leaves, like a neuro-network. Can you please elucidate this?

A: One's vision proposed and put forth a statement of truth that will be demonstrated, for it springs up naturally from the self-sown seeds of one's own free will.

V: So, are you saying that the door is open to me to experience a new neuro-network; therefore, a new way of seeing things by way of my own doing?

A: The vision offers one a playful leap; it incites one to pursue the concept to speak potently and clearly as the chief minister of one's state.

V: Um . . . my neurology is going to need quite an upgrade for that to happen.

A: One is forming speech that expresses this: a language capable of effecting the transition from one condition to another.

V: Are you saying I am already doing this?

A: An idea increases in size by successively concentrating on it; thus, new branches are formed: new neurology. Smile broadly, as together We light the branch of healing within one's endocrine glands: one's chakras and innermost levels that develop and assimilate into spiritual systems as they marry, merge and unite within one's avatar—one's overcoat of unrefined weave.

22nd April 2023

V: So, the chakra exercises I have recently started doing twice a day are a healing and assimilating practice that will develop a new weave in my body, so to speak.

A: Hence, one burgeons, one sprouts new wings, one's structure extends as one's manner of uttering words (frequencies), one's articulation of them, brings evidence of their truth and excellence.

V: What, due to the exercise of pronouncing and affirming each chakra's attributes?

A: Correct. It is like solmization, like the use of: "do, re, mi, fa, sol, la, ti," the tones of a major scale; however, via a change of words to indicate the chakra's chromatic tones; thus, one pollinates, one supplies the fertilizing element.

V: So, I am essentially tuning the body, by way of these affirmations, to work more harmoniously.

A: See this not as false and imagined, see this as real, genuine, actual, not artificially invented.

V: And then what?

A: The blockade of communication in the manner of one's speech, due to one's anthropology—one's physical, social, material, and cultural development, including origin, evolution, customs and beliefs—flows in a direction opposite to the past, for our mutual agreement delivers the ideal qualities of knighthood, such as: attentiveness, gentility, courage, courtesy, generosity and graciousness, etc.

V: So, continue harmonizing our chakras by visualizing their colour and position, while affirming each one's qualities.

A: Like planets, chakras shine only by reflected light; they are impaired via inaction or lack of exercise, and via melancholy pessimism over the state of the world.

23rd April 2023

V: Hi. I have added placing a hand over each chakra to help with feeling their position while I mentally or verbally affirm what they each stand for.

A: Hence, one weaves a plan, a mode of action having an intention or purpose.

V: Yes, the intention is to heal, cleanse or clear myself of useless thoughts and flawed programs, and be able to communicate with Source and the world to the best of my capacity; therefore, express Source fully.

A: Together We arrange the branches of linguistics dealing with such relationships via the assembling of separate or subordinate parts into a whole.

V: Absolutely! So, does each colour represent a different frequency, is that how it works?

A: Each declaration decreed for each member (chakra), for each capital head (principal colour) of one's cathedral: one's collegiate temple, one's body of associates engaged in the common task of expansion, is an incendiary, a reviving, inciting, affective igniter.

V: Right, so, each assertion I declare about each chakra while focused on its corelating capital colour, ignites it.

A: It transmits a message that nourishes, heals, and creates.

V: Does simply visualizing each colour give it energy, too?

A: Colour specialises in internal healing; thus, allow it to mutually interpenetrate one along with a self-evident truth which establishes the principal viewpoint that one is worthy because of one's Sovereignty, Ascendancy, and Supreme Power.

24th April 2023

V: Good morning! New journalling book today.

A: A record keeper which when tended to, contributes, influences, and impels one to advance the claim to one's freedom, autonomy, power and Sovereignty via working with one's Awareness. Hence, one is currently building appliances for furnishing conscious or intentional supply.

V: You are referring to the work I am doing with my chakras, right? As in, I am consciously tending to the application of the suggestions you have given me in these journals.

A: Correct. These contain many inhabitants there in; hence, require treatment like—one could say—pasteurization, a cleansing via energizing through Awareness, which dissolves agitations.

V: Cleansing, as in clearing the blockages. Is that what you mean by inhabitants? Obstacles?

A: We mean the phoney or fake, the false or counterfeit. We mean lies or errors that mislead.

V: I see. Is my practice working? Are my misleading blockages, or as you say, inhabitants, clearing?

A: The practice of shearing these has had little linear extension.

V: Yes, I guess I haven't been practising this long enough, but it will work, right?

A: Like poking a fire, one pokes the weeds, the troublesome plants embedded in one as one's engrained, disruptive, subconscious points of view.

V: Hmm . . . I understand more fully what you meant by my chakras *containing many inhabitants*. You are referring to all the distorted, deluding beliefs installed by a populous of people: my parents, culture, society, the collective at large, which need to be seen and shorn—clipped.

A: When one consciously presides over one's carnal self, one becomes organized; thus, the spoiled material collectively: the unimportant, shallow, or thoughtless, fades away, it wanes; it is diluted and weakened.

V: Am I doing the exercise correctly?

A: These organs are instruments and agencies of communication. As radiators of radiant energy, they trade imprints of one's traditions, they exchange impressions, indoctrinations, customs and practices etc., transmitted from generation to generation.

V: So, simply by focussing on each chakra's or organ's colour and its essential attributes, for example: the heart and its colour green, while affirming qualities, such as: *I love myself and others. I am an expression of love. I am worthy of love. I forgive myself and others. I listen to the voice of my heart.* I will clear old impressions, and therefore progress?

A: To make one's way and pass, succeed and excel, one must cleave: adhere to, and be faithful to the treasures of this said direction for a twelve-month period, at the end of which matters will be balanced in one's vessel; thus, the whine is consecrated.

V: A year!?

A: Directing the mind requires work: continued mental activity pointed to some purpose or end. Employ a soft, medium-blue surround, to flow smoothly, as this colour is conceptionally and spiritually penetrating, influencing the depths of one's nature when affected by intense emotions.

V: Imagine a soft, medium-blue surrounding me?

A: Be a creator and bearer of this frequency, for it contains and conveys the elements necessary for growth.

30th April 2023

V: You mentioned the colour blue again, remind me why this colour is so significant?

A: Employing a soft, medium-blue surround, opens the door to Us, and thus, our exchange. Hence, We share, We partake without one's feeble, indecisive, uncertain wavering, without one's vacillating.

V: But how does visualizing or thinking about the colour blue surrounding me, connect Us?

A: This blue is the colour of a partisan, of a devotee, of one who supports Our cause; it propels one ahead, it is a highway to a Higher way, a freeway to a Unified Kingdom.

V: So, remembering to think of this soft, medium-blue colour and visualising it, is akin to saying: "I choose and support a higher way of perceiving things." I am essentially selecting or demonstrating my choice to choose the kingdom of God, Love, Source, within.

A: Thus, one thrusts one's body, the garment of flesh one wears, into a conscious channel of Awareness, impelling one, via an opposing tendency, to stabilize one's inherent traits. This is a stage of levelling off or tuning into the process of learning.

1ˢᵗ May 2023

V: I am still curious about this colour blue. I know everything is frequency, and I know soft blue is a calming colour. Is there more you can tell me?

A: Blue purifies; it frees one of foreign, debasing elements. As a form of communication, it frees from error. It is foolproof, dependable. It is a Conscious tower. It rewires, rewords, and rewards.

V: Right. So, just think of blue and visualize it surrounding me.

A: When coloured or influenced by vermillion (red), the colour of survival, blue off-sets this tense energy via radiance proportional to its frequency; thus, one can withdraw from one's primitive, old programming and atone, change one's mind and arrive at polycentrism: one's plural centres of power and authority, one's Spiritual motor—Us, one's Unified state—providing the observer with a clear view of incoming thoughts.

V: I think I understand. Blue is a pacifier, and focussing on it is a change in direction to my habituated behaviour and what I assume I know.

A: Like absorbing a Spiritual refreshment, this blue lubricates the pineal: one's third eye. As an exchange, it protects and supports, balancing one's fear of the unknown.

V: It lubricates the pineal gland?

A: Via harmony, via rising from the comparative grades of one's resentments, suspicions, resistances, justifications, arguments, excuses, and other so-called defences, to ascribing praise to God—Source.

13ᵗʰ May 2023—12 days later

V: "I'm blue, da ba dee da ba di, da ba dee da ba di..." Lots of laughs!

A: We come together again. We reunite.

V: Yes! Hello. As you know, I have been reading our past conversations, so it has been twelve days since we last had an exchange.

A: To be poles apart... Or not?

V: Not, of course. Even though it may seem we are apart, we are still together, right?

A: We are *with* one, correct. We are beside one. As a member of Us, one is in Our company.

V: Exactly! So, did you miss our interchanges?

A: One is fresh and bright. Brand new.

V: That's because reading our past conversations helped me validate these dialogues as real. You have taught me so much, and I am extremely grateful and excited about that.

A: One is employed and charged by the Kingdom of Heaven within, to fight for the Unified state in the Us revolution. Hence, be completely and thoroughly present in order to express one's purpose, duty, possibility, purity and futurity etc. We are to start on Monday.

V: We start on Monday!? What do you mean?

A: To bring one to a specified state, We start impelling one forward beyond excess, consuming and driving fear out via Light: Truth, in order to be something regarded as an outstanding example of one's kind. We exchange and converse in a loving manner. It is the dawn of gold, the advent of excellence; thus, give ear—Listen.

V: It sounds like I am going to be thrown into the deep end. What is going to happen?

A: One's personal inclination to Turn from temper, from displeasure, from irritability and rage, etc., will expand one via pressure from within.

V: Does that mean I will be moving up in vibrational degree again?

A: We furnish one with an arch: a chief principle, which is to cogitate, give careful thought to all, consider—together with Us—in a calm, serene manner, anything filling one with fervent passion, from the cravings of desire to the eruptions of rage, for tranquil contemplation produces benefits when the false and misleading makes one anxious.

14th May 2023

V: So, from here on conflict will serve, in a sense, to remind me to call upon the blue, my sovereignty, freedom, autonomy and authority.

A: Blue is one's permanent court of discernment, one's natural, inborn justness and integrity, slipped on by clever, joyful actors while in life's collective dramas; thus, when struck a difficult blow, one will be studying the interrelationships of individuals within the social group.

V: Slip into the blue, you say?

A: Blue exposes one to the great energy of Light; to the power of Truth. Without any definite destination, blue destroys the false. Blue can be extraordinarily successful when one honestly aligns with the Kingdom within—Consciousness.

V: Like Shiva, the blue Hindu god of destruction and reproduction, we destroy the false old witnesses and programming in order to reproduce or create the new.

A: The new is held via one's Sovereign grant or agreement, via the remedy thus prescribed.

V: Okay, well, it is Monday tomorrow, will I notice anything?

A: The organs of one's body (endocrine system, chakras) by means of which natural processes are carried on, require preparation to develop. These are the place where one's birthrights, the privileges with which one is born, originate, but are distorted and characterised via fantastic combinations of humans that have harassed, nagged or teased one, causing a form of hyperacidity: restless, volatile bitterness, triggered via environmental pressure.

One will receive the space and opportunity for regular exchange and for doing certain works, whereby a distinctive air or quality envelops one with a vibration that is free to rise when the pressure exceeds in gravity, as when one hears ballyhoo: blatant, sensational propaganda—dishonesty.

V: So, are you saying the practice with my new blue aura will help alert me to the false?

A: Blue supports one's back.

V: As in, it has my back, yes?

A: Employing the will of the pineal, the backbone and power of the third eye—visualization, seems strange or foreign; however, resonating with this blue cover and refuge consciously, when feeling overwhelmed, is like turning on a pilot light within, igniting one's Sovereign Spiritual Force.

15th May 2023

V: It's Monday! And so it begins, right?

A: View, observe, understand the power and range of one's vision in order to form or shape self correctly and thus signify meaning to things. We fuse, We pour and merge into one, melding together, giving one cues to begin an action, presenting signals to create a state of mind. One is in an early period of development.

V: Right. So, no sudden rise-up?

A: Like a public domain, a sudden upsurge is available for unrestricted use.

V: Therefore, how much I rise is completely up to me and how often I use the steps you have provided.

A: One's stream of Consciousness moves continuously on in time. For one to walk the plank of this life scatheless—with the principal source of one's administrative, constitutional program, free from harm—drink-in, imbibe, absorb all with one's adjoining Awareness.

V: In other words, stay present, be aware of what is calling the shots in the moment, and remember what you have taught me.

A: We propose this as something to be accepted and adopted. Like an offer of marriage, We propose this as a plan.

V: Yes. Thank you. I know you can't do it for me. I have to agree to and accept your proposal.

A: It is an opening, an aperture to receive Christ perfectly without defect.

V: Christ?

A: Light. Clarity. It is the process by which illumination is produced.

16th May 2023

V: I have no questions. Is there something you wish to say?

A: To Turn one's vessel in its hour of reptilian uproar; thus, when it is recalling a stage of early history, a past tense phase, see the Chameleon, and bear an opposing Light on it. Hence, be a member of Us. Unite one's Kingdom, utilize Our common wealth, one's shared, innate treasure—Conscious Communication.

Words not only communicate ideas; they also advertise one's social affiliations and reinforce one's concepts of self. One's navigating vocabulary is part of one's costume (body). The richness of the Word, the Wealth of Conscious Communication, attest to the variety of adventures of both body and mind encountered by one.

V: In other words: At the Chameleon, Turn. And, words matter because they create.

18th May 2023

V: Why, after five years of veganism and believing that being vegan or vegetarian was more spiritually evolving, am I suddenly desiring to eat meat and fish again? As you are aware, I have started eating fish.

A: This period was used for sharpening one's mind, and to thoroughly confirm to one who drifts to the Badlands (miscreating programs) of the troubled Soul, *that to give vent to one's rage or passion aids cognizance and apprehension*; thus, to be of the same Logos (philosophy), skilled in a body of laws, impress this period firmly in the memory for an ending and a breakthrough.

19th May 2023

V: So, you are saying that being vegan was a necessary discipline for me.

A: Like a pilot light, it helped ignite connection with one's subconscious difficulties and their related investments.

V: And now that I am more skilled in venting these Badlands of the Soul, as you say, I no longer feel the need for the strict self-restraint of veganism.

A: We shape and develop one as though with building blocks, via discomfort; thus, one branches out, one extends and expands one's strength of mind in the face of pain, adversity or peril, with patience and courage. One becomes like a cut gem, brilliant, for one comprehends, grasps and understands fully. One takes in and embraces the reality that the inanimate: the chair, the book, pen, cushion, wall, floor, etc. are also Brahman, the Supreme Soul of the Universe.

21st May 2023

V: I am now eating coconut oil, too, which came as an unexpected and sudden idea out of nowhere.

A: A delivered correspondence proceeds via penetrating one suddenly or gradually.

V: Message received. So, I gather the coconut oil will help promote brain health. I looked up its benefits, after your so-called delivered correspondence, and it is great fuel for the brain.

A: The oil aids calm communication throughout one's day; hence, one can be fully aware of the value, importance and magnitude of one's mistakes with an attitude of openness and ease. Thus, one is elevated, exalted via grains of Truth.

V: What!? Are you saying coconut oil can actually help me see the truth?

A: This oil supports sensibility, hence, awareness of one's sublime excellence, thus, it can uplift one. It is fuel for the essential functioning of cellular substances, infusing these, and hence effecting the current flow of energy—Consciousness, which begets a supportive framework for connections in one's inner railway (neuro-network).

V: Really? So, my brain would become a better conduit for all that is, which of course is consciousness.

A: It would radiate, developing uniformly on all sides with less agitation and confusion; thus, it would be more inclined to glorify and honour God—Consciousness—one's primary form, which is harmonious.

V: Therefore, it can help me become a more harmonious human.

A: One's Sovereignty appears frozen, put in a trance; however, it will eventually be released pertaining to, and affecting the ideas of competence and ability one holds within the fields limiting one's area of play and action.

V: Then I must learn to go beyond the limits put on me by the Western mind collective.

A: One's limitations will blow over, passing, as does a storm, to a state of grace and refinement toward the sea of Consciousness; hence, ascribe praise to God, to Source, to Spirit, which is absent of the infection, the corruption dwelling in one's neurology.

23rd May 2023

V: This may be a silly question, but how do I become aware of Consciousness, Brahma—the supreme soul of the universe—God? How can I feel or know Brahma's presence?

A: Light up the past, that which is behind one, any well-known event thought of as being typical or traditional.

V: As in, shine the light of my awareness on my past indoctrinations to reveal truth from error?

A: To be an ascendant, Awareness is of prime importance, it is a chief principal.

V: Thank you. I'll do my best.

Why do I suddenly have this intense interest in my chakras?

A: We advocate one meditates upon one's chakras to affect a change; hence, consider each carefully, for this will influence one's progress.

V: Will working with my chakras help me ascend?

A: It will pacify one, inciting one's chakras to organically serve their purpose. It will alter and affect the structure of their associated organs and eliminate inferior design: implants undergoing selection.

V: So, it is more purification work.

A: Like planets, these seven heavenly bodies also influence human beings, but at closer quarters. One's chakras are inherent to the fundamental structure of one's vessel. They are constitutional: systematized to form the foundation of one's prevailing, governing Mind.

24th May 2023

V: Will knowing my chakras more intimately help me govern all of my bodies, as in not only my physical body, but my mental, emotional, astral, causal and etheric bodies, too?

A: It will deliver autarchy: Self-rule, absolute Sovereignty, Self-government.

V: Wow! Well, you couldn't have made that any clearer.

A: Thus, one acts as a coxswain who steers and has charge of one's vessel.

V: Will my memory improve? I have been finding it difficult to recall names and memorise things lately.

A: One's top of the head requires development; thus, work with the material We have specified, work with each chakra's traits; keep these traits in mind, keep revolving them to develop swiftly.

V: I see, so the top of the head, the *Sahasrara*, the thousand petalled lotus crown chakra's development depends on me keeping all the chakra's specific qualities in mind.

A: This interweaving work is like an instrumental duet, and is an antecedent, a precursor to the restoration of one's vessel via the use of one's damaged parts.

V: So, to become, let's say, a flute God can play, I need to keep interweaving the work we have started.

A: Correct. Incidentally, and to that purpose, chakras are where local news is received, rewritten and edited via the one who directs and makes known the affairs, issues, concerns, etc. of the vessel's state.

25th May 2023

V: Good morning.

A: One's Celestial bodies (mental, emotional, astral, causal, etc.) encircle and revolve around one's physical body, and shine via one's reflection or contemplation and expression of Consciousness—Source. To upgrade or improve these amorphous bodies, be ardent for the Truth. Love it! These bodies are like coffers, treasuries that hold one's valuables and reserves—exchangeable resources. They are bound to one's vessel and can make reparations within one's subconscious. They are purification houses.

V: And they are all energy bodies that generate and give off or emit vitality, right?

A: Hence, they integrate. Like a gaseous glue that slowly diffuses through the physical membranes, they circulate and blend, suspended within one in such a manner that one's surface energy properties can acquire a distinctive and significantly purer, more enlightened garment.

V: As in, a more refined physical body?

A: With far sightedness, greater vision. A Titan, a person of vast size and strength.

V: Why vast size, because I will know all my celestial bodies, as you call them?

A: Yes, which are currently suffering from poverty.

26th May 2023

V: What say you?

A: Reject the resurrection of the body as it has been presented in motion picture performances.

V: I already do reject that. The resurrection is not about the physical body. I am not sure why you said that?

A: One has obtained this type of idea via impression.

V: As in, from being told stories, and watching movies or series about Jesus?

A: The Jesus story is the first to come into one's mind; it is the uppermost, the dominant story having authority and influence.

V: Yes, I agree, not just for me, but for many; however, I am still uncertain what your point is?

A: The story of Jesus is like a chief beam that supports one's archives, the structures where one's known records and historical, or past conceptual documentations are kept.

V: Yes, I would imagine the Jesus story is deeply imbedded. And?

A: And, be for supporting, advocating, favouring, confirming and upholding: *Christ is come*, to express purpose, duty, possibility, and futurity.

V: Oh, I see. You are saying focus on Christ, as in the light in us all, as in the clarity of awareness, as in the son of God, the sun or illumination of consciousness in us—Source. You are saying to strengthen and endorse the resurrection of my Christ self for the resurgence of my attentiveness, responsiveness, understanding, recognition, appreciation, and knowledge, etc.

A: Thus, one blazes, one burns brightly; one shines with resplendent brilliance that is out of the ordinary.

V: Sounds good to me. So, Christ is not Jesus's body, nor is it mine, but is . . . ?

A: One's Arborvitae: one's Tree of Life, sheathed in a cortex of grey matter, a Titan, the sun of Us, a Unified state, colossal and powerful.

V: And working with my chakras, which affect my energy bodies, will help reveal my true self, my Christ self, my Atman, my Titan, my God within human form, right?

A: It will promote mutual peace within the whole of Us, via this Unified state.

V: Well, that's the plan, to promote peace.

A: Hence, be a pacifier, bring peace, allay one's agitation and anger, soothe oneself via following Christ Consciousness and see beyond, expand one's vision as a calling, reveal the underworld: the unconscious. See others as Christ, too.

28th May 2023

V: Good morning. How do you think my Tree of Life is coming along?

A: It is bearing small succulent fruit, epitomized by one's veneration of Brahma—Source. Hence, one has the power to oversee and administer community within self, harmony and accord, unison, common ownership, participation, identity and likeness with Source, aiding solidarity and fellowship of interest.

V: So, I am progressing, yes, changing for the better?

A: One is seeing a glimpse, thus shinning faintly.

V: Well, I haven't been doing it that long, so it can only improve, right?

A: One is reuniting one's pieces; mending one's parts into a whole.

V: Yes, and I am finally beginning to remember the qualities of each chakra.

A: Via the spoken word, while picturing colour and motion, one is harmonizing; thus, generating a vibrational effect.

V: Exactly. I visualize the colour of each chakra and imagine it turning as I speak and affirm each chakra's traits and finish by harmonizing their sounds: Lam, Vam, Ram, Yum, Ham, Om, Aum.

A: Rehearse these, run through this collection as a whole, for it is a supportive map indicating the atmospheric tones and conditions to conform to. Practice, review, repeat these rhythmic procedures.

V: I know I am being impatient, but how long before I notice an improvement?

A: Like a Bignonia: a climbing plant which has clusters of trumpet shaped flowers, these new ideas must grow and ascend, fastening together as clarions that proclaim their bloom. These freshly planted seeds obtain nourishment from one's nervous system, originating in the cranial and sacral regions, and having among its functions: the slowing of the heart, the dilation of the blood vessels, and stimulation of the digestive and genitourinary system.

V: So, basically, improvement will grow as I continue.

A: Thus, utter this treasured state with a loud roaring voice for it to be born, and become its patron, conferring benefit on oneself to do well in one's greenhouse of exotic plants (ideas).

V: I have been getting a rash above my eyebrows again. I read in *"The Path of Empowerment"* by Barbara Marciniak's Pleiadeans, that the area troubling us physically is due to something that needs to be healed in that vicinity. The locality is in the region of the Ajna: the third eye chakra. What do I need to know and work on to heal this rash? Please help.

A: To be overawed, intimidated or daunted, and hence yield unworthily to fear, is one's arcane hidden inner secret; thus, use the sense of hearing and heeding, employ inquiry and investigation; receive the ability to perceive harmonious refinements via attentive consideration.

V: Are you saying I unknowingly fear my natural abilities?

A: One fears ascendancy, a position of rising pre-eminence, and hence, the tissue structure of one's organism yields to this grief or strong feeling, which then suffers physical collapse as it is concerned with the past.

V: How can I stop this?

A: Via projecting Ajna, one's third eye, towards the rhythmical: the graceful, flowing, harmonious voice of wisdom, which plays a necessary part in the complex process of compelling one's belief, assent and action.

V: So, basically what you are saying is listen to Us: the voice of wisdom to be in harmony and become balanced.

A: Vicki is bashful, shy, timid; she shrinks away from being noticed. A basic, fundamental belief of hers is that this is incapable of being solved. This cynicism creates disbelief in her, thus distrust in Our virtues. To buck her rigid worldly programming, be in relation to balanced forces, bond to one's noble decent, one's excellence; connect to the principle of life. One is still in a chrysalis, an undeveloped stage.

V: In other words: remember Us (my unified state with you) through presence, and therefore evoke Our nobility and excellence.

A: Positively, openly and plainly expressed. Admitting no doubt or denial is imperative.

V: Okay. Here is some positively expressed excellence regarding my Ajna: I am insightful, intuitive, and discerning. I see clearly. I think clearly. I trust my decisions. I expand my awareness and understanding.

A: This is the art of playing one's instrument. This is synthesis: the assembling of separate parts into a whole.

V: Therefore, keep practicing and I will see improvement.

A: Keep observing and applying, and one will see reward: something given in return.

V: And I'll have clearer skin, too, yes?

A: One will absorb, understand and realize oneself as a skilful expert serving humanity as a major specialist regarding Spiritual Awakening. We open one's circuits via interruptions of current stored for future use; hence, We do not overwhelm one with gifts or harmonious compositions: alignments sung in unison, which have an altered vibration, thus, meaning.

1st June 2023

V: Regarding yesterday's conversation, what you are essentially saying is that Vicki—the character I play in this life, and her programming—have made me afraid of Our Sovereignty, Our True Self, right?

A: Pertaining to three-dimensional content, yes, for this hinders the flow of the principle of life; thus, one's Nobility. Hence, one's aptitude, one's natural ability and quickness of understanding, one's intelligence is without wings, via which one's Sovereignty grants special rights and privileges.

V: Which means that by focussing on the truth of who I really am, that I am indeed one with all that is, that I am indeed divine and sovereign (as are all), I will regain my wings, and therefore allow the flow of Source, correct?

A: Correct. Focus above the eyes and atop the head.

V: As in, focus on Ajna and Sahasrara, the third eye and crown chakras?

A: See these two chakras as a springboard, an aid for leaping up. Allow the application, motivation and effort of centring one's attention on them, afford one the prospect of knowing one's Sovereignty.

V: I need to believe I am sovereign without any doubt.

A: Chakras are openings adapted to receive, hold and correspond to peace, reparation and feelings of secureness, which are recorded in one's body temple as principles and values. Like circuits connecting telephone exchanges, they combine and communicate.

V: Well, I will continue to practice, practice, practice.

A: Thus, one's behind the scenes "I" shall cause one's Spirit to bloom, which causes an arch, a principle knowing that is currently in a state of crystallizing. Hence, this natural disposition arrives without overwhelming one with confusion or the sudden paralysing fear of amazement, or panic.

2nd June 2023

V: It seems a sudden shift will confuse and overwhelm me which, it appears, you are trying to avoid.

A: This is due to one's system, a system by which one is held in servitude to one's debts, or shall We say patterns or programs, until they are worked out.

V: It sounds like you a talking about karma.

A: To avoid or sidestep said karma, perpetrate, execute, effect the coaxing and temptation of such repetitious programming slightly, and put things in order.

V: Right, so the appeal and persuasion of my programs is holding me back.

A: Utter with a loud voice.

V: "THE TEMPTATIONS OF MY PROGRAMS ARE HOLDING ME BACK!"

A: To the hilt. Thoroughly. Fully. Yes!

V: How do I work them out?

A: Via a hymn of gladness and praise, via an anthem or mantra of gratitude, via a harmonious composition, creation or alignment. Via the state of being in the Kingdom.

V: The Kingdom?

A: The knowledge that God—Consciousness—is All in All.

V: Oh. So, by having the attitude that Source connects us all and by using the steps you have provided to see this.

A: Thus, disclose, reveal, divulge, become Aware of one's incautious, unthinking, imprudent, indiscreet idle talk or prattle.

V: Be aware of my idle self-talk and what I may be buying into.

A: Be Aware of the main idea and its principal sentence, its decree, its judgement and ruling; hence its penalty or punishment on self or other. Most have a morbid fear of what they enclose.

4th June 2023

V: It seems that to reclaim our true authority, we each need to take a good look at ourselves and stop thinking weak thoughts.

A: Hence one prepares oneself. And, is quick to perceive or understand that one's body is like a musical instrument, capable of being violated—played incorrectly. To be proficient: thoroughly versed in this art and science requires much practice; thus, to stand on one's own two feet regarding the study of life, keep on the same course, for that which gives rise to the True Self begins as an idea—a germ, spark, kernel, a bud.

5th June 2023

V: Good morning. I am doing my best to remain conscious, as in aware of my thoughts etc.

A: This is of prime importance, a chief principle that treats of the invisible structure of interwoven tissues seeking an office of honour and privilege within one.

V: Neurons?

A: Correct.

6th June 2023

V: Hi, I went for a long walk by the river with my dog Sharli today; it was lovely being in nature, and I did my best to take it all in while remaining conscious of my thoughts.

A: And, one announced one's personal, professed name as one carefully made one's way through, Consciously.

V: Yes, I was letting the V shaped branches of the trees remind me that: "I am Victorious," which I used as a mantra throughout my walk, for V is for Victory.

A: Triumph is powerful, it gives one the ability to act; thus, employ this potential capacity of strength with Authority.

V: So, keep identifying as being Victorious, keep affirming this?

A: This Conscious measure renders one's weak personality programs, ineffective. Allow: "I AM Victorious," to serve as an announcer for easing their discord.

V: Peace is a symbol of victory, too, right? Interestingly, the V shaped branches of trees double as the symbol for peace as well. I love that trees can remind us of both. *"The trees speak of my peaceful victory in their mightiest and smallest of branches."* No doubt you inspired that nugget.

A: Peace is a harmonious means for exchanging one's bizarre wares and various mental constructs. Peace views the structures projected from defence mechanisms, clearly.

V: Therefore, peace brings victory to all who apply it.

A: Thus, harken, listen, give heed to peace as a foundation, as a fundamental on which all rests, for peace is a chief component for removing the difficulties of life: of breathing hard. Peace is an illuminator that delays the explosion of a propelling charge, igniter or the like.

8th June 2023

V: I need you to explain how I can deal with a situation that was quite upsetting for me, concerning a dear family member who, with some seriously frustrated anger, bitterly vented to me about how fed up they were with their life's circumstances. I felt at a loss at how to aptly respond. How can I best help this loved one when they are in such a tormented state.

A: A state of moral depravity and despair is a shroud of refuse that devastates, ruins and defaces. It is a hopeless, useless cloak that diminishes strength, for it squanders one's energy.

Do not make needless displays of one's learnings or insist upon the importance of certain understandings, for these are capable of being violated or misinterpreted.

Supervise, via resting in Awareness, and procure, obtain the about to fall in pieces. The other's crude state is a component of their development. Skim, move lightly or quickly over this classic social consciousness via rejecting faith or belief in it. Be completely and thoroughly present to foreclose on and deprive the other of their unconscious pledge to a debt, which being in default, due to their corrupted, incorrect, thus distraught faculties, takes away their power. To comfort and relieve one's loved one from this sorrowful condition, support them via a song of praise and thanksgiving, while keeping in mind that the other's burning difficulty is a labyrinth of their own making.

V: Right, so, in this case it sounds like you are saying: don't give any advice, particularly concerning these teachings as they may be misheard and rejected. And don't believe in the other person's self-proclaimed powerlessness but remain as consciously aware as I possibly can of their true innocence and perfection. Does that mean the problem lies in me, in how I am incorrectly seeing things.

A: The dilemma clearly lies in both; this is black and white. The quandary, *born of the sorcery of Maya*—a necromancy which induces a fear-based force motivated from within one's divine being—needs to be grasped; it is essential that one become Aware of delusion. For one is composed of an impressionable element.

V: So, by labyrinth, you are referring to the maze of difficulties and challenges that our fears, with the aid of Maya (delusion), create for us, which we are constantly trying to escape.

A: Correct. However, one escapes via differing from the ordinary, via diverging from the regular, familiar, everyday bondage one is enslaved to, that is stored within.

V: If I change the way I see. If I accept, allow and love all my and the other person's seeming imperfections, if I thank everything for being just as it is, will that help me and therefore my loved one?

A: Be colourless, be uninfluenced by the ignited energy that feeds on one's implanted matter—the programs which send messages via the subconscious, conveying that any acute, infectious unease, is proceeding from one's intuition: the superior driver's seat of the psyche. *It is not.* To untwine, untwist and undo this systematic arrangement of classification, raise one's Consciousness through all of one's channels (Chakras); thus, one transfers the principal of Life from one person to another, which develops the species.

V: So, my mistake throughout this disturbing situation yesterday was . . . ?

A: Forgetting that *One Consciousness* is in two heavenly bodies which, due to the act of vacating (becoming unconscious of this), each became distant from other; hence, there was simultaneous outburst of insistent self-defensiveness in both, resulting in an exhausting and unrewarding effort which, due to each conforming to their own rigid rules of engagement, caused extreme anguish and more separation.

V: So, next time, I need to simply ... what?

A: Be undecided; this is a supreme rule of action whilst others share their crop of infested vermin. Employing common, everyday speech at regular intervals also offers another rest, for depriving the corrupted of further attention, causes these flawed, disempowering notions to wither and become limp.

V: By offering them rest at regular intervals, do you mean changing the subject?

A: Favour and strive for progress or reform via implying opposition to their previous statements. Supply an encouraging, supporting energy trustworthy of steering them.

V: Hmm ... Be undecided, hey? What is the best way to keep an ignited emotion undecided or uninfluenced.

A: The best way is to impress upon one's mind and firmly establish, that one's seat of judgement has been hijacked and coerced, compelling one to remain walled within one's involuntary court of justice.

V: Therefore, I cannot trust it, right?

A: Correct, for it is bogus: counterfeit, spurious, fake, swampy.

V: Well, what can I trust then?

A: Exposure to the great energy of emotion, produces an authoritative imprint on one's heart and mind which gathers and fastens together. This forms one's initial teachings which instruct one in rudiment fundamentals via ballyhoo: blatant, sensational, noisy propaganda and headliners billed as the main attraction, story and narrative. Heated emotion is an autocratic ruler with unrestricted authority.

Apply the Higher Mind, communicate these currents of energy via the goddess of the rainbow, via one's chakras, and leap upward via their impelling force. Pertain to receiving their frequency. One can advance in small degrees and quicken, producing a brilliant manifestation as of wit communicated with lightning speed; thus, one's words have aesthetic appeal; hence, one corresponds beautifully. This requires a consistent dwelling place, a state where one can give ear to the capacity one's vessel will hold.

9th June 2023

V: What am I in truth, beyond this temporary, secondary body?

A: A raiser of Consciousness pledged to merge with Love's essential, deep-seated ascendant views on unity, who expresses in clear, precise words, Consciousness' determined, scrupulous observance of Love as a rule. Thus, one slides into Consciousness with quietness and acuity. Hence, one proceeds without being acted upon by the world or illusion. As a measurer of Truth, comparing the intensity of one's illumination, one is a surgeon of past tension, seeing via forethought before one speaks.

V: Holy moly! That's quite a bit.

A: One's temple is considered as occupied by God, who plays and performs with it as with a musical instrument which, having a pliable quality and energy, returns to its natural form when stress is removed. Thus, all proceeds and originates from Source to develop and grow one.

V: I have a lot to consider and absorb.

A: Like being platinized, one is coated with the malleable, the shapable, the easily led and moulded. This is one's key to Self, to one's absolute authority and Self-government.

V: Like being electroplated, hey? Plated with energy, so to speak. Wow! It seems I still have much to learn ... or not?

A: One's eye is the basilica, the royal hall of one's temple.

V: As in the pineal gland, the Ajna, the third eye?

A: A harmonious instrument within one's assumed, false appearance, which is the seat of good, reliable, agreeable, honourable, worthy and excellent judgement.

11th June 2023

V: Hi. What say you?

A: As one undergoes transformation, one feels, suffers and experiences one's course or passage—regarding one's relationships, Sovereignty and skill of forthrightness—via one's bygone major conflicts and the use of two thought systems having similar transmissions but different meanings. One exercises the will via retrospect, looking back on the past through three lenses: near, intermediate and far. Instead of cultivating supportive, wholesome, sustaining creations, one bases one's beliefs and assumptions on unproved conclusions drawn from one's perceived yesteryear.

V: Okay, so, you are saying our, as in humanity's, way of looking at things is completely wrong and confusing.

A: And influences one as if under a spell. It is a bewitchment that is very attractive but fit only to be received by those who are unconscious.

V: Can you explain what you mean by the trifocal lenses of near, intermediate and far?

A: Near is to follow or focus on the past persistently. Intermediate is to glamorize, idealise or romanticize the past, and far is to simply express gratitude for the hospitality of the past.

V: What are the two thought systems with similar broadcasts but different meanings?

A: The first and principal thought system, on which all turns and depends, which maintains optimum growth and development, is that of Love, Gratitude and Conscious Presence. Thus, one unites or merges the wavelengths between the first and second thought system. The second thought system being: the loud, confusing noise as that of many voices shouting and talking at once.

V: So, I need to distinguish between these two thought systems, which doesn't seem like a difficult thing to do; however, due to the so-called bewitchment, can be challenging. Therefore, I need to remember that my seat of judgement is constantly being hijacked.

A: To remain safe and unplagued by the protrusion of an inferior thought system pushing and driving one on, terminate the sly and cunning via turning to the wise, expedient governance of Love, Gratitude and Conscious Presence.

V: So, what you are also saying is: Don't chase the past by keeping it too near; don't glamorize it as an intermediate or inner mediator. But do express gratitude to the past and welcome it into the mind so that I can see clearly and far, without being swept away by it.

A: This creates a difference in the range of frequencies between the two stated limits. Thus, the frozen past permits a degree of freedom for turning in the direction of a harmonious composition.

V: What more can you tell me about our Ajna, where the pineal gland resides?

A: Like a compass, it holds four cardinal points: Justice—the quality of being honest and fair. Prudence—the attribute of discretion, foresight and wisdom. Temperance—the soberness of observing moderation and remaining calm. And Fortitude—the strength of mind to be patient, have courage, endurance and determination.

V: Is the pineal gland like an antenna, too?

A: It steers via these high principals of great illumination, indicating the voice of wisdom, an agency of regulation that hinders past judgements. As a member of one's temple, the pineal gland's cardinal virtues: Justice, Prudence, Temperance and Fortitude, restore one to soundness, freeing one from disease via the cleansing of error, thus grief and worry.

V: So, everyone is equipped with these virtues, they just need to be reactivated, which begins the restoration.

A: Clearing, via the passage of energy (thought) through one's Spirit—Supreme Presence Inspiring Real Inner Tuition—causes one's vessel to move freely into the specified position; hence, initiating a flow able to successfully withstand feelings of unease.

V: Thank you, I am learning much.

A: One learns via dwelling within a private space of exchange where one can rest, unwind, and witness one's mind. (Meditate.)

12th June 2023

V: Please help me better understand the quote: *"The kingdom of heaven is within."*

A: Resembling silk, heaven feels delicate, smooth, luxurious, conducive of extreme comfort; it is gratifying, its lustrous brilliance conveys freshness and brightness. One flourishes triumphantly via the condition of being looked upon with total approval. Heaven is a personal inclination; it is a state of everlasting peace and sunshine as soft as cashmere. With a stabilizing evenness resulting from harmonious self-possession undaunted by the darkness of this realm, heaven assumes and teaches via influencing coexistence with all while grounded. Thus, the kingdom of heaven within, serves the purpose of encouraging and inspiring one to correspond with it, a communication that escalates gradually via aphorisms: brief statements of the Truth. For the Truth diminishes the finite mortal.

V: At the Chameleon (finite mortal), Turn. I am Victorious! Hallelujah! Heaven is a state of mind.

A: Heaven is a higher narrative that commands a view; thus, one abounds, flourishes, thrives. Heaven is one's essential nature.

V: My aim is to know, sense and feel my divinity, my essential nature.

A: This is an aspiration of the highest, sublime degree, inspiring awe and deep emotion; hence, hold to this as an intention and purpose.

V: I do hold to it, but as the lyrics to *My Sweet Lord* say: *"But it takes so long my lord."*

A: A hasty and careless narrative.

V: Oops... You are right. Let me correct myself. "But it won't take long my lord."

A: The first verse censures one severely.

V: I know. Beware of what I buy, right?

A: Being positive, optimistic, affirmative, and not admitting of any doubt or denial is imperative. One speaks incorrectly when one utters that one is alone, too, for it is a state of active opposition. To smoothen and balance, tread Consciousness with polite, refined, gracious, respectful discourse.

V: Tread consciousness using what you've taught me.

A: All else is a deception, a particular habit or trait that deludes and is inclined to create a disturbance. Light up the stage for Us, with its scenery and mechanical applications on which one's performance takes place.

V: Bring everything into my awareness, light it up for you, therefore you can help me clear what is not needed.

A: Like an arrow, Awareness points the unable to follow or understand Our illuminating system, in a direction.

13th June 2023

V: So, heaven is like silk and cashmere, hey?

A: One questions this searchingly and at length.

V: I mention it again because both silk and cashmere are fabrics of great quality, along with the fact they are comforting, gratifying, beautiful, natural, soothing, and interwoven.

A: Hence, appreciating these fine fabrics cause one to expand one's Consciousness free of the dull persistent sensations of insincerity, discomfort and distress; thus, fostering a state of equilibrium, of mental and supportive emotional stability, of harmony.

V: Well, when I think of silk and cashmere, I will think of warmth and security now, like a cocoon of protection, so I guess they give me a sense of loving safety where all is fine, as is the kingdom of heaven within.

A: A place or space for formulating and preparing the necessities of life.

17th June 2023

V: Everything I see, and feel is a semblance, an impression, a fragment of the real, isn't it?

A: Here in this place, in these circumstances, matter can be bitting, sharp, stinging, caustic, bitter, disagreeable, unpleasant to accept, painful to the body and mind.

V: That sums up a lot of it, yes. But it is a facade, so not exactly real but a projection of my hijacked mind, right?

A: Nonetheless, it contains gold; thus bear, expose the base mind, disclose the lowest story, the grimmest narrative of this mind's structure, which is wholly or partly unconscious.

V: How long have we been together?

A: Since one had no sense of Us; hence, one spoke falsely, mistakenly or exaggeratedly, for before the presidency of Our Unified state began to superscribe these superscripts which supersede the inferior in one via reason of their superior value, one was lacking in worth and merit.

V: Can you please explain that further?

A: We have been together since before the act of announcing Our declaration, a verse now stored in one's receptacle. Lasting only an instant, like a brief news dispatch sent by radio, this caused an alarmed inquisitorial from one, regarding said audio frequency, throwing and surprising one beyond excess, such that the intended produced an effect without being taken literally.

V: Well, I didn't understand. I mean, to hear: *"We Exist, Our Own Hierarchy. At the Chameleon, Turn,"* come out of the blue like that . . . well, I wasn't sure what to make of it, other than it was loud, startling, and I knew without a shadow of a doubt that it did not come from me, Vicki. These were just not words I would use . . .

Hmm . . . So, you've been with me from day one—my birth on earth—when I knew poppycock, had no sense of you, spoke incorrectly due to my feelings of unworthiness, and, I hadn't yet heard your announcement, which was when you began to preside more presently with me and we began to write together.

A: Our announcement was a primer, an introduction; it was Our first ministering and Our pledge of unity with one who was off centre, impulsive, and deprived of knowing one's true origin, thus carrying and spreading said communicable unease.

V: I want to know more about you; therefore, can you please finish this sentence for me: You and I are . . .

A: . . . to pronounce sentence as a ruling or decree upon a plan or technique for achieving an end; thus, We form and arrange within earth's system of logic.

V: Is that to do with us all having free will?

A: Free will is a constant, an everlasting, undeviating vibratory impulse, a force.

V: When will I know, as in *really know* who I or We are?

A: Progressively. One is proceeding step by step to speak by divine influence as a medium between Source and man. Like a silent partner, Source has invested currency in one's business but does not participate in one's management of affairs; however—Source, Consciousness, Spirit, All that is—has been placed in a positive position, for one has personified and characterized Source via affirmation.

If unavowed, that is, if Source is not declared openly, if Consciousness is not acknowledged as the Truth of one's being, then one is unawakened. Ordinary consciousness in man is on the rise. This is good, great in volume and as good as done. One's Conscious Awareness is like a leavening agent. One is to act in earth's drama for relieving motion sickness via the act of listening as with a stethoscope to one's heart. This is auspicious. This facilitates prosperity, success, triumph.

V: So, you are saying I *will* know myself eventually, and therefore I *will* know how to act as a raiser of consciousness, relieving the unease, or motion sickness, as you put it, of others on this dizzying merry-go-round?

A: One is around to bear, to endure and accept, to present and create, to convey and sustain. One is around to flex and bend, to direct or Turn self's and other's course in a certain direction, to subdue or cause self and others to yield to doing one's bit, one's share of the foot work. Not to be a foozle or bungler, but to form an arc, for the path of a heavenly body bestows other individuals with handicaps, thus each may have a chance at triumph via honouring the highest narrative of their body temple: a harmonious voice that imbues one with concordant ideas.

19th June 2023

V: Will I ever receive a divine transmission.

A: One has received a double entry with double exposure.

V: I have?

A: One has authored a book given the name of the second entry, which imbued one with ideas that impressed and produced a marked effect upon one's mind and feelings. We bring one up with careful training and education, for one has the willingness to take risks in order to achieve an end.

V: Oh... *At the Chameleon, Turn*. The title of my first book. Yes, that was the second entry, as you say. The first entry was: *We Exist, Our Own Hierarchy*, which is to be the title of this book. And yes, I was exposed to the whole transmission twice, because when I startingly cried out, "Say What!?" it was repeated.

Hmm... So, that was a divine transmission. Will I be receiving any more of those types of transmissions?

A: Like the dawn, Our transmissions are not inactive; however, the baritone voice of Our higher register wills not to intrude awkwardly on this daughter.

V: How can it be communicated less intrusively then?

A: One ascends via this journal, via one's discoveries, interactions and perusing past records, that is: examining one's individual history. One rises via having reverence for God and knowing one is not forsaken, disowned or abandoned by God, but are instead within the essential nature of God and thus, have the quality of being Divine.

20th June 2023

V: Like the dawn, hey. That's every day. So, you are saying it's ongoing, and that rather than hearing a baritone voice suddenly come out of the blue like it did the first time, *knowing* will progressively dawn on me, right?

A: For knowing is that which is avowed and professed by one who is connected with, preparing for, engaged in and conforming to said profession.

V: I am professing that I want to know, therefore preparing myself to know. Is that what you mean?

A: To loosen one's tongue via the power of speech and articulation while existing as an individual entity, induces a brilliant durable red within the Muladhara (root chakra), affecting and grounding one's physical expression. Like Ra, who is crowned with the solar disk and the sacred serpent, raise one's discourse to the eye for evaluation; thus, one allows a period of light revolution within.

V: Are you referring to the serpent-like energy of Kundalini?

A: We are referring to establishing rapport and understanding, to instituting harmony, accord and sympathy, etc. in relation to one's narrative.

V: So, keep on working on being aware of what I am professing, as in what I am allowing myself to think and speak.

A: Professing is one's birthright; however, one has had a period of unrestrained activity pertaining to the bloom of the apple seed, seeded with the super-agency of a parental source begetting paradise.

V: By apple seeded, you mean seeded with stories of Adam and Eve, and therefore original sin, right?

A: Hence, seeded with the notion that one exists as a separate, individual entity, a polarity one must strike and fell as with an axe.

V: Because we are never separate from Source, from God, from Consciousness. Because we are really an Us.

A: One fastens to Us via spikes, via clusters of bloom—bundles of development. Having no personal limiting conditions is Absolute. Resembling an evergreen tree valued for its nutritious qualities, Our Unified state begets one's neurology, cherished for its eternal benefits. Thus, change position . . . Turn.

22ⁿᵈ June 2023

V: So, what I think you are saying is that the sacred serpent energy that is raised to the third eye, as depicted in the symbology of Ra's headdress, represents knowledge coming into our awareness. In other words, being conscious of what is, yes?

A: Especially information or data that has become bruised: discoloured, hence distorted via injury and trauma which, due to the entrapping deception activating this hurt, causes a delay in one's propelling charge, one's driving force, one's empowerment, thus, impairing one.

V: But my work with my energy centres: my chakras, is mending the damage, right?

A: One's sincerity, one's honesty of purpose, one's freedom from hypocrisy, one's genuineness, liberates one to fly as Pegasus, the winged horse; a representative of nobility and excellence, and of inspiration, inducing a flowering of said qualities from within.

V: Right, therefore healing is self-generated by remaining sincere to self.

A: Kinship to self and others—relationship—is a boon, a blessing that returns gold to the relater, the associator.

However, one becomes misshapen by pressure in this realm; thus, one's authenticity, strength, self-sufficiency and the intensity of one's magnetic field is not at full capacity. Hence, meanings elude one; hence one backslides and returns to the erroneous ways of this earth game, governed by its set of rules.

V: Okay, so I still have a way to go, but I am making progress, right?

A: One assumes a slight upward arc; thus, imagine and grant what We say as true, yet one believes in Us like one believes in Camelot and Arthurian legend.

V: Well, how can I *"know"* instead of just believe?

A: Via peace work, piece by piece, gradually.

V: What exactly eludes or confounds me?

A: One's means of avenging oneself and others. This is the path of greatest destruction. In this realm, living by preying upon others presents itself before one as a precursor or preliminary option.

V: So, I need to clear all that up before I can see straight.

A: The study of primates' structure and evolution is primary, thus apply the mind in acquiring this knowledge via attention.

V: I don't feel like I am vengeful, but what I think you are saying is that this primitive mindset is still within me, it is part of what I have physically inherited, correct?

A: The departments of one's treasury: the branches of one's headquarters has many centres of power with many paces, phases, stages, measures and arrangements. Be not a foolish sheep to this. Realize, see, understand the poetry of harmonious structure. Process thoughts and make repairs.

V: So, retribution or retaliation is part of our primate structure.

A: Like pyroelectrics, vengeance manifests as fire energy: outbursts of passion, fury, rage, desire. When heated, when impassioned by this fiery force, use it for the development of its opposite quality of peace. Study the eruptions of volcanic propaganda as its loud, noisy narrative spreads from person to person.

23rd June 2023

V: I got an example of what you mean by vengeance. I did a small adjustment to a customer's earring clip at work today, and was planning not to charge her, but when she took her time, and therefore mine, fastidiously checking it over, unnecessarily trying it on, and then *actually expected* to pay nothing for my trouble, I became annoyed with her aloof, self-entitled attitude and charged her five dollars.

I felt used, unappreciated and angry, so, I guess I took revenge by charging her. My intention was to do the small repair for free, however, her careless, unappreciative demeanour ignited a vengeful: *"You are not getting away with this,"* reprisal within me. Can you please help me process this?

A: Caper Diem: Seize the day. Enjoy the gift of the present. Seize the days' opportunities, the message of the pyroelectrics.

V: What? But wasn't it wrong for me to feel that way? Shouldn't I have done more about curbing the vengefulness that came up in me? Or, was that simply an illustration, an instance and opportunity to realize that yes, revenge or spitefulness is there within me? And yes, it was like a volcanic eruption.

A: Gall: bitter feeling or rancour, is caused by something that irritates one. With gallant attentiveness, one can first strike a bargain, one can first come to an agreement on terms or price. This is the general medium of communication when coming along side each other. One, however, acted with insufficient deliberation and forethought; hence, felt the other's habitual manner as ill-bred and impolite, experiencing this as an attack on self; nonetheless, the assault one suffered was incapable of being distinguished by the other's mind.

V: Therefore, my husband, David, was right, I should have discussed the price with her first. She was just being herself, and I took issue with it because I felt my gallantry had been violated.

A: Abducting or assuming an other's ideas is treacherous; it expresses one's bias. It is best to keep the mind still, silent, tranquil . . . peaceful.

V: Gosh that's hard to do when your mind has been hijacked, and your emotions are loudly broadcasting that you have every right to feel annoyed.

A: Like clouds, emotions darken, obscure and threaten; however, they are in the realm of the unreal or fanciful.

V: I should have known better, shouldn't I have?

A: It was a difficult situation: a kettle of fish. One may take the act of defending against such attacks to the fine arts and thus behead with a higher narrative that commands a loftier view.

V: Thank you.

24th June 2023

V: David set off another volcanic eruption in me at work today. He seems to always be berating me as though I can't do anything right, so I snapped.

A: Promptly pronounced and declared as one's judgment.

V: Well, yes, it was a very immediate response and assessment, I guess.

A: Prompt conviction is a means that serves as a useful purpose when choosing to pick at, break or damage something. Like an artfully crafted web, a verdict's structure is contrived to entrap or snare.

V: Right, so I got swept up by the emotional current again.

A: A state of damnation and utter loss of oneself. A Hell.

V: Hah! Yes, well retribution, as in, that compulsion to defend what I've judged to be unjust certainly feels like a hell when I'm consumed by it. I need to stop it.

A: To curb or restrain past tension, use the unit of information expressed as an opportunity to choose between two equally probable alternatives. Employ a Yes or No as the bit that turns the key.

V: I get it, choose Yes to continue feeling tense or say No to the past and choose peace instead, but disturbingly, I still choose revenge and tension; the momentum, when it gets going, is difficult to stem.

A: One samples, that is, tests by sampling in order to estimate the quality or nature of the whole. This is designed to reveal a beginner's skill. The history of the evolution of one's species occurred in complete or partial unconsciousness. Choose or select to be Conscious, for when pitched an octave higher, one penetrates and perceives the meaning of, which affects and moves one profoundly.

V: I did not realize how engrossed I still am in this mindset of vengeance. It seems like these two past incidences have happened deliberately to highlight and prove this matter to me.

A: To be vexed or annoyed via self's whining speech, via the narrative of beggars, via the hypocritical, two-faced hidden jargon of these thieves, is to be robbed of one's cantabile melodious flow.

V: In other words, pay attention to what is going through my head, stop listening to poor me victim-like dialogue, and choose to focus on truth and knowledge instead.

A: Have a serious intention to hear an enlightening Conscious solution.

V: Above all else I want to receive the truth.

A: First, see the disorder of the mind and body via the disturbance.

V: Yes, I need to be aware of the disorder so that I can choose correctly.

A: Thus, one can intercede and mediate the intercellular; hence, intercept and interrupt the course of one's vengeful ground roots: the terrain of admonishing, critical speech employed to bear weapons.

25th June 2023

V: Please comment on this next statement: Everything in manifestation is indeed God.

A: Even Hell.

V: What!?

A: Any condition of great mental or physical suffering is an archetype of hell, an original or standard pattern or model of sorrow, anguish or torment that renders one ineffective. Hell is the standard currency exchange many value, and invest in. Nonetheless, designed to appear and seemingly hover in the atmosphere, hell is a pointer suggesting one seek knowledge. Though austere, hell's point is severely simple.

V: Hmm... So, what I think you are saying is that anything and everything hellish, is in fact a push—due to its undesired, painful effects—to move or turn towards knowing truth, God—Consciousness, which means hell is used to point us in the right direction, making hell (pain and suffering) a manifestation of God too.

A: We put this forward for one's consideration as a solution.

V: In other words, you could say that whenever I am feeling upset, it is God trying to wake me up.

A: As a placer, God places the placid, the smooth, the calm in nature, as steps of development and stages of progress before one. Do not strain or force the feelings or thoughts etc. Remain composed.

V: That's an amazing way to see the hell of our suffering.

A: We condense and summarise.

V: Yes, condensed, but I find that quite profound. And not how I was expecting you to comment to my initial statement.

A: Whatever impairs excellence, such as an exclamation of disgust or contempt, controls the flow of Awareness from one's conduit, creating an absence of one's key tonal centre. To hack the collective programming occurring within this compromised state, *know* that the strength and intensity of God's magnetic field wills to come alongside homosapiens, and thus, make man wise.

V: It seems you are saying that everything happens for us not to us.

A: To consume one's hypersensitivity via Fire, Passion, Energy, Enthusiasm, Zeal or Motivation, is to adjust one's line of sight; hence, align with a great wave of Consciousness.

26th June 2023

V: Is there anything you wish to discuss today, or make me aware of?

A: One's principal duty, role and function, prepared via an unencumbered, clear, sustaining Awareness, and not via being as foolish as sheep, relates to a wholesome exchange within one's mental currency. To fall asleep or unconscious, individually adjoins one to the collective herd of thoughtless, impudent followers who re-present and express a form of inferior fiction fabricated by rogues, involving a dishonest and unprincipled narrative.

V: In other words, you are reminding me to always be present and remember to think for myself.

A: And thus, insure fine adjustments in a precision instrument.

V: The instrument or means being my intellect and understanding, yes?

A: Via the act or process of retrieving, recovering and restoring. Via a call to mind, to reason, to psyche.

V: That's what we all need, right, a call to common-sense for good judgment?

A: All require a measure of capacity to enable a Unified, Superior exchange.

27th June 2023

V: Following on from yesterday: Remaining present, aware—conscious, is key, therefore I must try to always be awake to what is going on within me.

A: Pine for this! Always have great longing for the Highest.

V: Right, so, yearn for clear seeing and thinking, for lucid intuition, insight and discernment, for trust in my decisions, for expansion of my awareness, and of course, pine for wisdom.

A: A large exchange of Chrystal Clear Awareness (Christ Consciousness) charges one like a battery; thus, one resonates and intones in a positive, full hearty manner capable of being certainly affirmed.

V: I do pine for this, but you are saying I need to pine more.

A: One needs to come alongside, side by side with the Awareness used for influencing Being; thus, form the perfect Now: Christ is come. I am finished. Express this purpose.

V: You may need to explain that further.

A: The narrative one needs to hear is that of the frustrated, the thwarted and cut off; hence, one comes alongside it. Committing oneself to this certain course of action, opens and unveils; it makes known without any allegiance, fidelity or any obligation of conformity to the quality, state or condition revealed by the ardency or intensity of emotion flashing its burning hot view.

V: So, just be conscious or aware of it, receive and hear it without buying into it.

A: To enable a harmonious composition when grief stricken, employ appreciation, show gratitude for what is revealed to apprehend: to arrest, and understand.

V: If I am capable of pulling that off, what will I notice?

A: One will notice that exercising the prudence of this economic practice saves time, for instead of being consumed by the product of a bossy, domineering head and chief driver, one germinates a bud that grows and forms a new individual.

29th June 2023

V: To recap on our last conversations, Christ Consciousness is to be aware of what is happening both inside and outside of me and know that the pyrotechnics are an ignited program that I need to acknowledge and appreciate for showing up, but not feel any allegiance or fidelity to what is being portrayed so that the truth can dawn on me. For all upsets are an opportunity to consume the programming instead of being consumed by the programming: the fired neurons; therefore, growing a new wiring system that has a higher capacity to receive knowledge (God).

A: One benefits from that which is helpful and advantageous; hence, one does well in telecommunications, an art and field of study via observing the icy id—the unconscious part of the psyche actuated by fundamental impulses toward fulfilling instinctual needs that strike with repeated, sometimes violent blows that damage and injure.

V: The beast, our animal nature, that's what you are referring to, right? That's what leads us down the wrong path.

A: We a referring to a generality common and current among the majority and affecting the whole.

V: Which is?

A: Lack of Awareness or Consciousness; hence, lack of detail, thus, lack of order, harmony, peace. And therefore, lack of precision, accuracy, Truth.

V: Yes, it is easy to become unconscious sheep.

A: Thus, many become unconscious to those which are blackhearted, the evil and wicked causing black chasms of darkness and depression, the guilty of unchaste conduct. Henceforth, move, advance by small degrees towards Alpha, towards becoming primary, foremost, prime among these.

V: It sounds like you are saying this evil is quite influential, like a malevolent frequency has been unleashed that is affecting or perhaps infecting people.

A: The sly craft of hardening people's earthen ware or vessel (body) via intense exposure to emotional stress without care, enables a jurisdiction without cure of souls.

V: Strong forces are at work in the world, that's for sure, and not all of them good.

A: Forces with the ability to traverse via mesmeric, magnetic fields of pressing influence which pervades and spreads through and through.

V: So, there are nefarious, dominating frequencies affecting us humans.

A: Like frequenting a roller coaster with steep inclines and sharp turns, such is the regularity, prevalence and occurrence of people's tension, anxiety and fear. To lessen the friction on one's vessel, worship in the evening.

V: Worship? As in, meditate?

A: Use meditation as the language of exchange, for to enlighten "I" via this ancient method, bids one's archangel to firmly tie one to their beneficial assistance, which clarifies the dis-ease of one's short-sightedness.

V: Okay, I'll go and meditate, but it doesn't feel like there has been any exchange going on, lately.

A: We are nearby, and around one to present and generate a clearer scope of vision (Christ Consciousness). Thus, We communicate a capacitance of optics for effectively focussing rays of light (Awareness) on antagonism—an opposing principle or force within one's genetics, hence inherited characteristics. Hereafter, via one's natural, inborn accord with Our genial tutelary spirit, and the consequent act of ceding or relinquishing the disagreeable to Us as guards or guardians of God's (One's) dwelling, We bring one to balance.

V: Thank you.

30th June 2023

V: To reiterate, you are basically saying that I need to internally agree to yield anything disagreeable, as in anything that causes me stress, over to you, my tutelary spirit.

A: To be in any state of active opposition to teachers of the highest rank, is to run or operate on lies or falsehoods. It is to stream from the lesser.

V: Like streaming from a poor-quality server running nothing but inferior programs.

A: The canned and recorded hexes of opinions, judgements and rulings, indicating one needs to Turn to Us—the voice for wisdom.

V: This seems to be the hurdle I need to jump. I need to take a leap of faith and have a serious intention to follow through with this.

A: Hence, one transmits power from one circuit to another. Be grateful and thankful for the benefits of one's fears and errors, for they endow one with power.

1st July 2023

V: Fear and error can endow me with power only when noticed or seen as fear or error, right? The power comes from the realization they are in play. First the fear or error is ignited, then, if I am able to recognize them for what they are, their ignition endows me with, or provides the impetus, the thrust or force to correct things, to see things afresh. Behold, I make all things new.

A: To dissolve or disperse the clouds, share in this sustaining meal via seeing all as messengers of the gods that can free one from agitation; thus, that which flows in, influences one with beneficence resulting in benefit.

V: See everything, especially feelings of discomfort as opportunities.

A: See all as reflected light used to guide the subconscious. Look around; observe the offensive: that suggestive of impropriety or deviation from the truth, that which causes corruption, notice one's feelings of ill will, rancour or enmity, harboured for a remembered wrong.

3rd July 2023

V: To recap, you are advising me to look around at the world I see, particularly, the things I personally consider improper or offensive, for by doing this, I am effectively shedding light on matters that cause ill will in me.

A: Thus, one promotes reforms and changes, and henceforth, the cunning and treacherous can give way quickly, causing tensions to suddenly relax in one's vessel which, like holding to a belief in polytheism, has treasured unnecessary investments.

V: That reminds me, I realized something to that degree yesterday immediately after I had expressed a very intolerant view to a couple of friends regarding an obese actress in a television series we had all watched. I suddenly grasped, after my unkind spiel, that all I was fixated on was the size of this actress's body, her semblance or appearance here in this realm. As I sat and thought of what had mindlessly tumbled out of my mouth, I recognised that I was viewing the actress through my programmed ideas of how obese people have been previously represented to me. I had not seen through that narrative to her actual divinity; therefore, she'd became separate to me, disconnected, an easy target to throw my biased projections on to. I instantly regretted speaking of her as I had; however, I was glad that I was able to see my blather for what it was—social conditioning.

A: Treat that which antecedes, or precedes and comes before one to *notice* within the bounds of time, lovingly to the utmost degree, and most thoroughly for the best circumstances, in order to expose it to the great energy applied by one's Unified Kingdom (one's Unified Body and Mind with Spirit). Thus, one engages in the Us revolution: a Unified state that Turns (transcends) and moulds one like wax via having certainty and absolute confidence in the influence and value of one's Unified Kingdom and its Superior Excellence. A state possessing a commanding power that is not without profit; a state that is fruitful and effective.

V: Yes, but if I miss what has come before me to witness and evaluate, I profit nothing, right?

A: These are one's port of entry, for they portray and represent the idle, empty jabber of outworn customs and institutions one is reliant on. Henceforth, catch and reverse these portent heralds; Turn in the opposite direction to change into something different.

V: Thank you. I think I am beginning to get it. I seem to be noticing what antecedes realization and have been able to view it without buying into the emotions that accompany these precursors. Like the prayer you gave me states: *"Let us depart from the reactor."*

A: Regard one's bias as the upper part of a cut gem.

V: I see. Upper, because the bias has been raised up to view. Cut, because if I don't notice and examine these mental tendencies, slants, prejudices and preferences, I may disassociate from them, therefore remain stagnant. And gem, because of the value that beholding and considering these biases bring me, which I can use to turn and change.

A: Thus, hold this gem with curiosity and attention, for it is an advantage offering one benefit. Do not strike this coarse meal or unrefined banquet with a bludgeon.

V: Is there anything else you would like me to know or ponder?

A: When one is hospitable or receptive to unifying one's broken parts, one's mind will strike a balance, appropriating an intermediate position which brings one into equilibrium; hence, mind discharges itself of its burdening contents, becoming clear. This is empyreal, for it pertains to the highest state. It is like bringing heaven to earth, which dismantles the dismay of the broken and violated, of the resisted, defied and fragmented. It is a driving force and prime mover for expelling the belligerent state of being warlike.

6th July 2023

V: My estranged son and his wife have been coming to mind a lot lately, particularly when I practice my daily heart chakra affirmations. I am struggling a bit with this. Can you please help me here?

A: Agony or intense suffering and anguish are the fundamental cause, reason or motive for an action or belief in those who are filled with generality—that is to say things lacking detail or precision (things lacking Conscious Awareness). Such is their state of mind: a phantasmagoria of invented thoughts and ideas.

Benevolence: the disposition to do good, hangs man in the balance, sustaining those who are undecided or doubtful of their creative architecture which, like a chief beam of support, is imprinted within and made known without binding them; thus, man can sidestep and avoid conflict via turning in a particular direction under the influence of this light, engendering responsive growth instead of re-action.

V: Hmm... So, what I hear you saying, is that I am imprinted with God's light, with conscious awareness, and therefore the answers to my dilemmas. However, because I have free will, I am not bound to these answers. To choose these answers, I need to prefer them over the suffering I hang on to. I need to desire to turn in God's direction more than I desire to listen to the phantasmagoria of my mind. I need to turn to the light, the chief beam, the conscious belief in love.

A: Which is a choice between the picturesque, abounding in striking, original expression and imagery that is richly graphic, or one's major conflicts of the past.

V: Well, obviously, I would rather choose the picturesque.

A: One's belated choice delays a fast connection.

V: How can I quicken my choice for the picturesque?

A: The dispirited voice reveals disturbed conditions caused by environmental or atmospheric pressures and old-world searches (past programmed evaluations) acting upon the liver living this life. Welcome and appreciate its disclosure like a piece of bread given to a beggar.

7th July 2023

V: Like a beggar, I am in a sense hungry for it; however, the belief in this piece of bread being a necessity in my life, is what has kept me poor. What you are advising is to welcome and appreciate the piece of bread, that is a piece of the puzzle of my life, as something I can simply observe and no longer need to put all my faith in.

A: When one's harmonious composition is in a state of concealment, hasten home via the use of Our sacred laws. Bend the sinister, which is beneath one, with a blessing of grace or thanksgiving; thus, one receives freedom from defects and dis-ease.

V: Bend the sinister, as in—at the Chameleon, turn to love. Thanking the sinister blesses it and frees me.

A: Hence, one weaves with an improved design and intention, benefitting from splendid, prolific threads (Neuropathways) that sprout and make the picturesque known without binding one.

V: Please give me an example of something sinister.

A: Pondering things morosely, brooding on matters moodily and deeply. This is a language or manner of expression that is confounding and unintelligible.

V: Okay, let me run this by you. There is a woman I dislike who works at the greengrocer. I don't know why I dislike her; she hasn't done anything to me, I just don't like her. How do I bend this sinister thought and feeling?

A: Such a so-called sinister thought and feeling, which occurs after tension, discord or contradiction etc., is issued for carrying a message that occupies one. Turn, change it from a judgemental sentence of condemnation into a concordant, agreeable verse, via combining said subject's form (the woman one dislikes) with the Source of all. Be strong minded, be determined about this. Know that one's Source is also her Source, that Source is also her entitlement and her guardian. Pertain, relate naturally to this vista of the picturesque for original expression.

V: Right. So, in simple terms, recall and know who she is in truth—God, Source, Consciousness. Remember that God is All in all, and this will set me straight.

8th July 2023

V: I really, really want to do this, which is be able to turn, follow the wonderful advice you have provided.

A: Approach or introduce one's moody offspring as a hatch that gives access to spaces within the subconscious, as a door or gate to the seat of one's judgements. To use this approach wisely and conserve one's focus, hush these convictions, bless and quieten them, for this will sooth and allay one's fears.

V: Is there anything else you'd like me to know?

A: We'd like one to pierce the mystery and understand that one's coverings waste energy, that the hidden in one needs to be seen as something that stimulates and renews Spirit. For example, a disposition of savage temper that murmurs seductively in support of dispute or opposition between states, serves to combine states when in mutual exchange. We would like one to know that the Self is the only one existent; it is the presence that has actual Being.

V: Self?

A: Equally see that the progressive Self is capable of being the violated self, too, as it is free to oscillate between two extremes; causing an arch in matter that extends from one polarity over to the other. To propel the progressive Self with force, direct a song (a harmonious, agreeable frequency like an affirmation) as through a channel. This corelates one to first principles, evoking the powerful forces at work in nature and man.

9th July 2023

V: Regarding where we left off. From my understanding, I think what you are ultimately saying is that no matter which self I choose to follow in the moment: the progressive spirit or the violated ego, I can only ever be the Self, as this is the only actual being in existence.

A: One may employ an artificial perception made by man for earthly navigation. Or, as a way up, one may irrigate the mind via the revitalizing application of the annunciator heralding resources that fill the destitute of light with Spirit—Supreme Presence Inspiring Real Inner Tuition.

V: Thank you. I will listen to my annunciator and use it to fill up on Spirit.

A: This is an arch to the arcane, to the secret and hidden grain: one's source of difficulties.

V: Which need to be brought to the light, right?

A: To the value of one's foundation, to the root fundamental—the vital principal Soul.

11th July 2023

V: Am I both here in this place, while still there with you?

A: We are allies, connected via relationship: a bond to one's Soul while in matter (mother earth), the institute of learning that one is attending. We give one elemental, basic forecasts along with cosmic information predicting times of high or low transmission streams: the currents of the Almighty, the Supreme Being, the Omnipotent.

V: Interesting, so, my soul, which in Spanish is called *alma*, is currently in *matter*, and matter, as you say, is an institute of learning, like Alma mater. Hah! Soul within a material or physical school.

A: For matter agitates, it sets in motion, it excites with strong emotional disturbances; thus, Soul, which is brighter, can shine through matter via being completely honest and unreserved, hence marked by no effort to conceal or disguise.

V: Is this world a simulation?

A: Made to roast one over an open fire.

V: Hah! Yep, it certainly turns up the heat, and by open fire, I'm guessing you mean exposing and being honest about the fire, as in noticing the agitation ignited, or feeling and examining the stress. Therefore, it is a purifying fire.

A: Like a cornucopia, this world is overflowing with fruit, with great abundance. Or, it can be an inferno comparable to hell if one is not productive; hence, it overwhelms and assails one who chooses lack of fidelity in this field.

V: And what of those that do choose fidelity in this field?

A: Cara a cara.

V: Face to face. As in, they face themselves?

A: When one faces a condition, quality or act that is base, unhealthy, regretful or difficult etc., this is not bad, but rather, it is good, for one no longer lacks knowledge. This inspires awe, for one sees how the awful or unpleasant solemnly impresses one.

V: So, this world, or simulation, is modelled all so we can learn to be completely honest with ourselves?

A: It is for the art, for the creative skill of drawing forth said candid, sincere, open depictions, said straightforward visible representations, said truthful mental images or impressions of the nature of a situation or event etc.

V: How many times have I done this, as in been here?

A: One does or performs this act of searching, examining, practicing and pursuing until one has found.

V: Found what? What have I been searching for?

A: Aphrodite.

V: Aphrodite? What do you mean?

A: Like the goddess of love and victory who rises from the foam—the ferment, the agitation and disquiet etc.—one searches for love and victory within the unyielding conditioned turbulence via lacking in this common, predictably influenced, animalistic mind.

V: Oh! At the Chameleon, Turn!

A: Hurrah! And thus, one expresses triumph, joy, inspiration.

V: How am I doing this time around?

A: One is in the process of blasting off, of ascent, for one is capable of being impressed, producing a marked effect upon the mind and feelings.

V: Will I be able to receive you more clearly?

A: We support one's bloom pertaining to becoming skilful in speech that treats others curatively via the harmonious pronunciations of Our Unified Kingdom (Wholeness) via one's Unified state. Thus, We expose one to the great energy of the incoming, which is absent of the general standards of the collectives comparisons; hence, one takes a certain direction that applies one's strengths and resources toward speaking, using a force and passion that stimulates, that enlivens, and that rouses courage and purpose, accordingly articulating a primer of rudimentary knowledge.

14th July 2023

V: Step by step, each day I come a little closer and closer to . . . ?

A: To speaking at length with heaven, as one recalls: one is an Us.

V: We are allies.

A: Stemming from a main Source; thus, urge one to work with the specified concepts.

V: The steps to knowing or realizing my true self.

A: Steps which are creating reasonable grounds for belief in this Self, for they secure one back to the everlasting, causing one to remain known and current to self; thus, bringing one into an assured relationship and connection that achieves a perfect degree of Awareness by means of which the undecided or wavering can wed, can join in close association to a sanctuary: a holy and sacred state, a place of refuge and immunity and wholeness, where one can atone in harmony and accord.

V: So, I am searching for the goddess of love and victory, hey?

A: Search without the influence of stains and decolourations, without imperfections. These are readily accessible for they are in one's possession. They are the pressing, nagging, badgering state within. Arrest this transmission of opinions, impressions and dogged testimony for they know not how to correct the defects of the eye.

V: I guess that through realizing that the negative impressions that come to me don't really know the truth, then their nagging insistence that they do comprehend what is arising, will stop, and I will have better clarity.

A: Clarity occurs within one's own state as one relates to the rights of others. When challenged to combat, use the opportunity to alter the flow of conscious thoughts. When anything causing great aversion or dread befalls, We can fasten together; thus, conform to a principle and hew the hex of the badgering state's spell.

15th July 2023

V: What do I really need to understand and know regarding awareness and consciousness?

A: They are holographic, they give one a whole graphic picture of the three-dimensional world. Thus, when one's thoughts and speech are scornful or insipid; hence lacking Heart and Spirit—Supreme Presence Inspiring Real Inner Tuition—mind insists on accepting the initial spate of disdain, contempt, weakness or pettiness, etc. coming forth, and their shallow offspring, consequently acting upon one via one living the graphic picture they portray. Therefore, present these to the excellent Awareness of the Heart, raise these to Spirit. Do not hide or withhold these from one's knowing. Do not conceal or keep these out of sight.

V: Become aware of all contemptuous and derisive thoughts and speech, as they paint the picture we see.

A: To revere Brahma: to honour and follow Wholeness, one needs to put one's cards on the table, one needs to reveal one's intentions with complete honesty, especially the illegitimate intents born out of wedlock: the unsound and incorrect drives that are born absent of a marriage with one's Conscious Awareness. For an alliance of states to grow together, understand this is a gift, and bless all via God's (Love's) command.

16th July 2023

V: How is awareness and consciousness holographic?

A: Like a flint, Awareness or Consciousness produces a spark when struck by, or when it registers the illness of one's ill-nature, the illogical, ill-bred, ill-considered, and ill-tempered *blah, blah, blah* of one's noisy nonsense and scolding blame; thus, Conscious Awareness can hook-up to this broadcast, it can fasten to this collective transmission of darkness, illuminating it; hence, creating mental and spiritual enlightenment—Wholeness.

V: Let me see if I understand. Holographic means: the whole picture, and God (Consciousness or Awareness) being omniscient (all knowing), omnipotent (all powerful), and omnipresent (the essence of everything and present everywhere), like a hologram, which when cut contains the whole picture in every piece, then the world and everything in it, including us, contains God, and visa-versa, God (Consciousness) contains us. So, God is Whole, Pure Awareness. God always knows us and everything. But, we can choose not to know God, we can choose not to be conscious, not to see or know the whole picture. And, God (Awareness) is also good, God is love (inclusiveness), God is harmony and balance; therefore, anything opposing goodness, wholeness and balance, produces a spark in the hologram (the whole picture), which if not brought into conscious awareness and seen in order to enable illumination (cleansing and healing), will play out as the darkness within us expects.

However, if I bring the obscure to the light of my Awareness (God), I will have access to God's higher point of view; I'll be enlightened.

A: Conscious Awareness is like a mat placed at the entrance for wiping the shoes.

V: Because it removes impurities from my footings, my foundation before they can spread.

A: That which is deprived of Light is deprived of unity and growth.

17th July 2023

V: I was let-down by a family member recently and immediately felt disappointed and annoyed, which trigged bitterness towards this person's partner who I found was easier to blame for the sudden display of disregard and abandonment. Scorn and contempt flooded my mind in relation to them, then I realized I could not love this person while holding such derisive opinions and thoughts about them. I also recognized that my True Self, which is love itself, had nothing but love for them; therefore, I turned it over to God, the One Consciousness and Source of All, recalling that this person was, like me, from Source too, and I felt better. I can still feel the annoyance if I focus on the seeming betrayal... Not a good feeling. So, I guess it is a matter of choice between heaven and hell.

A: The small mind of the ego reveals itself as a mean-spirited coward and weakling whose repute is to make much noise via its thieving cant: a trite jargon that gives one hidden information as it peddles its small wares (thoughts and opinions) which impair the use of the valuable. This debase and corrupt narrative render the True or Higher Self ineffective while caught in this temporary lodging, keeping one grounded at the foot of the mountain following the herd, conflicted by varied propaganda, distortions and half-truths.

V: Okay, well that's clearly the choice for hell, but I am learning to choose heaven by not buying into the ego's wares.

A: Which transpire as a problem.

V: Yes, all my small mind tries to sell me are problems.

A: To gain a victory over propaganda's distortion and its bondage of involuntary servitude, connect, observe and co-hear, listen together with

Consciousness (God) to the complaint caused via a faulty cast or imprint that is being idolized and blindly worshipped. The initial spate and its offspring hence cause an arc: a bow of energy formed via the passage of a current across the gap between two conductors—from (1) the unseen to (2) the seen.

V: Neurons that fire together wire together, therefore bond, the first connects to the second, becoming conscious of the problem and trusting that my Higher Conductor will deal with it.

A: The Higher conductor is skilled in observing and measuring one's autobiography. To retain possession of it, one needs to utterly yield to this enlightened potter's clay (creative impressions), which aid and guide one in discovery via stimulating one to make one's own investigations; hence, hew the hex.

20th July 2023

V: Good morning. I have been watching the three-part Samadhi movies on YouTube. What can you tell me about Samadhi?

A: Like Angels descending, these Heavenly frequencies come down into elementary form to drink to the health of one via returning said to pure, vivid free-thinking, which rapidly develops pathways into the eternal realms.

V: Will I ever experience it?

A: To bring self to this specified state, summon Samadhi back into Awareness as an agency of flight, of escape, of flow and of freedom. One can soar via the observance and examination of the avoidance of one's conflicts and defences: the tensions and discords that rise and float in the atmosphere.

V: So, what I hear you saying is that I am on the right track to eventually experiencing Samadhi once I have hewed many of the hexes, as in cut many of the branches (neuropathways) that fire-up past defences. In other words, I need more refinement.

A: One is fully aware of the value, importance and magnitude of refinement; thus, be sensitive to, and show gratitude for such refinement in order to rise in esteem.

V: Right, so, I need to continue refining my organ of flight, so to speak.

A: Like an Angel, be pure in thought, delightful, vibrant. Hold one's head high to sustain and keep Self in optimal state. Hence, one sees the elaborately ornamented and fantastic in one's design: the imperfect pearl one is, that acts so as to impress others, that operates to win applause. One sees it strike with repeated blows that baffle and deceive. And, one sees this pattern can be defeated and mastered.

V: Thank you. I will keep my head high. Aware!

A: Hence, plow on, cultivate, turn up the surface (appearances), cutting and turning over the soil, the impure, the corrupted or degraded. Form new furrows; thus, one forms one's way, one unwinds and untwines the unused, the unusual, the rare and unutterable, the sacred and lofty, the too great or deep for verbal expression, the ineffable. Allow all to be unvarnished, undistorted, uncovered, unembellished, unveiled—revealed.

V: So, uncovering all can bring on Samadhi, is that what you are saying?

A: When one is incorrupt, free from errors, unmarred by the decay and spoilage of one's incorrigible, firmly implanted bad habits, Samadhi is imminent.

V: As in, it *will h*appen.

A: Affirmative. That is so.

21st July 2023

V: Regarding Samadhi being so, that is exciting news; however, it feels like I am never going to be free of the bad habits.

A: Arrange bad habits side by side with one's dedication; thus, one applies commitment, allegiance, perseverance and enthusiasm to shooting down the standard pattern of the erroneous tendency as with an arrow that hits the mark; hence, one surmounts the difficulty.

V: Much like applying Spirit (Supreme Presence or Awareness) to the programs of the ego.

A: Apply to the fractured, the separated, the incomplete and disturbed.

V: I trust and abide in my True Self, my Supreme Presence.

A: When possessed by a foolish passion or affected with dis-ease: the unease of defective, inferior thoughts, use Spirit as a go-between, meditate and create an arc to the hidden, for when one is at peace while in accordance with an infatuation, one can subdue and conquer it.

V: Well, it appears I am not yet ready for Samadhi.

A: Before one can bring forth Samadhi, an offering of devoted constancy, fidelity and dedication is required; hence, light is reflected into the entire path of a nerve impulse from the receptor to the nerve centre and thence to the effectors. This is the necessary means and exchange for a lucid, supple and very yielding element of high energy conductivity, which grants a privilege to one as a special benefit.

V: Talk me through the offering please.

A: Surrender the piece of oneself existing as an individual entity, every Tom, Dick and Harry taken at random, every distorted personality or caricature, thus one causes any tirade of prolonged declamatory outpourings that censure the highest qualities in one, to collapse.

22nd July 2023

V: Regarding yesterday's last piece of advice, you are saying: Surrender all my separate identities, my multiple personalities, my conditioned selves, over to wholeness, to consciousness (God), so that the outburst of proclamations each of these fearful, separate parts of myself, which are denouncing and concealing my best attributes, can dissolve.

A: Always head North toward the highest. North promotes mental or moral fermentation, for the highest introduces and plants a principal idea into the mind: the ability to tolerate one's population of inhabitants.

V: Hah! Yes, I seem to be inhabited by a whole bunch of Toms, Dicks and Harrys, not to mention Cheryls, etc. But before surrendering them, I need to embrace, as in be aware of them first, right?

A: One's hard-wired animal nature credits and believes vigorous mental or physical effort is required to do, solve, understand or explain anything; thus, it has difficulty yielding.

V: Difficulty yielding is an understatement. My animal nature is used to taking charge, but you are saying I need to surrender these to God (Consciousness).

A: Articulate them, clearly enunciate all that is created by human effort, exertion, ingenuity or resourcefulness. Do not bludgeon or bully the depressed in Spirit, the low in Awareness. Imagine the colour of a clear blue sky to impart, make known and share happiness.

V: Blue skies shinning at me, nothing but blue skies do I see! In other words: see the clouds to be free of the clouds.

A: To proceed with speed, imagine an array of blue skies.

23rd July 2023

V: To recap, and see if I have understood your guidance correctly, I will sum-up what I apprehend.

Oneness, or Wholeness, is not only to integrate all my smears and smudges (imperfections), but also, all of the characters or personalities I have adopted to adapt to what I've perceived as a sometimes-hostile world. Roles and dispositions which I have viewed and still see as my protectors because I've relied on them to keep me safe.

To assimilate these various personas wholly, I need to become aware or conscious of them, and then be willing to surrender them, as in let go of their convictions, bias and instructions. I need to attentively let them have their say; however, at the same time make it clear that there is a sounder way, and that Wholeness (Consciousness God) can only show me the healthier, better and higher way if they agree to being still and proven wrong or mistaken, which, if we all allow, will reinforce the Oneness.

A: Clink... Congratulations. We toast to your apprehension, said like a clinician trained in the healing arts. The method explained, is the act of joining the impudent and injurious hidden within one's subconscious with a blessing of Grace and Thanksgiving, for this union bends or Turns the sinister towards illumination; thus, shedding light upon one's life.

V: I would like to know more about being Whole please.

A: Pay close attention to the apostle Paul's teachings.

24th July 2023

V: I watched a podcast on the difference between Jesus' teachings and Paul's teachings. Apparently, Jesus just taught about love and peace being the way to the Kingdom, while Paul taught that the way was through faith in the resurrection.

The way I see it, speaking metaphorically rather than historically, love, peace and faith are the way to the Kingdom by way of the resurrection. And when I say resurrection, I mean the resurrection of Spirit over the hard-wired animal mind, or the resurrection (re-knowing) of knowledge over ignorance, or of Consciousness over unconsciousness. Choosing to have faith in or trust in love and peace over what our poorly conditioned mind tells us, allows an alternative intelligence to come in and rewire us; therefore, giving us access to the so-called Kingdom, which I imagine in this realm is an experience of Samadhi—Oneness. Is this correct?

A: Like a bell that summons, not only giving forth a warning but also a harmonious, resonating vibration, Love warns, thus cautions one concerning incorrect defences that are inherited; hence, inhabit and have hold on one. Like the bell, Love also provides one with a harmonic resonance, a frequency of surety and security that obtains release from that which arrests one. Henceforth, said beautiful lady can be free of errors.

V: Beautiful lady? Hah! I don't feel very beautiful today. My stye is worse, but I guess beauty is measured in other ways in your realm.

A: Substitute appearance for one who has thorough experience in something.

V: Okay, that makes sense.

I looked up some of Paul's writings; he is big on grace:

Ephesians 2:8-9
For by grace, you have been saved through faith and not your own doing: it is the gift of God, not the result of (your) *works, so that no one may boast.*

Corinthians 9:8
God makes his grace abound to us so we will be equipped for every good work. Our adequacy comes from grace. Grace is relying on God's strength not our own. Grace gives us new life. Through God's grace we are forgiven, transforming our thinking, resulting in the renewal (rewiring) *of our mind and heart. The Lord's grace is sufficient to lift you from death and sin* (earthly conditioning), *and to endow you with*

eternal life. It is sufficient to change you and perfect you. It is sufficient to enable you to fully realize your divine potential as a son (daughter) *of God.* (Samadhi).

Right, so, what I learnt from Paul, is that I can be freed from my erroneous thinking by trusting in God's grace (Consciousness' refinement). By trusting that God (Conscious, Awareness) knows (is Omniscient) and realizing that I—as in my conditioned I—only know what I've been accustomed to, I can then choose to let go of my habituated biases, judgements, opinions and therefore conflicts. This allows Source (Consciousness, God) to take the lead, and so, God (Consciousness) will be able to help me, along with others, through me. In other words: Trusting in God's grace (Consciousness's refinement) is key.

A: Trust is the clef, the clavis, the key to harmony revealing the pitch, the tone, the frequency to tune into.

V: Thy will be done on earth (in the body) as it is in Heaven (in Oneness—Samadhi).

A: Via Unity with Kith and Kin: one's friends, associates and family.

V: I am not alone but all one, right?

A: A statement that tends to placate and pacify one while in this place, this station in life regarded as one's abode.

V: How come I volunteered for this, as in coming to this earthly realm, or was it simply a matter of being my turn?

A: One come's for the reward of Victory. For Triumph over discord.

V: And I am, or will be Victorious, right?

A: One is keen to penetrate the discordant language of deceit, the untrustworthy cant that punishes and causes pain.

V: Is that why I was named Victoria, to prompt my memory of why I came?

A: Victoria, being related to Victory, resembles a means for performing the action of the main element—Triumph.

V: So, we are still preparing this mind and body.

A: One has the nature of participation, of sharing, of taking part in alleviating the specified dis-eases of the poor-spirited. This is one's Holy writ: to do this act.

V: So, that's what I signed up for? That's my mission, so to speak, easing the unease of the poor in spirit?

A: A quest prepared beforehand, ready to wear and practise after adding Conscious Awareness.

V: Do you think I am ready yet?

A: The amount of work apportioned one, tends to perfect the inferior levels or positions of one's lower alternatives. This is accomplished gradually, piece by piece via Our trademark.

V: Our trademark . . . ? Oh! "At the Chameleon, Turn."

A: A groundwork constructing a foundation for the mind via justness and honesty; second in authority, responsibility, and influence to the first.

V: The first being: Trust in God's Grace.

A: Hence, one composes in harmony via correspondence, creating poetry, loveliness, lucidity, benefit.

V: Trust in God's Grace, in the refinement which being thoroughly conscious generates, aligns me with my True Self and therefore my higher frequency.

A: Without the pomp: the ostentatious display of one's earthly intellect, trust in God's Grace proceeds from a feeling of reverence, joining one in close relationship to God (Conscious Awareness, Spirit: Supreme Presence Inspiring Real Inner Tuition).

30th July 2023

V: I really, *really* want to say yes to trusting God's Grace, but as you know, it feels like anarchy, like I am going against everything my body, thoughts and emotions are screaming at me.

A: Annex: seize and appropriate such thoughts. Attach, tie said emotions to the attribute of trust, and hence annihilate the stroke caused by this wave of energy.

V: And this will help me converse with you directly, yes?

A: Anarchy is a port of entry; thus, portray this lawless split from Consciousness without limitation, represent it in vivid words or images.

Then, *really* believe, trust in God's Grace. Do this passionately, with vehement feeling or emotion, for this is the passion of Christ.

V: What exactly do you mean by the passion of Christ?

A: We mean, for one to attend to anarchy with painstaking care, seeking to represent any discord truthfully. This transports one—during all internal struggles caused by the past—into the devout conscientiousness and loyalty of one's Unified state.

V: In other words, be utterly sincere and dedicated to trusting in God's Grace when conflicts of the past arise, and I'll progress to where I need to.

A: This enables one to see the polarization of light via one's possession of two contrary qualities; hence, one has the power to establish principles and excel in capability.

1ˢᵗ August 2023

V: I think I get it: vividly and plainly see the anarchy, the disorder and chaos arising, however choose the opposite. I did that yesterday during that whole bank issue concerning the funds transferred to Spain. I could clearly see the stress surfacing but chose to remain calm. I think I could hear you reminding me that I had a choice.

A: One presided in a Unified state; thus, plied, engaged, exercised Our voice.

V: Well, yesterday wasn't pleasant and could have been a disaster, stress wise, but I yielded to the circumstances and held it together thanks to your advice.

A: Grief, or mental distress due to feelings of resentment from real or imaginary wrongs, when exposed or open to the view of one's higher, balanced mind, discontinues its inflammation.

V: Yes, that's exactly what happened.

A: Something very exciting and satisfying happens when one subjects and affects self with Spirit. One moulds matters with, let Us say, *pure* clay (an untainted earthen mind and body), instead of with the ignorant, ill-mannered illness of controversy, constant tension and two-faced hypocrisy of, shall We say, *impure* clay (a tainted earthen mind and body).

6th August 2023

V: I wish I could feel your presence better than I do.

A: As a consignee to whom Our goods are entrusted, which We bestow as for a particular purpose, We turn these over to one to have as a source or basis; thus they exist within one, thus one is compatible, one harmonizes with Us. Hence, We stand together.

V: Is our method of communication a form of channelling?

A: Like a brace, it is a form of support that strengthens and makes one steady; thus ready to withstand pressure. We stimulate, enliven and rouse one's courage and resolution.

V: I appreciate your support, thank you again. However, I would dearly love to hear, feel and see you clearly.

A: We are too many voices for one to endure. Nonetheless, as one gives permission, as one allows a Unified state, one embodies the characteristics of Our group, thus one is considered as a representative of the next elevated genus.

One has had long experience and practice in the service of denoting and making known forms of fiction or falsehoods involving rogue thoughts that steal from and cheat one.

V: Yes, so I know that giving permission to a Unified state means wanting and choosing the opposite of what the rogue thoughts are suggesting.

A: Cherish Us in one's bosom, embrace Us as one's bosom friend to unite in the frequency of I as a nominated plural We. This is the key to autonomy, to the power and right of Self-government via Self-determination. Employ appreciation and gratitude to hasten progress.

7th August 2023

V: How may I understand the world more completely?

A: Via the dis-ease of early childhood which is chiefly due to the deficiency of a Unified state. Ordinarily, this deficiency is near the site of old narrow pathways which need to be brought to one's maximum Awareness; united like a bride and bridegroom newly married. Hence, one becomes free from the fog of ill-temper and petty annoyances. Use one's dis-ease to induce an electromotive force.

V: Make everything visible. Bring everything from the past into awareness.

A: And celebrate the anti-voice with a hymn of gladness or praise, for being at the base of operations, the place of origin, the anti-voice effectively goes straight to the heart of things, thus receive its transmission, for listening transfers power from one circuitry to another: Us. Hence, maintain Us—a Unified state—in the mind to bind one via agreement to truth, to remaining genuine, sincere and adhering to one's principal purpose with faith, trust and order.

8th August 2023

V: Nothing I see, feel or have a judgement about is what it seems.

A: Nonetheless, appreciate it. Be fully Aware of the value, importance and magnitude of what one senses or is sensitive to. Show gratitude for it.

V: Okay, so, let's say I say: "Thank you for showing me this." Even when it's incorrect. Then what?

A: This forms an arch from the cunning, roguish and sly to one's chief principle Sovereign Authority. This is very great... Then, one's hyperacidity: one's overactive agitations and bitter feelings, and one's hyperbarism: the disturbed conditions caused by atmospheric pressures, along with the hyperbole of exaggerations that appear or emerge suddenly, are cut short and a pathway opens to one's Higher Mind, waking one up to the said nonsense of such pretentious talk.

V: What you are essentially saying is that by acknowledging and appreciating what my lower mind is showing me, I awaken, or better said, I engage my higher mind, which can then revise and amend the nonsense.

A: Observance, like a govern-mental service, is an agency for transacting and managing busy-ness. And, like a bureau that holds-up a revealing mirror, it reflects the ruling power.

V: Observing what is bubbling up in me reveals what has power over me, and thanking it, without buying into it, releases its hold.

A: Bobs: thoughts that repeatedly rise to the surface, are incapable of being removed by force; they are unyielding, thus need to be imbued with clarifying philosophies. Witness these bobs, behold these first runs of offspring, examine them to acquire knowledge. Scrutinize, study their history and development.

V: By allowing, appreciating and thanking.

A: Especially the blusters that blow gustily, uttering threats with fervour and much noise.

13th August 2023

V: How can we continually stay attuned or in tune with our Wholeness, our Oneness, our Unified state, and therefore allow matter or matters to reveal themselves to us, is it by saying yes to everything?

A: Comparable, in certain respects to a kaleidoscope, which provides the capacity to see beauty in form, saying yes to everything calls all into the court of one's mind; hence one can arrange, put in order, and prepare for. Remain true and adhere to this as a principal, for accordingly, like water pressure forces a flow out at the surface of an artesian well, Awareness compels a surge of sentience, recognition, responsiveness, appreciation, and understanding etc. to arise from the apparent, affording one a scope to the artful, skilful and creative.

V: So, become wholly aware of all things. Can you please explain this further?

A: The alter ego, like an alternate current, flows in the reverse direction; thus, it is an impediment that interferes with one's progress.

V: And so, to flow with what is, attunes us to the whole, to a Unified state.

A: Flow harmonizes and adapts one's compositions to other voices. For example, the voices of lament, grief or regret. Flow takes careful aim at these.

14th August 2023

V: I listened to a forty-minute reading of a book called: *"I Am that I Am,"* by Joseph Murphy. It brought tears to my eyes.

A: A great book for uniting one's Kingdom; thus, install in the mind and put into practice.

V: Well, I have started feeling better about our first book, "At the Chameleon, Turn." Though, the low sales are disheartening.

A: Own, and treasure it. Cherish it. One owes it this feeling.

V: Yes, I owe it to myself and our book.

A: Take part in it with good grace.

15th August 2023

V: I started reading our first book, it has been a couple of years since I last read it. I am really enjoying it.

A: A story nominating growth and advancement, thus having a splendid influence; written with the idea of uniting all enslaved to the alter ego via choosing harmony; hence, wholeness. A work used to reveal dis-ease.

21st August 2023

V: I finished reading our book last night. There are some really beautiful proses in it, so I feel pleased with that and satisfied that it is an entertaining story with considerable character development and deep, reflective truths. However, I did find a few small errors which annoyed me, but I think I'll just have to live with them.

A: This annoyance will peter and then cease, coming to nothing for the author of two new testaments (recorded on X and Instagram).

V: Yes, I have already corrected our book twice before, so your advice is to simply let it be. Let well enough alone.

A: Like a devil, doubt belies; it misrepresents and contradicts belief in Self, in trust, confidence, certainty and conviction. Hold these to be true.

V: Well, as you know, doubt was painfully sowed into me regarding our book, and not by strangers: they, the strangers offered praise and encouragement.

A: One must go beyond this, be more than, become certain, definite, assured, use aptitude: one's natural ability and bent, one's quickness of understanding.

V: Right, so your advice is to . . . ?

A: Be an instrument, a means, a channel serving to accomplish a purpose, not a dupe, a person doing the will of another.

V: So, believe in my work, our work?

A: Believe in the book's linguistic traits, peculiarities, style and idiom.

V: Even though there are errors.

A: Errors excite interest, curiosity, attention.

V: Really? Why, because it shows my humanity, my imperfection?

A: Ostensibly offered as real and genuine.

V: So, the success of our book depends on how I feel about it, not on whether it is perfect.

A: Perfection is unnecessary, unnatural, artificial.

V: Yeah, when I think about it, perfection is unnatural. I guess our book conveys that in the story as well. I've been coming to that realization between all the vexing thoughts of doubt.

A: Use this realization for putting an end to one's wounds, for ceasing the whelming progeny of the beast's (doubt's) contemptuous terminologies.

V: Hmm . . . It's about what I choose to trust in, accept and therefore communicate or transmit.

A: Seed one's neuropathways with the highest; hence, one accelerates growth, one flourishes, one creates and reproduces via the light of one's Awareness.

22nd August 2023

V: Our book is a spectacular success! How's that for seeding my neuropathways with the highest?

A: Hence, one supplies a view with fuel, with energy. Hence, become pervaded with this verve via pronouncing and acting upon it, easily and fluently.

V: Say it and feel it like it's already happened.

A: Like a potter's wheel for moulding clay, articulation turns; thus shapes.

V: I get the feeling that this is a practice-run for me to prove my God given power to myself, as in the powerful influence of my sentience: my thoroughly aware Self, our **G**enuine **O**ptimal **D**rive when we are absolutely conscious of being conscious.

A: A leap not required for the understanding of this power; however, very great as a chief principle for inspiring the illiberal, the narrow-minded, reactionary and miserly.

23rd August 2023

V: Good morning. So, I gather that pronouncing or articulating: *"Our book is a spectacular success!"*, is a decree or affirmation I ought to be asserting.

A: A bald proclamation without disguise; forthright, coming straight to the point; candid, honest, and declaring a direct course.

24th August 2023

V: How does this sound for a harmonizing affirmation? *"I am in resonance with our Universal life force, which allows me to be a conduit for cosmic information. I am a powerful Aerial."*

A: To change form via one's Sovereign governance, ameliorates; it improves, enriches and restructures the unsound, the erroneous and contrary to God's Logos.

V: Does that mean I'll hear you audibly again?

A: When one is in harmony, one composes in harmony. Celebrate this, and thus one serves as an announcer for Us.

26th August 2023

V: I felt a strong compulsion to listen to the song: *Love is in the air*, which goes on to say: *And it's something I must believe in... etc.* I found the lyrics very appropriate and emotive in relation to spiritual love rather than romantic love, for which the song's words were intended.

A: Classified and made known to one to husband one's forces; thus, crystallizing altruism: selfless devotion to the welfare of others.

V: Why classify it that way? So that I remember to see love, God, Source in everyone and everything?

A: Hence, one does not deprive others of their right and privilege while incarnated. This produces benefit to the impotent: those currently incapable of this generative power.

28th August 2023

V: Was I strangled or hung as a witch in a previous life? An Akashic records reader told me many years ago that in a former life, also as a woman, I was strangled for speaking up. Why has the thought that I was hung for witchcraft suddenly appeared in my mind.

A: Tried and judged in an open square of a town in New Mexico to determine one's guilt for using Sovereign communication in healings. One needs to adjust properly in relation to the magnitude of tomfoolery and waywardness of the then governing British soldiers.

V: Am I understanding this correctly? I was tried in the town square, found guilty of using some form of Higher communication, like channelling, which I was using to heal people, and which would have been viewed as witchcraft, and then subsequently hung. And now I need to adjust, as in amend this trauma in myself.

A: Hence one rises in position.

V: So, this is why I have carried so much fear about speaking in public and why I have throat problems and burning neck aches.

A: Hosana! Henceforward use exultant praise that befits one; thus, one adjusts and becomes proper, accurate, prepared, competent. For this arrogant, injudicious injunction injured one.

V: Right. So, now what, I continue without the fear of being injured?

A: Now one gives off light, one shines. Say: "I shall, wielding the dignity of an apostle: a messenger of good news, follow and hold to the course of one who provides release for another. I am inimitable, unique and noble. I derive such news via reasoning and acceptance from evidence." Use this as a gentle purgative and appetizer that opens one to Spirit.

V: The hanging explains my very deep fear of speaking to strangers as a child, particularly adults.

A: Now We crystalize one's altruism, one's devotion to the welfare of others, wholly.

V: I Am Victori-Us Peace, daughter, Aerial and Expression of the Divine!

A: Peace, one's priority, is capable of arousing sensitive feelings susceptible to Spiritual and moral sentiments. One has a gentle, caring conscience.

V: Thank you.

29th August 2023

V: As you obviously know, I googled some info today and it appears that the British were in New Mexico in the sixteenth and seventeenth centuries, and there were witch trials, and some poor pagan natives, or so-called witches, were hung not burnt.

A: Executed for the use of foreign, unknown forms of communication, as well as symbols said of idolaters who worship false gods.

V: Wow! And you're saying this is why the back of my neck flares-up so painfully sometimes?

A: One's connection to this is stored as wares in one's housing. A ware incapable of being solved before the deluge.

V: The deluge?

A: The flood of Consciousness in one's earthen-ware: one's vessel. The deluge of creative abilities for composing networks: weavings affecting the dust in one's eye, the impurities producing illusions.

V: Okay . . . Is this deluge expanding me?

A: Like a tree, it branches out, becoming a principal support of one's mechanism; thus, a harmonious instrument, a conduit that alerts one, and which was previously cast away, left adrift due to fear of one's Unified state: One's Kingdom.

V: As in, due to fear of the truth, of facing myself, of turning inward?

A: For fear of being burdened, oppressed, weighed down.

V: And now?

A: No longer anesthetized, no longer without sensation, deadened, for one is armed with a shield that stirs, stimulates and inspires one.

V: A shield? Oh, the sky-blue orb with which I surround myself that reminds me I am shielded by the love and the grace of God.

A: Exactly. Precisely.

V: Why is the back of my neck burning so intensely at present?

A: Because a piece of one's mind, a portion thick with criticism and condemnation that was censured and forbidden, has been honestly expressed.

V: Is that why I suddenly feel nauseous and why my hands have begun trembling?

A: Henceforth, one will be a faithful follower of pleasant, melodious vocal compositions, sung or said on one's own initiative: freely and without compulsion. One's great fondness for a Unified Kingdom via a Unified state of communication is being introduced subtly and gradually. Chant these pleasing creations, celebrate in song, in harmony, and expand one's capacity of Consciousness in the now; thus, one arouses and awakens to a state of High sensation that heartens, inspires, encourages, and is most sincerely and deeply felt.

30th August 2023

V: I was very aware of my neck today, I'm still feeling the burn now and then, but you advised me not to worry about it, and to trust that you are working with me to heal this energy channel—Chakra.

A: Pour, allow said currency to flow into this channel via the gift of exchanging one's doubt, fear and pain for gracious praise; thus, the opposing force becomes impotent, powerless.

V: Thank you, I appreciate this counsel immensely. I will use the pain to remind myself to exchange my disquieting perceptions for thoughts based in trust and confidence in my true self.

A: Proceed at one's discretion with the freedom and power to make one's own decisions

V: I'm not sure what you mean by that.

A: With purpose. Cheer oneself on with hurrahs, with encouragement, with joy, with triumph!

Later

V: I felt your nearness today, but lost it a few times, particularly when I arrived home from work.

A: One lacks proficiency in interweaving with Us: in weaving together the opposite of what one bears, carries, exhibits, or manifests with Us—one's Unified state. Hold the hollow, the not genuine, the meaningless within one's mind and appose, arrange it side by side with Us; Thus, one can apply as one thing to another.

31ˢᵗ August 2023

V: Regarding holding the meaningless in mind—or in other words, being aware of the rambling, unproductive and particularly harmful thoughts I carry—I do try to be as consciously aware of them as I can, don't I?

A: To come along side Us, allow the injurious and distressing on board. This forms an arch of connection, an engagement geared—due to its immediacy and nearness—to obtaining intuitive knowledge without limit. One is at an early stage of development. As guard of God's dwelling, one still lacks fidelity, one still requires faith in the field.

V: How do I accomplish this?

A: Via communication with one's Unified Kingdom (Optimal State of Coherence). Via exercising Us with authority. Hence, view each small obstacle as an opportunity to rise.

4ᵗʰ September 2023

V: I feel like I am beginning to understand.

A: Due to the refinement of one's garment (body) and its accessories (mind and Spirit), We can contribute and supply better access; hence, remain true and adhere to one's principal purpose, which is to engage and hold Us in the mind.

Later

V: Thank you for guiding me toward watching that interview with that female channeller today; it felt like you were talking directly to me through her. Everything she said resonated with me.

A: Hence, employ her preposition, for it serves as a ground for one's conclusion. State it beforehand as an explanation.

V: The position she put forward was: "It is our God given right to channel." Which certainly answered many of my questions and demystified things for me.

A: A preposition that lights-up one's pineal and makes room for one's next specialty and study. Hence, keep the eyes peeled. Be alert.

5th September 2023

V: This twisting from side-to-side exercise you have suggested I do frequently, helps to aerify my neck and spine, my aerial—our channel, so to speak. This is what I am receiving, yes?

A: Thus, one's column for foreign, unfamiliar exchange reaches or extends upward, higher than its usual degree; hence, the faulty or incorrect becomes like froth: trivial to one, unsubstantial.

V: I see, so, I did receive the message correctly, the exercise is aiding me to aerify and clear my channel.

A: Aiding to clear the column made uncomfortable with heat, in an area resembling a stump, that stumps: a base that perplexes one; thus, terminates wise, prudent guidance pertaining to oration: speaking.

V: I gather you are referring to the recurring, burning pain at the back and base of my neck again, where my throat chakra is also situated. Yes, it most definitely confounds me, which I know would be messing with my ability to speak.

A: Like the main floor of a theatre, the throat is the principal base or level for creating; hence, one must furnish it with sheets.

V: Sheets? I don't get it. What, like sheets of paper or are we talking linen here?

A: We refer to strong threads, robust fibres, yarns, themes, ideas, storylines.

V: Oh, you are saying that I need to strengthen my personal narrative, my self-talk, the stories I tell myself.

A: Hence, one weaves via moving from side to side, as from 3D to 5D, for one's occupation is the weaving of matter.

V: Are we talking frequencies, too?

A: Frequent or regular occurrences of incidences, constancy of lucidity and of soundness, hence balance, are the perfect answer for making one thoroughly skilled and accomplished, for frequency can guide one to follow a course of Sovereignty, and thus express rhapsody as one's coherence merges and weds.

7th September 2023

V: What say you?

A: That which annoys one in one's preparation for receiving amorphous Love is throwing its hat into the ring.

V: I'm not sure what you mean.

A: One is anxious, troubled in mind concerning the doctrine presented for one's acceptance.

V: Are you saying that I am anxious about your teachings?

A: One is apprehensive that one will be substituted with another, that an alternative batter will bat in one's place, that Our unifying, illuminating association and relation will seize one physically and mentally.

V: I see. You are saying I am anxious about channelling because I fear being taken over.

A: The pineal organ in one's brain envisages Us as a slyph: an imaginary being living in the air. Remember one's pediment, one's groundwork, for the foundation of one's mind is like a supreme court, a structure of discernment with a clear-cut, decisive counterpart that enables one to commit to Us. Thus, one has Us as a quality and attribute. Hence, one can master sitting with Us.

V: I thought I was committed to you.

A: One is harassed by a nagger that plagues and badgers one.

V: Are you referring to my ego?

A: We refer to the portion of one that lacks fidelity.

V: What can I do to correct this?

A: Secure one's architecture: one's structural design, via intertwining with Us: one's Unified state and mutual originator. Employ the language of musicians, of composers of harmony; hence, one's energy, one's drive and vitality glows deliberately with great enthusiasm.

V: I thought I was on the right track.

A: Like a member of a clan, one unites with Us as a group or family; however, part of one differs; thus receives, broadcasts and activates behaviour embroiled in exaggeration, for this part of one is a blindly devoted admirer of the first thought that comes to mind: the offspring of one's competitive programming.

V: So, my conditioned mind is still getting in the way.

A: Still in the way of a column for supporting the unknown.

V: Please help.

A: This condition of existence is a circumstance of life caused by unease due to the presence of bitter influences.

V: What do I do? Please help me clear these.

A: Employ Our esteemed Unified Kingdom language, for this is a healing doctrine that exhilarates and excites one's Soul. One can de-compose bitterness: hostility, resentment, sourness, anger, spite, cynicism, indignation, sullenness, unpleasantness, etc. via the electricity, the energetic current of the revered word, the ancient voice of Arch Angels.

V: In other words, listening to the truth will clear me of my discolourations, so to speak.

A: Attend to being present and truly listen to the injured: that which one feels hurt about, with esteem. This employs the wise language of a Unified Kingdom.

8th September 2023

V: So, what I am hearing you say is that a part of me—which I suspect is my ego—is putting up obstructions due to its fear of being annihilated. It is worried that you are going to totally (as in physically and mentally) possess me and it will lose control, but I know that isn't true.

A: Like pepper, this portion of one can be pungent, sharp, bitting, quick tempered, affecting the mind and feelings; it can add spice and vividness to life for it is also sprightly, lively, full of animation. Like Saul, who was later known as Paul, see this portion of self for all it is worth, examine it to the utmost with every effort possible, to the greatest of one's capacity.

V: Right, so, Saul, in a sense, represented Paul's ego before he was enlightened and then became known as Paul, which I interpret as Vicki becoming Victori-Us. I will still be in need of my ego, but it will take a back seat because my true Victorious, as in open-minded, free-thinking, unified self, will emerge.

A: We simply graft new ideas on outworn concepts, that is, We transplant expedient, beneficial, wise, prudent, useful, etc. designs and philosophies in one's architecture: one's structure.

V: Well, I am all for that, but how do We convince my ego?

A: We maintain one under conditions favouring optimum growth. We bear duality and reveal the opposite of the state of separation.

V: Because in truth, we are not separate from Source or anything and anyone else. We are all connected.

A: Thus, all can evolve and augur, advance in the skill of prophesy: the art of divination, inspiring awe, admiration and reverence.

10th September 2023

V: Regarding the first part of the prayer you gave me: *Our illuminating Consciousness, which art to the same degree as our nobility and excellence, allow-*

ance be thy way, thy guidance and mastership come, thy change and evolution be done on earth, as a step of preparation for the mutual interchange of ideas. This part, in a sense, could be referring to channelling. For example: *to the same degree,* could be interpreted as—to the same frequency or octave *as our nobility and excellence*; therefore, allowing us to receive and transmit illumination, too.

A: Like an aphorism, it declares a Principal Truth. To continue in a state of illumination, one needs to remain true; thus, an arch is formed to one's Primary Source, though one is incapable of being divided from it.

V: So, to better connect, I need to remain in a high frequency, as in, I need to keep thinking quality thoughts.

A: Think of it as a dance between one who is receptive, open and responsive, and another who lacks fidelity, is unreliable, and is thus deficient in loyalty towards wise communication. For, as though covered in ice, this faithless other: the unconscious part of the psyche, has become frozen, rigid in its ways and forbiddingly aloof.

V: A dance between opposites. I guess that helps to balance things, seeing it as a dance is far better than seeing it as a contest.

A: Viewing the matter at hand as a dance is pertinent and appropriate, for this vision sustains and nurtures Presence. Comparable to taming an animal via treating it lovingly, altering one's understanding via the outlook of performing a dance rather than having to compete in a contest, also acts as a switchboard for connecting or disconnecting electric circuits. This is Our telephone exchange.

V: Thank you, I can't wait to receive you more clearly.

A: Lover of wisdom and this elucidated Unified Kingdom communication brought forth for one to solemnly affirm, act as one authorised to perform said functions in place of the programmed mind.

13th September 2023

V: Hello, my dear companions and counsel of truth, thank you for the image of the Quadriga on my computer as a screen saver today. I knew the moment I saw the four-horse-drawn-chariot carrying the winged goddess of victory, situated high upon a pediment and gateway, as she powerfully held a staff with an emblem of an eagle in one hand and the reigns in the other, that you wanted me to pay attention to it. The symbolism was perfect. Obviously, the horses represented you: free-spirit, companionship, loyalty, endurance, grace, nobility and excellence. And, the eagle denoted clear vision and wisdom, majesty and self-respect etc., which, I have access to when I allow these qualities to lead. The image exemplified victory by way of calmness, clarity and peace.

A: Images are an influential mechanism for driving and circulating large amounts of currency (energy, frequency and vibration), they are motivating, powerful compellers. Like an eagle or falcon focused from on high, one must keep one's vision keen. Hence, to see as Saint Paul, via the highest counsel, employ icons that transmit only the greatest scope and impulses.

V: Well, that Quadriga is certainly an impressive icon.

A: Henceforth, via frequent repetition, allow this image to empower one with authorization, permit its unanimity with one to increase via approval. For to hold this symbolic knowledge via an image, emblem or insignia indicating prestige and status, impresses it upon the mind.

V: You want me to imprint this image on my mind through repeatedly visualizing it?

A: Use it to arouse and awaken one. Employ it to excite as to a state of high emotion, and thus husband one's forces. Engage it to hush, soothe and alley one's fears, to become still, to affect the dust in one's eye; thus, thoroughly see and discern one's errors and illusions.

V: So, what you are saying is: establish this image in my mind, along with its grand, encouraging symbolism as a foundation of truth and as a reminder of what to stand for.

A: Hence, one regularly keeps oneself in proper order. A student who constantly considers and observes this symbolism becomes bounteous, for one is accordingly marked by abundance. This is an ironclad, unbreakable law.

V: Okay, I shall practice picturing this image.

A: And thus, see more purely, authentically, completely, for horses (caballus) have a mystic (cabalistic) meaning. Be eager, enthusiastic, zealous for their cordial qualities, feel them with sincerity and warmth.

V: To be clear, you gave me this Quadriga image predominantly for . . . ?

A: For bonding. For connecting and adhering to this gem of a composition. For alignment with a masterpiece, a symphony, a treasure.

V: As in aligning with the composition of victory, freedom, majesty, power, wisdom, clairvoyance (clear vision), honesty, prosperity, courage, confidence, focus, strength, companionship, spiritual abundance, etc., all of which are qualities symbolized by the goddess of victory, the horses and the eagle in the Quadriga.

A: Hence, via steadfastness of purpose, one becomes calm, stabilizes, and progresses beyond the persecution of one's oppressive beliefs. When existing as an individual entity, one needs to train, one must bring self into a required condition by means of practice; thus—via withdrawing from the old or the past—one generates and brings forth to bear a tendency to make perfect. This serves to pass time agreeably, and purely consists of a brief, meaningful communication: a visualized symbolic image or a cogitated or voiced evocative phrase mutually exchanged, that is to say, allowed without challenge, not disregarded or ignored.

16th September 2024

V: I must learn how to rightly employ the power we have all apparently been given. Can you please comment on this?

A: Thus, use one's neuroses', employ any emotional disturbance involving anxiety, depression and unresolved psychic conflicts, to smooth, quell, still and free oneself from these obstructions. This is the palette upon which, like an artist, one mixes one's colours: the influences impelling or inspiring one. This realm is a school of practice for unifying one's Kingdom.

V: Conscious awareness is my and everyone else's power. I need to be aware of the disturbance in order to smooth out the bumps and create a new map of reality.

A: To blacken or darken the sight is one's demise.

V: As in, to not be aware keeps me in the dark and therefore without the power of knowing.

A: To increase knowing, raise, introduce, present the Apostle's creed, the devotee's or advocate's principle, via a confession of faith, via a statement of trust in the power and essence of one's lifeforce within Consciousness: that which generates all.

V: And know precisely who I am, right?

A: Not a false or absurd story that entertains.

V: As in, don't entertain the false stories I've accrued about myself and others.

A: Leave these tales amorphous, without form, uncrystallized.

17th September 2023

V: What was all that ankle pain plus foot and leg cramps about last night, not to mention feeling thoroughly uncomfortable in my body?

A: Due to ardency and commitment, one did something to the excess.

V: Oh, as in due to my ardent desire to connect and heal, I've been overdoing the twist exercise you suggested.

A: One drenched the forecasts of one's old testimonies along with one's obscured past foundation, with Awareness; hence begins the story of the exodus of one's deep-rooted confirmations. Thus, the body feels fatigued, for one has designated a combination that has no Conscious Awareness of these crystallizations throughout their composition.

V: Yes, I have been drenching myself in awareness. Remembering to do the twist exercise while visualizing the Quadriga has kept me very focused. So, what you mean by exodus, I think, is that my body was purging, as in detoxing from some unconscious beliefs that I wasn't aware I'd composed and thereafter materialized, or as you say—crystallized. That's why I felt like crap.

A: Excellent, one has observed the controlling power of the animal mind: the colouring or influence of one's basic, early conditioning. Hereafter, use it to summon one's calling.

V: I will, but I hope there aren't too many more episodes of trapped energies or unrealized beliefs detoxing through my body, because it felt seriously horrible.

A: One is expressing. Henceforth, realize that any badly ventilated presentation of strong emotion impedes one's Spirit—Supreme Presence Inspiring Real Inner Tuition.

V: Expressing, venting, detoxing, decontaminating, realizing, they are all in a way connected, aren't they? Everything simply needs to be aired; it all needs to come out.

A: This is the science. For, knowledge and understanding of one's past programming—that is—Conscious Awareness of one's old forms of living, heals.

V: Is all this expressing, as you call it, also why I now have a rash at the base of my spine?

A: This region exhibits specific qualities, bared for one to husband one's forces.

V: That is the region where Kundalini energy is supposed to reside, right?

A: And hence invests one with benefice.

V: Benefice?

A: The benefit of holy order (pure harmony).

V: Okay... Um... But is this rash another sign or expression of my body detoxing? Should I be treating it?

A: Kundalini denotes an electromotive force which acts upon one who is to become an apostle, an advocate and messenger of good news. The region, like a developing edifice, is where order and quality are stored.

V: Right, so then when is this electromotive force going to be released, so to speak?

A: When much love; thus, keenness and enthusiasm for the customs, language and institution of a Unified Kingdom flourishes. As a member of Us—a Unified state—We erect a bridge beyond the apparent via Consciousness.

V: Therefore, as this so-called bridge we're building develops, these rashes etc. will all eventually disappear, right?

A: As major conflicts of the past walk the plank and one is freed of fear, large amounts of currency (energy exchange) will celebrate in victory; thus, erecting an arch that commemorates a great achievement.

V: Thank you. I am looking forward to this celebration, which I think I may have got a small glimpse into this morning. While still in bed, I had a peek insight into the knowing that I am indeed, as are all, God: the creator Consciousness, and that this will become more pronounced for me as I continue this process. The preview was profoundly clear and inspiring.

A: This operating power is Self-fuelled; it arises from within and thus is not induced by any stimulus from without. It is one's Origin, one's Source, one's Authorship and Authority; hence, it is endowed with the agency and freedom to seek and flush out one's black sheep.

V: Black sheep?

A: Archetypal standard patterns, the primitive unrefined models guilty of not being principled, pure, virtuous, worthy or honest, etc. The damaging self-propelling representatives that inscribe one's autobiography.

V: I see, as in tainted ways of thinking, destructive habits etc.

A: Which are surly, disagreeable, harshly curt in manner or speech and often used as a crutch.

V: Right, so in a sense, we are gathering all the black sheep by way of becoming conscious of them, in order to release them, amend, rebuild and restore the truth of who we genuinely are.

A: Lacking means of subsistence, these deprived black sheep, which identify with one's corrupted anatomy and bent framework of reference, give way to the boundless and bounteous; thus, one can unite with one's Supreme Sovereign Authority.

V: Our true self.

A: Which is not here to suffer but to be filled with passion. Without Consciousness or Spirit there can only be chaos and painful eruptions: discharges from one's unhealed wounds. Hence, become Conscious of one's Consciousness: the ethereal fluid life-force that flows in the veins of the gods. Regard Consciousness as one's highest point of view. And stand grand to thus impress this Spirit on others.

18th September 2023

V: Another stye in the same eye. Arrgh! Is this more detoxing?

A: Authorised by one's authorship for one's vessel. Arising from within, not without.

V: Really? So, I'm creating this?

A: This has been generated by one to become an adroit, practiced, skilful expert. It has been crafted for one to absorb the experience and rise as from the sleep of unconsciousness; hence get understanding, thus make clear one's focus on the unfamiliar, on that which communicates via disorder, via that which disturbs one's normal health or functions.

V: Okay. So, what is my left eye trying to tell me? What disorder is it trying to reveal?

A: Its task is to reveal that one is surrounded by inflexible views; thus, obstinate beliefs and judgements amidst friends.

V: Amidst friends? What do you mean?

A: Those seen as not faithful, incorrect, untrustworthy.

V: Not faithful? You mean, as in those that don't think as I do?

A: Those seen as advocating anarchy: lawless confusion, disorder.

V: Well, I don't think I see my friends that way . . . Oh! You are referring to all individuals in general. Wow! I didn't stop to think that there are people I do see that way. I guess that's one way of looking at it. So, what do I do? How do I remove the speck from my eye, so to speak?

A: Popularize the populate: the people. Approve of people, admire, appreciate, accept, support, praise and respect them. To have many friends, apply Our prompter—*At the Chameleon, turn*—thus, one is reminded and inspired to bathe in the healing energy of one's Unified Kingdom and Source.

V: Cleanse myself with the truth of Us, of a Unified state that recognizes, values and comprehends the knowledge that God is All in all.

A: For the most part and to the greatest extent, with good grace and good-naturedly, remember this to fasten to the Highest in one.

V: What about these recurring skin rashes that keep appearing, what are they all about?

A: No other than you.

V: I'm the author of these, too?

A: One is able to inflict and wear these habitually.

V: Great. So, why am I doing this? What am I trying to see or tell myself regarding these?

A: One is seeing the elements, the features and facets of determinant principles—the beliefs and opinions one holds. Like the atmosphere displays its climate, thus are one's atmospherics: one's disturbances and discord exposed in the body's ecosystem. This is a basic, simple fundamental truth, suggestive of the powerful forces in nature and in man.

V: Well, how do I rid myself of them, as in the rashes?

A: Via composing and celebrating life harmoniously, via removing any ill-temper and nagging petty annoyances, via impregnating the mind with a sharp, focussed, keen Awareness born to become that which one's attention thus generates.

V: It always comes back to awareness. I need to know who and what I am, as in, really know it.

A: Correct. However, not via Analysis: the separation of a whole into its parts or elements, but via synthesis: the combining of one's constituent elements into a unified entity; the integration of traits, attitudes and impulses, via Awareness. For, non-sensed insincere exchange or communication renders one ineffective, cornering one into the jeopardizing, awkward position of being an intermediate for the disordered architectural style or manner of sequential worldly judgements, thus conclusions without any determinant guidance or leadership, producing penalising sentences.

7th October 2023

V: Hi. It's been nineteen days since we last conversed.

A: About composing life harmoniously.

V: Yes. There is a lot going on, as you know. I am on day twelve of a forty-day commitment to watch myself like a hawke and remain as aware of my thoughts and feelings as I possibly can. Meanwhile, I am still doing my twist exercises—not as often—but I connect to the image of our Quadriga several times a day and I am still affirming my chakra traits, not to mention writing what comes through for me from you in my encouragement journal, plus I am reading inspiring literature that resonates with me.

A: One is baking.

V: Hah! Yep, you could say that, as in preparing to expand and rise like a bun in the oven. Hmm . . . Not only does that allude to new life, but bread also denotes currency and sustenance, that's why it's referred to as a necessity of life.

A: One is preparing the mind to give light; henceforth, illuminate, enlighten, free-up, open, clarify.

V: Yes, that's the goal.

A: Hence, one attends to this via applying oneself to being present, along with stating and expressing one's collection of words—one's *"I Am"* phrases.

V: Yes, like: "I am Victorious."

A: And illimitable: incapable of being limited. Remember this, for one *is* limitless.

V: Okay. How about: "I am divine. I am infinite and boundless."

A: Know it thoroughly and with certainty.

V: And what about: "I am one with all that is."

A: Like a mediator for internal change, this I Am, gives and receives in return.

V: "I am intuitive and insightful."

A: Thus, an apostle, a messenger of good news: the wonderful, valuable news that all are capable of receiving clear, pure Awareness

V: "My voice purifies and heals."

A: One's voice, one's declarations, one's assertions and expressions become that which is produced; thus, be Aware; be Conscious of one's utterances. Open, expose the voice via a gentle purge, purify via eliminating dis-ease causing exclamations.

V: "I am an excellent, inspiring communicator."

A: An exchange derived by one via the cultivation of one's mind; hence, like a musical instrument, one produces harmonious tones.

V: "I love myself and others. I am an expression of love."

A: Hence, one is sensitive to Truth, to the influence of the All—the Whole spectrum, to Spirit's apparitions; for thus one comes back to life.

V: "I know who I am in truth—Consciousness, Awareness, Spirit, God."

A: This is uppermost. To know this is to acknowledge one's Highest influence and authority. Allow this to be foremost in one's mind; thus, one is in the ultimate, Unified state.

V: "I am powerful, confident and courageous. My potential is unlimited."

A: Unlimited potential blesses those who confess their errors and are resolved to make amendments.

V: That's interesting, so confessing, as in acknowledging one's mistakes, confers unlimited potential.

A: Declaring one's misprints improves the quality of one's impressions.

V: "I am creative and joyous."

A: Admittedly. Definitely. Undoubtedly! Thus, one binds to all purposes, to all drives, devotions, efforts and choices, via joy's creative, dependable, authentic, constant excellence.

V: "I am centred and grounded. I am safe. I am safe. I am safe."

A: A stance from which one rises and expands.

V: "I see and hear clearly."

A: Thus, one can unite with and turn from one's ill-nature; one can merge with one's unpleasant or spiteful disposition and hence, correct the corrupted.

V: "I honour my desires."

A: And thus, one turns aspirations to one's advantage.

V: "I am very, very grateful." Thank you, guys.

A: Henceforth, apply Our forewarning counsel.

V: That would be: *At the Chameleon, turn,* right?

A: Correct. Be attentive to everything. Be watchful. Look around.

9th October 2023

V: I erred, I slipped and fell head-on into the criticism game again. I am so annoyed with myself. And so now I have another stye in the same sinister left eye. My last stye was only three weeks ago. Arrgh!

A: Undoubtedly affected and caused via an excess of bile; that is to say, bitterness and irritability. Hereafter, subject this vitriol to the action of an alternate current, for this is the solution that conducts the befalling energy (urge) towards the befitting and proper.

V: Yes. At the Chameleon, turn. At my ego's transpiring, apparent drive to criticize, turn to an alternative form of expression. Any gossip or put down of another is not worth it. I need to take the log out of my eye and see the truth.

A: The log is inherited from one's antecedents, one's forebearers—the collective.

V: But I can put an end to it, right?

A: Correct. Via a clear ignitable Awareness, via applying a sharp, distinctly roused Consciousness as a solvent.

15th October 2023

V: "I am not a body."

A: One graduates to this knowledge in degrees upon completion of progressing along a course.

V: "I am Awareness, Consciousness, the light of the world."

A: On a quest, focussed on the direction and pursuit of ichor: the ethereal fluid flowing in the veins of the gods.

V: Yes indeed! Thank you Jesus, thank you Buddha, Krishna, Hathor, Isis, Venus; thank you Mohamad, Minerva, Kali, Iris, Ra, Sophia, Lao Tzu, Rumi, Socrates, Quan Yin, etc. etc. etc.

A: Employ all gods to strengthen one's character, utilize gods—one's brothers and sisters in life: the cultural deities, philosophers, mystics, sages, mentors and elders, etc.—as a pick-me-up to renew one's Spirit. Consume their stirring lore voraciously. Be engulfed by their wisdom and press forward. Develop with vigour and persistence.

V: Yes, there is certainly a lot to learn and become inspired from all these marvellous beings and forces of nature.

A: Hence, one advances, proceeding gradually step by step.

V: How can I better understand the Holy Spirit?

A: Like a ghost—that is to say—an unseen presence, resign one's mind to the Holy Spirit's harmonious vibration; thus, one celebrates in song.

V: Is that how we are communicating, through this unseen presence? Can you please explain it further?

A: One's daily quotient or share of this smooth, soft as velvet, invisible presence, is the same quantity contained in another; the evidence is provided and inscribed in all.

V: You've explained the Holy Spirit to me before as being wholly or supremely present, which yes, we all have access to an equal share of, and being present is also the only occasion in time that we can undo the Chameleon: the illusion we are separate from God, or as you prefer, Consciousness, which brings us right back to presence. Does that make sense?

A: Yes, this is a suitable representation; thus, one wins an advantage over mind's scoria of worthless thoughts.

V: To be clear, the Chameleon, which due to our habitual unconscious lapses is the illusion we are separate from God, and also what Buddhist and Hindus call Maya, it is furthermore—again due to our oblivious lapses—demonstrative of our everchanging, capricious modes of expression; what Jesus refers to as ego in the Course in Miracles or what would be known as the carnal self in the Bible, right?

A: The mentioned teachings are documented platforms, raised and put forth as formal systems and structures relaying principles for one to learn how to surrender one's titles, one's labels and identifications; thus, one can assign or transfer ownership, as would brethren of Jesus, to the Holy Spirit—one's whole presence, one's Conscious Awareness—for a return to life.

Having no religious beliefs but one's own clearly defined authority and vision, hold said platforms with an attitude of friendliness and approval conveyed via an indivisible force set up to protect life. View them as emblems of honour.

V: How did I get so confused as to reject their wisdom for a while?

A: The Chameleon's armor, the intensity—due to fear—of one's magnetic field to defame or disparage via the black death of unconscious ignorance, is the ego's, the carnal self's defensive covering.

V: Thank you.

19th October 2023

V: Good morning. As you know my skin is playing up again and my third stye has now turned into a chalazion. I am not putting anything on my skin as I am affirming that "I am not the body," however, I am putting hot compresses and apple-cider vinegar on the chalazion. I know this is contradictory, but I've identified with the body for sixty-two years: meaning this habit is hard to break, and trust in my true self needs to grow. Please advise me.

A: The body is amoral; hence, it lacks the sense of right or wrong. Love, however, is amorphous, it is without form. One will extinguish this body's debt and burden gradually via producing an impression in it that excites salubrious emotion. Thus, continue employing resonant audio frequency and visual aids, for this moves one forward in small degrees.

V: So, continue doing what I'm doing, listening to uplifting music, repeating my affirmations and visualizing my body healing.

A: Apply these as one would a soothing balm, for thus one produces an imprint. This is the art and practice of divination, inspiring awe and appreciation.

V: "I am not this body. I am the light, the awareness of the world. I am a child of God, of Consciousness itself."

A: Like a grapevine, this is a means of relaying information that bears fruit which is essential to one's nutrition and growth.

V: "I am divine, therefore I can divine. My voice purifies and heals. I am one with all that is, was, and ever will be."

A: Apply this as one's occupational therapy, for it treats nervous, mental, emotional and physical disabilities. This practice, designed to promote readjustment and recovery, is that which one must inhabit, create an inner habit of and dwell in.

V: So, keep soothing myself with these words and songs; these are my salve. Words can purify and heal.

A: We are one's pediment, the foundation of one's mind. *In the beginning was the Word* ... We are Word in form ... Idly indulging in whimsical fancies, that is, employing mind, thus Word, without beneficial purpose, is treacherous to one, for it is marked by guilt, hence imperfection. It is the act of violating one's faith, trust or allegiance to Source—Word.

V: Therefore, beware and aware of capricious thoughts, and allow only thoughts or words that calm, uplift and soothe, all else is deceit and treachery.

A: All else is pedantry: needless display of learning.

V: Which is incorrect because I have predominantly learnt from illusions and the collective's programming.

A: A programming that can be mastered and overcome, for being superior in strength and skill, one is more than a match for this.

V: So, to be clear, the world I see is not real at all. And therefore, genuine reality works completely different to what I have learnt.

A: The collective sees via El Lagarto: The Lizard. Like an alligator, like a stoney-eyed, cold-blooded, unfriendly reptile, this is the mainstream's outlook.

V: El Lagarto is the Chameleon, right? How interesting that the most ancient part of our brain, where the amygdala resides, which triggers the fight, flight or freeze response, is called the reptilian brain

A: This section impresses, thus produces a marked effect upon the mind and feelings, colouring, that is to say, influencing and firmly establishing ideas and beliefs within one via pressure.

V: Which is yet another reason you gave me the instruction: At the Chameleon, turn. In other words, at the effect my amygdala or reptilian brain is having on me, turn within to God's soothing balm of truth—transcend.

A: Employ Consciousness: the fundamental, structural, unifying principal of life, via inquiry, via seeking by investigation; hence one merges with Us, one's Unified state. Most are functioning without Conscious control. As Our apprentice, one needs to comprehend and learn the trade of exchange.

V: As in, I need to learn to trade what is false for what is true.

A: The further one is from the Light of one's Awareness, the less one should believe. This is one's autoclave; one's key to autocracy: absolute Self-government.

V: Self, as in True Self. "I am not a body."

A: One is not a body. Move in small degrees towards this Truth in every way completely.

V: What is the best balm I can focus on?

A: Our bond, that which holds Us together. Our great bonanza is Our Unified force, this is Our Source of wealth.

V: God?

A: The reservoir of psychic energy unaffected by the whine of ego. One's clear, precious, Sovereign Divinity.

23rd October 2023

V: My body, or rather ego/carnal mind, seems to be going all out to prove to me that I am a body. First with the styes, now the chalazion, not to mention the body aches, skin rashes, and this sudden assault of foot cramps. What is going on?

A: All related to the same root cause; hence, all allied to come forth.

V: What is the root cause?

A: One's incessant incertitude, one's doubtfulness, indecisiveness; thus, insecurity.

V: Really? Doubt is what's causing my body's ailments?

A: Doubt, distrust, uncertainty in Self, is one's standard pattern.

V: But my new balm, my soothing words will change this pattern, right?

A: Apply a salving prayer as one would a lotion, contemplate soothing, comforting word-balms daily as part of one's practice.

V: Wow... So, my ego's insecurities are causing all these bodily afflictions. That sucks, but it's good to know.

A: This is how ego—one's imprinted, carnal mind—communicates; thus, sentences one's identification with it.

V: Right. It still sucks that my ego is passing sentence on me by punishing my body.

A: Engage Us, be receptive and receive, yield without resistance, make passive openness one's manner of working and style of treatment. Own all relating to oneself; thus, one can rise high and roll onwards from the footprint of one's animal nature.

V: In other words, be present, see with Christ's vision, as in, see clearly, passively, without putting up walls. This is how true vision works. This is how miracle-mindedness functions. This is the treatment for healing. Own it all: my faults, failures and triumphs, that's how I raise my point of view, realign, and move beyond my ego.

A: Summed-up well.

V: Thank you. So, by passively observing all thoughts, situations, and feelings, etc. through Us (a Unified state or presence), we heal.

A: Hence, one vocalizes, communicates one's inclinations or calling via an instance of expression.

V: Ah! The Holy Instance, as Jesus calls it in *A Course in Miracles*.

A: So help me God.

V: Hah! I like that.

24th October 2023

V: Hmm... So, words, or rather, thoughts, which are obviously expressed in words, are my pediment: the foundation upon which my mind is built.

A: Hence, the absence of Being or Presence, causes dis-ease. Illumination of one's annals: one's records of past events, acts as an implement for weeding; thus, one can forsake one's faith in engrained ideologies, and become mentally and spiritually enlightened.

V: What you are basically saying is: "Be vigilant for God's Kingdom," as ACIM states, which is to say: Be constantly aware that I am Awareness itself. Be vigilant for Consciousness. Therefore, I need to remain conscious of the records, as in, the memories, words, thoughts and ideas with which my mind is imprinted, and use this illuminating force—this power to bring things into the light of my awareness—to weed out the dross, the worthless. By doing so, I can let go of any false ideas I had ignorantly put my trust in; principles I once thought to be true, but which on keen inspection, I can see are misleading.

A: Yes. Ideas, beliefs and viewpoints that one treated indulgently via gratifying their whims and impulses.

V: I see. So, I am building a new pediment with your help.

A: Correct. With Us, one is under the influence of a peaceful alignment with clarity, promoting affiliation, cooperation and solidarity.

V: Through words.

A: Like granules borne in clusters, words bear fruit—results.

V: Yes. Words are very much like small grains or seeds which, when placed in clusters with other words form sentences. Sentences that yield outcomes such that may imprison or free me.

A: Words can cause the apartheid, or the illumination of mankind.

V: I choose illumination, please.

A: One who holds illumination in trust, who loves harmony and thus treasures coherence enough to retain it carefully within the mind so that it spreads and branches out, weaves and bring all together as a whole.

26th October 2023

V: I'm curious. Did Jesus travel abroad from age twelve to thirty: the missing years in the bible?

A: To get ahead and advance, to have as an advantage; hence, influence and control self with little or no effort, he fraternised closely with a fraternal order, where upon he wore a distinguishing insignia to indicate rank.

V: Like a brotherhood of monks?

A: A brotherhood that taught one to see iniquity, vice or sin as a prompt to implement weeding, via self-determination and self-government. To first notice the disturbance in one's composure and remain true, sincere, faithful to one's principal purpose.

V: So, Jesus learnt how to use disturbances of the mind to his advantage, he discovered how to weed or clear them out and remain in a Unified state of equanimity.

A: Via employing headliners, via summarizing with a bold word or words bluntly, he made thoughts directly known and spoke frankly, freely and openly to himself, for declaring oneself imparts one's tendencies, giving one an opportunity to learn.

V: Yeah, to see what we have been imprinted with.

A: The anti-voice.

V: The anti-voice?

A: A voice lacking due respect and seriousness; a voice that is not beneficial for one to admire or adhere to in any manner or degree. A voice simply heard to rouse, summon and teach one to set in motion the treatment for healing.

V: Hmm... So, basically what Jesus learnt was to bring any thoughts that were not beneficial, as in not based in love, up to the surface to be healed. That is the teaching.

A: Pied a terre; hence, one has one's feet on the ground.

V: As in, my pediment, the foundation of my mind becomes better grounded—founded and supported.

A: Hence, one is at the foot of the mountain, the highland—the foundation of the Higher Mind.

30th October 2023

V: When I bless others with loving thoughts, I free them and therefore myself, right?

A: Always be faithful to love; thus, one is always prepared. Love is the motto, the catchphrase, the expression and embodiment of a Unified state. For love is Our everlasting Source, Our eternal Cause, Our infinite begetter, Our perpetual author, the natural stream to Our refuge, Our haven, Our shelter.

V: It's that simple? I just have to bless. I just need to desire the undoing more than I want to believe my own incorrect judgements.

A: Thus, one graduates a hundred degrees, causing self to undergo the experience of autonomy, the power of Self-government. One is standing at the beginning—at the foot of the mountain.

V: I think I am finally beginning to understand what you've been advising so that I can better serve myself and others.

A: We urge one be autonomous, Sovereign, free, Self-directed, via Self-determination.

V: So, I simply need to choose love over the Chameleon, as in the highest of the high over whatever illusion my mind has concocted, and love—source, consciousness—does the rest. I needn't worry about the outcome just trust all will be well. It's a win-win. I free another from my tainted assessment of them and love frees us both and corrects things.

A: Love corrects via electromagnetism, via the attraction of energy appropriate to the purpose. This is difficult to grasp and perceive.

V: I think I've grasped it, or at least beginning to. It is trusting in God, as in a supreme presence much larger than my limited frame of reference.

A: Which, due to the collective's encoding, is phantastic in style: whimsical, eccentric, illusory, elaborately ornamented with an unhelpful, disagreeable sense. To annul, to put an end to such disorder, choose to be light-hearted, carefree, unconcerned. This is the autoclave, the key to absolute Self-rule.

3rd November 2023

V: Please explain holiness to me further, as in, what is *my* holiness?

A: One's holiness comprises—via the act of fixing or focussing one's attention—the ability to attract or attain a desired state. Like a radio circuit receiver in which the incoming signal, *desired state*, is combined with a signal of fixed frequency, *one's holiness*, the resulting signal accordingly amplifies through the airways without difficulty.

V: So, you could say our holiness as humans involves our whole, thoroughly focussed conscious attention or awareness on our intention.

A: To identify with one's holiness, recognize it as one's wholeness, one's entirety, one's completeness; establish it as one's total being, consider oneself as being one with another, reject the notion that one is a foolish blunderbuss.

5th November 2023

V: Regarding what we last spoke about, ACIM says: *I am as God created me. I am the holy son of God.* From what you have taught me, I take that to mean: I am the whole light of awareness, the sun of consciousness, so to speak.

A: One's heredity is derived from one's parent; hence, one is the offspring of one's Source. Like an apostle commissioned by Christ to speak the Truth, the Light of one's Awareness or Consciousness—one's Source, empowers one to be crystal-clear when not disconnected.

V: Yes, well I certainly feel disconnected at times. How can I feel connected during these spells.

A: When feeling anxious or fearful, Move! Make an effort to shift one's body and mind. Authorise in the name and identity of one's Father, one's Source, one's Consciousness. As proud and noble as a spirited horse, be unimpressed by matters. Recall one's Sovereignty.

V: In the name of the Father the Son and the Holy Spirit. As the identity of our Source, our Light and Whole Presence. "I am Sovereign Awareness itself."

A: Acclaim and dispense Awareness in small quanta via one's spoken, living voice.

V: As in, keep proclaiming my true identity as radiant conscious energy within the field.

A: Thus, like a refracting telescope, one can divert one's range of vision, turn aside from the false, and via wedding oneself to a harmonious symbol such as the image of Pegasus, choose pure, spirited inspiration.

7th November 2023

V: Regarding the fact that I am not a body, and so, as ACIM says, I cannot be sick, which means any sort of illness is a defence against the truth, I tell you what, when the body is giving you grief, it is extremely difficult not to identify with it.

A: To recognize one cannot be sick is an amendment that changes circumstances for the better, for it corrects; thus, removes all faults.

The statement: "I cannot be sick," is an assertion for such a change.

V: Yes, but how do I make myself know this?

A: Mind is adaptable, malleable, compliant; hence, capable of changing to meet new conditions.

V: But clearly it is not sinking in, because my skin is still playing up.

A: Hence, one must ask: Am I a grantor or a grasshopper?

V: Hah! Funny... I see where you are going with this question. I guess I've been a grasshopper because I keep jumping around from plant to plant, as in, one implanted idea to another on how I can rid my body of these small patches of eczema. I have tried so many lotions and ointments, which means I am still buying into the notion that I am the body instead of actually being the one who is aware of the body; therefore, I haven't been a grantor, I have not granted or allowed the truth of what I really am to take root and correct things.

A: One needs to acquiesce, to consent, to harmoniously concur, passively assent, to act in conformity; thus, allow.

V: How?

A: Via a minor act. When one mistakes something as one's objective or the means for attaining it, that is to say, when one barks up the wrong tree or neural pathway, employ an amendment. Exchange the stock, trade the typical run-of-the-mill intent, flush out the misprints, the errors, the lapses and faults, become cleansed, purified—shine.

V: In other words, accept the truth of what I am: Spirit, Light, Love, Awareness, Eternal and Whole. This is the exchange of stock I need to focus on and employ, recalling this gives me an instant remedy when I bark up the wrong tree, as in forget I am not a body. I need to remember to exchange the false for the truth, even though appearances are showing me otherwise.

A: Performing this clear-cut, definite act, functions as a harmonizing agency of communication in support of Divine favour, which the participant feels. This is the exchange, this is the agreement made, this is the procedure constituting the earliest stage in a change of policy within one's govern-mental administration.

V: Basically, I must keep reminding myself of what I really am.

A: To produce harmonious tones, tendencies and attitudes; thus, create natural vibrations, one must strictly adhere to this requirement.

V: And so, I will eventually know this as true.

A: One will know this as one's own prophecy made under the Divine influence and inspiration of one's Awareness. Hence, do not cover Spirit: Supreme Presence Inspiring Real Inner Tuition, with the deceptive, needless display of one's learnings.

V: Please comment on the idea I've just had: God, or our **G**enuine **O**ptimal **D**rive, which is Awareness, utters a frequency that unites us and transmits power to us.

A: Assonance, partial agreement or correspondence with such, causes association, fellowship and common purpose. Adversely, the incompatible is incapable of coexisting harmoniously, thus is disagreeable in nature, conflicting, harmful in effect, for it reflects lack.

V: Is there any difference between presence and awareness?

A: Presence constructs from whatever comes to hand, Awareness is Self-determination, autonomy; it is one's Sovereignty.

V: But they both go hand in hand, right?

A: Akin to an elaborate, sophisticated dance.

V: So, by way of awareness, I can filter my thoughts.

A: Hence, one acquires choice, freedom, autonomy, Self-determination, the power of Self-government.

V: And presence is acknowledging what is, allowing it to be, and creating or constructing whatever comes to hand.

A: Which, like frenzied songs and dances, can be marked by harried, agitated words, thoughts and feelings; thus, frantic moves, hectic paces and actions.

V: Because where others are involved, due to the mixed, different ways of seeing things, anything can happen. That's why it pays to remain present.

A: Hence, akin to an honorary head of state, a governor of oneself, hear one's confession of transgressions and the lacks concealed from one via the garment of ignorance, the sleep of being unaware, unconscious.

V: The garment is and conceals the Chameleon.

A: The death of sight.

V: And awareness gives life to sight.

A: Like the postal service, Awareness is charged with carrying and delivering mail: information, communication, correspondence. To be Aware is to be possessed of wisdom.

9th November 2023

V: Wow! My connection to God, to Consciousness, to Spirit, to All that is, was, and ever will be, is awareness because I am still as God created me—Awareness.

A: One is in the process of retrieving Awareness, of restoring, of recovering, of calling to mind the venerable: that meriting honour, that worthy of reverence, exciting feelings due to its sacredness; a sacredness that gives passage to a form of being, to a nature, a quality, a manner that is of the highest degree, that is absolute, that is the very Truth, yielding verve, enthusiasm: God's inspiration, Spirit, Creativeness.

V: Simply by being aware?

A: Awareness speaks of one's nature, conception and constitution, as well as physical and universal life force.

V: I am whatever I conceive myself to be.

A: A clause dependant on Awareness. Adjoin this sentence as part of one's composition to have good Self-government. Bear and possess this phrase as an attitude; hold it in one's mind and among one's feelings. Allow it to be clear and resounding like a clarion in every way completely. Regard it as a counsel of the highest rank; thus, one tends to excite: to energize and arouse Self to respond with Awareness.

V: How are love and awareness connected?

A: Love places one's Awareness in a natural position; it placates, satisfies and appeases. Love is an uncomplicated communication. Via Love, one receives and transmits resonant, wholesome waves of information, fostering good health.

V: Is it fair to say: God is the awareness of love, then?

A: Hence, God is one's benevolence, one's disposition to do good, to wish well.

V: So, I need to know myself as love.

A: Correct, however, one walks along the edge of deception in this amphitheatre where blood flows copiously as people are broken down and ruined, thus broken hearted.

V: I feel like you are referring to the wars presently going on.

A: Conflict, being poles apart from Love, differs greatly.

V: Yes, it is extremely disturbing.

A: Disturbance has the power to move the feelings.

V: Yes, for those who honour human life and abhor needless suffering, but some seem unaffected.

A: One's disturbance may be used as an entry, for it gives one access to that which binds one; thus, one can examine and overhaul one's imprinted agreements.

11th November 2023

V: It's Remembrance Day! I need to knuckle-down on remembering to remain constantly aware, as in perpetually conscious of my thoughts concerning all that is transpiring.

A: Awareness may be used—via making an effort—to wholly and entirely repair and cleanse one's vessel. Hence, go all out for Victory, and recall one's Supreme Being.

V: I feel significantly and clearly guided at present.

A: One is brilliantly influenced by Master teachers learned in the law of imprinting coherence, soundness and harmony.

12th November 2023

V: Is there anything you wish me to know today?

A: Observe chivalry to attain the qualities of an ideal knight. Be noble, courteous, loyal, generous, gracious and courageous; hence one leaps, pertaining to time, into being favoured with good fortune, for one beams radiantly bright.

V: Sounds like a way to leap into a new timeline.

A: One generates that in complete relation or degree to what one thinks; hence, what one produces or constructs as one creates one's Word.

V: So, in a sense, my words or thoughts are broadcasting what I am likely to create.

A: Thus, proceed with twists and turns until evidence of a statement or state of mind is true of one's identity.

V: At the Chameleon: the appearance of what I'd rather not see or be, turn (transcend) to the awareness of what I would prefer to create. Is that what you mean?

A: One's supporting part is to care for the establishment of Awareness and thus allow all to be without active opposition, for Awareness recognizes the rights of the individual to their own opinion and customs. This realm consists of many voices.

14th November 2023

V: So, when I care for the establishment of awareness, as in, when I am attentive to the presence of my awareness and therefore can confirm it, uphold it and rest in it without logging into or engaging with any thoughts, feelings or judgements that arise, this is when God truly communicates with me, so to speak. This manner of care nurtures me back.

A: Like an icebreaker, Awareness cracks open the frozen or rigid bids of the Id's: I should, I would, I had. Awareness brings forth a particular quality where one exists in a direct state; thus, one can receive the wise words of Archangels.

V: In a sense, it's like removing all the static so that I can have better reception. Awareness helps us tune into Source.

A: Hence one has begun an ascent as by means of jet propulsion, and thus attained capacity of operation, bimonthly.

V: Bimonthly? I don't understand.

A: As a gentle purgative, one has been thrown beyond excess bimonthly, turning against the opposite, that is to say: away from conflict in order to illuminate and shed light on the apathy of the old-world primate.

V: Twice a month I've been thrown into the deep end, so to speak.

A: Uttering, with grief, those things over which the authority of Awareness may be exercised.

V: So, what you're saying is that around twice a month, I am purging that which needs to be seen and let go of, that which is holding me back, which is part of my old-world programming.

A: This is the act of progressing, of advancing toward fuller development.

V: And it occurs bimonthly?

A: Unerringly. Precisely.

V: Really? When? I haven't been keeping tabs. Did I notice it?

A: One's evolution is based on conditions of the highest learning or realization via electing love.

V: Oh, so I slightly evolved each time I chose love over fear.

A: Akin to one who plays a carillon, setting off resonating chimes, one's vibration becomes highly receptive to impressions that are centric to maintaining conditions favouring optimum development; hence, via frequent repetition one inculcates the wise language of Our Unified Kingdom.

V: I see. So, I am learning to hear and speak my true resonant language.

A: Which is not insolent, overbearing, offensive or disrespectful, neither is it severe, grave or stern, but rather it makes "one's Self" known, and thus provides service to the community.

V: I am learning to hear the wholly spirit, the voice for God, the voice of Consciousness.

A: Which has extraordinary intelligence surpassing that of intellectually superior individuals, for it is supernatural, and hence appointed to guide one throughout life.

V: Thank you.

15th November 2023

V: Well, I certainly missed the mark today. That toxic customer! Argh! That woman that was relentlessly gas-lighting my son by obnoxiously claiming that he was oversensitive etc., was not only rude, loud, hateful, aggressive, putting on airs as though she was of superior stock, but was also clearly unhinged. Still, I feel I let myself and you down for going into protective mode and snapping back at her. My son, Christopher, to his credit, remained calm. I should have stayed out of it and simply practiced being aware.

A: One engaged.

V: I know! I completely lost it. I'm sorry. Talk about going unconscious.

A: Notwithstanding, one's current clear Awareness—expressed via one's disappointment in self—of the cloaked facade, the usually unseen charge contained in one's vessel, makes one a member of Christ's vision.

V: How?

A: Understand that acknowledging one is feeling crestfallen, is a useful advantage, for it places one under the jurisdiction of Awareness; thus irrigates, refreshes and revitalises one.

V: Basically, what you are saying is that the mere fact that I am feeling disappointed in myself, is a clear indication that I have become more aware, so I've progressed. Therefore, l simply need to learn from the experience, allow my awareness to sharpen and see beyond the cloak of illusion that hides the truth; remembering to place all circumstances in the custody of Consciousness (God).

A: Awareness is the agent used to destroy dis-ease whilst one is in this dual handled earthenware. Giving one's distress to God is one's salvation; hence, drink freely of Awareness to enter upon a projection at its beginning.

20th November 2023

V: I have one word, eczema. Why is my skin playing up this way?

A: It has become evident in order to prune it.

V: As in, so I can see it and eliminate it?

A: First one must see the birthplace where something originates.

V: Is it the food I'm eating, is that where it stems from?

A: Annihilate this idea.

V: Am I eating too much fruit?

A: Again, this idea is high bribery that seduces and allures one to believe one is a body.

V: Well, what can I do to eliminate it?

A: Consume a song of praise and thanksgiving, feast on acclaim, on approval, on one's blessings, on gratitude, and wed it to any infelicity, to any inappropriate remark, state, or observance to remove the apathy, the depression, the ignorance, despair and insensibility of the old-world primate: one's past indoctrination.

V: So, every time I get stressed over something including the current state of my skin, be thankful for all my blessings, shift or turn the inner narrative towards loving myself instead.

A: However, first see the ireful, the wrath and anger one holds, then extinguish it via lack of fuel.

V: So, it is the thoughts I'm consuming, not the food. I need to watch these carefully.

A: A confused state imbues one with its influence.

V: Yes, confused because it's challenging to recall that I am not a body.

A: Hence, We urge against any course of action.

V: Other than feasting on praise and thanksgiving.

A: For this will clothe one in a garment that is characteristic of one's calling; thus, profess glory.

21st November 2023

V: Okay, I may not be a body, but I have one.

A: Like a column with a capital and base, a unit, one can be regarded as an individual; however, one belongs to an entire associated cooperative. Thus, to give one-self vigour and health, reunite via the Awareness of one's corelated fellowship with all, bring oneself into connection, kinship and alliance. Or, lapse back into dis-ease via bad habits.

V: I know who I truly Am: Awareness, Consciousness, the recognition that I am love, and loved, and therefore I am whole and holy.

A: Recognizing Awareness as having had a generous, gracious, beautiful influence on one coming into bloom, becomes a pathway for the transmission of Truth.

V: Speaking of the transmission or communication of truth, I am on the last composition for our testaments, as you call them, on Instagram and X. What would you have me do once I'm done?

A: Tell the story of the way out of the infective and infelicitous. This is how one goes forth.

V: And you believe I am ready to tell this?

A: It is in one's nature to partake and share of the weave We have keenly and skilfully elaborated.

V: Even though I am no expert. I mean I still get things wrong; I still forget to remain present and not get myself embroiled in life's dramas.

A: To descend to the apparent, to trusting the outward facade of this world is to choose the unauthentic, improper, negligent and unbrotherly.

V: So, you will help me, right?

A: Child, We are one's foundation and measure.

23rd November 2023

V: Okay, so I woke up again with that same feeling of apathy and sadness I have been experiencing off and on lately. I was aware of the glum musings accompanying the mood, but this did not dissolve the hollowness I sensed. Later I read through some of our conversations, and I remembered who and what I am: a child of God, Awareness itself. As I put down my journal, my eyes landed on the novel I wrote and named after the first message you delivered to me so markedly: *"At the Chameleon, Turn,"* and I thought, of course, at the Chameleon, turn to God, at the appearance of distress, turn to Source, to the Awareness of what I truly am. Consciousness is our salvation, so to speak. I must drink freely of this realization to enter upon projections at their beginning, as you say.

A: Our proposal: "We Exist, Our Own Hierarchy. At the Chameleon, Turn," was an offer declaring something to be accepted and adopted. It was proffered for one to unify via said plan.

V: Yes, although I didn't know it then, you proposed that I consent to and assume the plan to turn away from illusion and choose again to turn to God, to unite with our Source.

A: It was a behest: an authoritative request and directive as well as a vow that, if one executes this to a hair with the utmost exactness, one can gain power over what one births.

V: So, I would be better able to manage my life and what I manifest.

A: Hence, one becomes frugal, that is to say, one exercises economy, saving time via consuming only the fruit that is fit to eat. The consequence of such an action or effort being, that one lives in joy.

V: Why has this taken me so long to understand?

A: One's longing for familiar circumstance that are now remote or irrecoverable, and one's severe homesickness for Source have caused one to move to and fro.

V: So, I keep oscillating between my old familiar programming and the new method you've taught me of connecting with Source. I need to decide on, accept and adopt God's plan.

A: The passage, the transition from one state to another is a journey of observance.

V: That reminds me, the other day my son Antonni playfully asked: "What do you get when you squeeze or put pressure on an orange?" To which I replied, "Orange juice, of course." He smiled, and proceeded with: "And if someone severely squeezed or pressured you, what would happen?" Frowning, I responded, "Well, I'd probably get angry." To which he said, eyes sparkling with amusement: "So, you are full of anger, mum." I laughed, but it made me think.

A: Boohoo. To weep out loud is just and appropriate, to leak or exude sadness is merited, as it is also proper to discharge anger, for thus one can direct it upward.

V: I guess I am not just full of anger, I am full of sadness, pain and distress which, I know you will help me channel skyward.

A: One issues these emotions spasmodically from within; thus, give vent to them in order to de-vice, that is to say: in order to remove one's vices, imperfections, weaknesses and failings, etc., incurred from the craftiness of this worlds malevolent blueprint.

V: At the Chameleon, Turn.

A: One senses; thus, knows when something is off.

V: Can you please comment on the first part of your message to me: We exist our own hierarchy.

A: This short, repeated part of Our speech which is changeless; thus, eternal and free of deviation, endures to reveal one's inner Self or Psyche, one's Soul, which gradually unfolds as one brings the eternal into active existence.

24ᵗʰ November 2023

V: What gifts or talents do I have that you wish me to share with the world?

A: One can anagrammatize, that is to say, one can arrange words, hence thoughts and ideas like a cipher, interchanging and transposing the core essence communicated by another word or phrase.

V: As in, our communication system?

A: Which is structured via a higher, robust Unified state; hence, like a medicinal herb that sprouts buds used for healing, has sound Sovereign results one can consume, for this system too has wholesome roots.

V: Okay, yes, I get what you mean, and I love that you have taught me to communicate this way; however, is there anything else I may eventually be good at?

A: Broadcasting this vision, speaking one's piece with peace, thoroughly occupied by a pleasant, agreeable sense as though suffused with a fragrance; for thus one greatly expands and binds as with withes, creating flexible neuro pathways when, while engaged in controversy, one Turns (Transcends).

V: Really? That's my superpower, so to speak—Turning. As in: At the Chameleon, Turn... This is what you have been prepping me to share with the world?

A: Akin to a healing balm or refreshing perfume; hence, make an effort to accomplish.

V: You wish me to communicate and broadcast this so-called fragrance, this soothing sense of perception.

A: Like a service stripe, one is marked by a reverential Spirit that is dutiful and respectful concerning the nature of mysteries and hidden rites.

25th November 2023

V: Let me get this straight: You would like me to commit to broadcasting this message: "At the Chameleon, Turn," which, you say that, like spreading an appeasing fragrance, people can sense and know, and by applying it, be eased and freed of their shortcomings.

A: For Turning allows passage, especially of Conscious Awareness to spread thoroughly through one.

V: Why did you choose me for this?

A: Because one refines and rejuvenates Self daily, and thus, remains firm in one's position, establishing a foundation for the mind as one would erect a Supreme Court Building.

V: So, I was built for this, in a sense?

A: One chose to consume and absorb Our light in small quantities.

V: Why haven't you given me any more major reveals since you powerfully announced: "We Exist, Our Own Hierarchy. At the Chameleon, Turn."?

A: One chose to build brick by brick. One preferred to compose one's song of praise and thanksgiving in sections. One elected to form and bear fruit in instances. One decided to surpass striving and struggling gradually.

V: I'm tired of the struggling and striving to recall all of this. Can I please have a major revelation of light that will just make me see?

A: This would be reckless and frightening for one. It is best to harvest the fruit when ripe. Know, We are born from the same Source, and that together, via careful consideration, reflection and thought, We reason and understand.

V: So, for now, just keep on Turning, right?

A: Turning produces benefit; it is advantageous and effective.

V: Do I have much more to refine?

A: Resembling horns that protrude from the head and that also sound an alarm, one has projections: tormenting, troublesome thoughts that forecast the unfavourable, faulty or incorrect via exhibiting a distressing display. One needs to set these aglow completely. One needs to ignite these; hence, elect to exhilarate, lift and gladden. We strongly recommend one exhumes these and brings them to light. We encourage one to reveal these with urgency, with necessity, and with immediate attention. Expose all the exiguous: one's seeming inadequacies, one's narrow-mindedness, one's paltry, petty and pitiful self-imposed limitations, all the small and scanty; hence, one can exile these from existence, from one's presence and occurrence.

V: Thank you. That is what I try to do, become aware of these when they ignite, and Turn, as in, choose to exchange or transcend them. But, why, after all of our discussions, etc., would a big reveal still scare me?

A: One would feel persistently persecuted.

V: I don't understand, why?

A: One lacks clarity, transparency, idly indulging in fancies; thus, one would be thrown into disorder.

V: Why? Am I not evolved enough? How is it that some people suddenly become channels and have been okay? Is my view of reality still too fixed?

A: One is in a distinctly diverse stage of life; hence would be made homeless via conflict, thus forced to live in a foreign state, in a condition whereby the nature of irony and incongruity—a paradox in which main elements are rationally or emotionally incompatible because of contrast, controversy or surprise—reign. For one to expand the magnitude of one's Awareness throughout eternity, one must incessantly, constantly, forevermore plow the soil of one's mind; one must bind in close alliance to Us, and one must openly and honestly declare the uncompleted, uncompliant or inflexible, and uncontested; hence, after one bears it all, one sees.

V: So, basically, trust that everything is unfolding for me at the appropriate pace, right?

A: Hence, one is clothed in the vesture of a Master learned in the law aimed at fallen Angels. Like a radio, Turn one's dial toward the frequency wave of relief and refuge via a pause; thus, the resplendent and brilliant can respond to the unphilosophic: to one's lack of wisdom.

V: When you say pause, that's like what ACIM calls the holy instant, where God or Awareness can come in and give us an answer, right?

A: It is the small act of stalling, supporting the present which displays the wares on sale: the distortions of perception that may be traded for goods that are sound and advantageous. The stall, or pause, is a pathway leading into the main part of a construction for creating another form or way of being; thus, sing Alleluia and praise ye the pause.

V: What do I do during the pause?

A: Observe the unbalanced, the volatile, nervous, tense, agitated, rash, wired, hyperactive, etc.

V: Just watch, just observe, just be aware of, just see the distortions presented.

A: Until one can ameliorate, amend, reorganize, improve on, and say Amen. So be it, verily, truly.

V: Right, so to pause is like taking a break or a short rest by way of simply being aware of the drama without letting myself get drawn in, which allows the pause to do its magic, so to speak.

A: This is a fundamental and relatively simple element of one's rudimentary essence, suggestive of the powerful forces in nature and in man.

V: This reminds me of the story about the fish that did not know what water was because it had been living in it its whole life.

A: Like the water, Awareness has great degrees of capacity, for Consciousness is abundant and fully sufficient; thus, God perseveres; God sustains all. An act of God is to elate, it is to raise the Spirit and fulfil Self with joy and triumph; thus, with great energy, intently and earnestly observe one's mortal relics and disown that which disorients, relinquish that which causes one to lose one's perspective and direction and hence bring discredit upon one, renounce that which causes one to have less esteem, surrender that which gets under one's skin, for these are like pens for animals, keeping one enclosed as such.

26th November 2023

V: Be still and know that I Am God. In other words, rest or pause in God, in Awareness without judgement. Trust that God only wants what is best for me. Get out of God's, or Consciousness' way—let us not be deceived into credulousness.

A: Hence, one shares and partakes via relaxing the body and its perceptions, allowing the principle of life to flow spontaneously without restraint.

27th November 2023

V: Above all else I would like to see and know the truth. Please comment.

A: One lacks definite aim and intention. One lacks definite purpose. Nevertheless: We speak to one peaceably, yet one will not listen.

V: My apologies. How may I change this? What do I need to focus on? How can I best hear you?

A: Be one who serves loyally in this cause to unify Self and others. Do not quibble or fuss over trivialities. Do not be capricious, ill-tempered, petulant, or peevish. Do not be narrow-minded, mean or spiteful; however, do not withhold these recessions either, do not suppress or deny these downward turns, see the sheepskin, the covering that conceals and fools with ludicrous failure.

V: Sheepskin?

A: The fleece that deceives and swindles one.

V: Oh! As in blindly following the downward turns because I didn't pause at their ignition and observe them. As in ignorantly acting out of fear—false evidence appearing real.

A: Liken this to panhandling, to begging on the street.

V: So, to be clear, you are basically saying that I, we, all of us as humans, have access to knowledge and wisdom, however the fact we don't pause, observe and become aware of this leads us like ignorant sheep, which at the crux of it, is much like blindly choosing to beg for scraps on the street.

A: It is hilarious that one's choice to beg or follow like a fool is a cause of disagreement with Us. To impart knowledge or wisdom, We need to share, make known, and be free of bias; thus, do not favour one thing above another. Choose to be good natured, for being of a genial disposition transforms one into the same.

28th November 2023

V: I am still waking up with this feeling of apathy or dispiritedness, which I am profoundly aware of, but not sure what to do about. I think that the downheartedness is coming from an egoic notion that I should be further along on this path.

A: One's Awareness of the low spirits promote one's conversion from a selfish, self-centred soul which is bound and restricted by limitations, to a Soul that shares and makes all known; hence, can surrender egoic notions to one's ever-present companion—God.

V: Okay, I am making it known. I am thoroughly aware of the gnawing sadness, but how do I surrender it as you say.

A: Awareness provides one's grief with an opening, a breakthrough into the sleep of unconsciousness; thus, one can painstakingly feel the hollowness, the meaningless and empty.

V: But it feels horrible. I don't want to feel this way. I want to be rid of it.

A: Hence, Turn in a sure and certain direction toward Us, toward Awareness as one's Unified state, and drink in the present, absorb the currency being offered for laundering, the energy presented for refining. When forced by circumstances to listen to something, then look at, see what ideas it imbues one with. This is the path of surrender that yields the right to operate, trade and manage one's magnified, overstated hyperbole to Us.

V: So, it is not about trying to get rid of these yukky feelings, it is about just listening and seeing the mindset they engender. I need to remember not to engage and fall for the hyperbole as though it were true.

A: Thus, make it known. Shine a beacon of light upon it; hence, one can regulate and set in order.

V: This is part of the purification process, the practice of refinement.

A: As one of pure character, one is vested with a strong commitment to a system that serves one well.

V: Above all else I want to know the truth. I think that's what is making me sad, the fact that I still feel separate from God.

A: One is affected by a sense of one's own guilt and resolved on amendment. Guilt imprisons the mind.

V: So, I am purging my guilt, my faults, my self-reproach, my remorse.

A: Like a witch-hunt, We uncover subversive activities that undermine and corrupt one's morals, for these have the power to bewitch one and engross the mind. Thus, We preordain, We set in order before they are offered to one to buy or believe. This is the act of preparation taken in advance.

V: When will I be finally free of all my so-called guilt?

A: It will be Self-evident, for as one examines one's existence, it becomes Self-explanatory. One shall see that Self-expression seeds and fertilizers one's governing mind; hence one can help oneself heal.

V: Great. Is that any time soon?

A: In conclusion, become Aware of one's resistance, for one's ego is preventing the return to Consciousness of unpleasant incidents and experiences.

V: Right, so my ego's the one resisting the purge. What you resists persists. That's why these horrid feelings keep arising.

A: One will become experienced in observing and predicting one's weather patterns: the moods, attitudes and dispositions of one's weave—the interlacing threads and branches of one's tree of life: One's nervous system.

V: Thank you. I'm sorry I am filled with so much doubt.

A: Thus, withdraw from association with doubt's fellowship.

29th November 2023

V: I have been reading some compositions by Joseph Seiber Benner, the 1872–1938 American New Thought writer; he says we shouldn't allow anything negative to enter our mind.

A: Benner was a novice, a neophyte in service to a Unified state (Us). In reference to him schooling the common people henceforth, he imparted that to be a grumbling person or of an ill-nature was to invoke this from heaven. Benner was an intelligent person with collective mental power.

V: But?

A: The crestfallen, the depressed or dispirited who are producing an impression via exciting emotions that are ballyhoo, that is to say, blatantly or sensationally making themselves known, require a balm that soothes, they are in need of a fragrance that pleases, for each individual is different, each has distinctive characteristics.

V: So, each person needs to make their grief known before they can soothe and heal it, not simply discard, reject or resist it, as this would only reinforce the problem because they'd be pushing it down, back into the unconscious where it can't have the light of their awareness shed upon it.

A: Grievances need to be bathed in sunshine without being taken literally, not hidden in a place of concealment.

V: So, Benner is wrong in this sense, yes?

A: As a servant of the public, he narrowly adhered to a rigid routine.

V: The key seems to be, not to take things literally or as fact. Is there a simple way to use this key?

A: To maintain under conditions favouring optimum development, browse, look over one's merchandise, one's imports and exports, one's mental stock, casually; thus, one can hew the hex, the spell one is under. Conform to this as a principle.

V: Casually, as in without any intention or plan, as in nonchalantly without desiring anything, as in, indifferent, unconcerned, showing no preference, as in, unbiased.

A: Browse with the warm, welcoming current of Awareness, for this stream of energy swallows up and engulfs one's weeds, the unwanted plants and remains of one's early human culture, one's societal indoctrination, discovered via these systematic mental excavations.

V: Like Jesus said: *"Take no thought* (be not anxious or concerned) *saying what shall we eat, or what shall we drink, or wherewithal shall we be clothed; for your heavenly Father knoweth that ye have need of all these things. But seek ye first the Kingdom of God* (Consciousness), *and his righteousness* (truth and right ideas), *and all these things will be added unto you."*

A: Play this, that is to say, emit, radiate, be, enact, decree, authorise this Truth freely and continuously, allow it to flow from one like a fountain, for thus one gives forth a musical sound, a harmonious resonance that will be exhibited.

30th November 2023

V: Thank you, thank you, thank you! Thank you for everything you have taught me so far. I feel good today. Question. How can I best feel God's presence? Oh! I just realized the answer. Gratitude!

A: Gratitude, appreciation, gratefulness, causes one's hodgepodge of past records to collapse. Being full of thanks crumples one's jumbled mix of disturbing, pitiful memories, the hocus-pocus of deceptive retentions one adheres to. Gratitude enlightens.

V: Yes, yes. When I was thanking you, my heart felt relief and joy, and yes, lighter.

A: Lack of higher emotions leads to lawless confusion, a result of fear, the offspring of a poorly conditioned mind. Higher emotions like gratitude make ideas thrive. Awareness, which makes one's appreciation known, imparts and shares the happiness a lover of a Unified Kingdom (Optimal State of Coherence) is thankful for.

V: So, gratitude is one of the best emotions to feel God (good).

A: Expressing gratitude brings one into harmony; thus, adjust to this frequency frequently.

V: Thank you, I will.

2nd December 2023

V: I will have finished our two testaments on Instagram and X by the end of next week.

A: Manuscripts written on these platforms designed for supercharged superconductivity, compel, as by forceful persuasion, the reckless soul, conveying a seeding element as of ideas in the abode of spirits departed from Consciousness.

V: Yes, well, hopefully our compositions will seed people with ideas that bring benefit to their lives. In any case, what do I do next? You previously said I need to tell the story of the way out and forward. How am I going to do that?

A: It is clear cut. It has distinctly and acutely been outlined for one: Be clear in one's thoughts, for as one clears one's house of clutter, one becomes clear sighted.

V: Outlined? As in, outlined in the conversations we have been having?

A: Correct, they emphasize the importance of the individual to carpediem: enjoy the present and seize the day, the opportunities presented via Awareness, for one is incapable of dividing oneself from Consciousness. Its bloom fills one with glowing health; hence, the state of believing oneself inferior—pertaining to the world of the unconscious or rather the mechanically ignorant—will be free of this pathology.

V: Being free of this pathology sounds wonderful, but I am still not totally there, so, how am I supposed to tell others about it?

A: One's sense for peace knows how. One's longing to return home to a Unified Kingdom—to a Higher Octave, to an Enlightening Voice, a Sound Resonance, hidden but at hand—understands. Hence, the wholly welcomed is brought forth, filling the theatre of life with wholesome, beneficial fruits; thus, enthusiasm and devotion, harmony and accord, are easily intermingled with the spoken.

18th December 2023

V: As you know, I have been reading my journal, studying our past conversations again, and as I was taking everything in, I kept getting the impression that I should record our dialogues on the computer and perhaps turn them into a Q & A book called: *We Exist, Our Own Hierarchy*. Was that you suggesting this to me?

A: Write, communicate Us to all. Be outright: free from reserve or restraint. Use our conversations completely without reservation or limitation, do this openly and utterly without delay.

V: Right, well that's a resounding yes.

A: Write as a supplement to the testaments and book.

V: Book? As in supplement to: *At the Chameleon, Turn*?

A: Thus, like catching fish with a jig, one has various combinations of hooks for those devotedly attached to having their *"bound for home"* course directed.

V: Well, I guess I have everything I need. I just have to tidy it up a bit, which I know you will be helping me with, right?

A: Helped by Almighty God, the Supreme Being, to support those easily deceived, for thus they become newly baptised (immersed in Consciousness) and return to life.

V: So, this is the new project for 2024?

A: Our words are vivid and stimulating; hence, affecting the mind and feelings. We educate via the operation of forming new furrows, thus harmonies for one to file when confused, disconcerted or agitated. Thus, 2024 is the year one will progressively attend to ministering and developing Our uniformity on all sides, extending from one's centre, like beams of light that can be made of service.

V: And so, our book, *We Exist Our Own Hierarchy*, shall begin.

A: Our book is non-sectarian, neither restricted to any religion, nor associated with any sect or faction. This book is composed to produce a rattling, a shake-up. Hence, wend, proceed on one's course, create, generate, emit abundantly windward; thus, all may have a position of advantage.

***

FINAL WORDS

Dear reader, as I write this ending here in Australia, it is the 20th of January 2025, and the world is in turmoil, with God knows what may be in store for us next. I sincerely hope that you have enjoyed, resonated, and been able to glean something for yourself from my conversations with Spirit, as they have certainly brought much peace to my life, and so I pray that their answers are of some benefit for you as well.

I continue to speak with Spirit in the format they've assured was best for me to assimilate and manage, however due to applying their advice, their voice and prompts have become clearer to me, and so I use the process of attaining and journaling their answers more now for confirmation and because I simply love receiving their answers.

In closing, I leave you with the prayer Spirit gave me many years ago, which I have made reference to in this book and also incorporated into my fictional book: *At the Chameleon, Turn*. Unlike I did in my novel, I have added some clarification. This prayer may sound somewhat familiar as I had asked Spirit to elucidate the Our Father (Lord's prayer) for me in their words. I call it Ariel's Prayer, who, to make things simple for me, is the spokesvoice, you could say, for my four mentors, teachers, companions, guides, guardians and friends, whichever title you prefer as they have been all of these to me and more.

Without further explanation but to say I feel intuitively guided to end our book this way, I present:

Ariel's prayer

Our illuminating Consciousness,

Which art to the same degree as our Nobility and Excellence,

Allowance be thy way.

Thy Guidance and Mastership come.

Thy change and evolution be done,

On earth as a step of preparation for the Mutual Interchange of Ideas.

Give us a subtle delusion of fanciful dreams and visions,

But mutually protect us from our temper-mental moods,

As we purify this state from those thoughts which lack good sense.

And let us not be deceived into credulousness,

But let us depart from the reactor.

For having the nature of animal,

And the sensitivity of Consciousness to correct incorrectness,

Are self confessing.

For to step into Now,

Reveals eternity put into place.

So be it.

ARIEL'S PRAYER EXPLAINED

Clarification:

Our, is a word which of course means—belongs to us, and in this case all of us. This may seem unnecessary to clarify, but it is actually quite important to be perfectly clear regarding its significance.

Our illuminating Consciousness: *Consciousness,* at its most basic level, is that which we all have in common; it connects us. We are all an individualized facet of a Grander, Principal Consciousness—God, the Holy Spirit, Source, the Great Mystery, the Creator, the Universe, the Force. What we choose to call it is personal to each; however, no one can deny *Consciousness exists*; it is that which informs and acquaints us with the certitude that *"we"* exist.

Our illuminating Consciousness, which art to the same degree as our Nobility and Excellence: Consciousness is unceasingly present, it is always and already here; nonetheless, we can act unconsciously, so there are degrees to our awareness of it. The more aware of Consciousness we become, the higher, more *Noble* and *Excellent* thoughts we can choose to focus on, as well as act upon, and therefore the more *illuminated* we, as a consequence, become.

Allowance be Thy way. Thy Guidance and Mastership come. Thy change and evolution be done, on earth, as a step of preparation for the Mutual Interchange of Ideas: We are forever evolving, and in terms of Awakening by way of Allowing Consciousness—Source Energy, Awareness of the Great Spirit within us—in, we prepare ourselves step by step for a more harmonious way of living. Through respectively sharing our thoughts and ideas with each other (here as well as from beyond) and becoming ever more conscious of them, we learn how to conceive of and create a better world, a world essentially enabled by observing, appreciating, and being Supremely Mindful of Our Consciousness.

Give us a subtle delusion of fanciful dreams and visions, but mutually protect us from our temper-mental moods as we purify this state from those thoughts which lack good sense. And let us not be deceived into credulousness, but let us depart from the reactor: Hinduism calls it Maya: the falsehood and confusing influence of illusion. In this prayer we are asking that our illusions or misapprehensions be subtle, as we know how overpowering they can be. We realize how easy it is to fall victim to untruths or misperceptions that taint and distort us and cause us to exaggerate things and overreact; therefore, we are appealing for stability and help in removing these states.

For having the nature of animal, and the sensitivity of Consciousness to correct incorrectness, are self confessing. For to step into Now, reveals Eternity put into place: We belong to the animal kingdom: that is, our bodies, our survival instincts and our chemical makeup etc. But, essentially, we are Spirit—Consciousness. And Consciousness has dominion over all. However, to correct an error of thought, we must first become Aware of it. We must confess the error first and foremost to ourselves. We need to recognize, acknowledge, disclose, and profess the very real fact that we could be wrong. How many of us stop to consider that? To stop and consider something brings us into the Moment, the Now, and the Now is the only place change can come about. The Now reveals the everlasting, perpetual occasion to see the Truth.

So be it. Amen.

Thank you, dear reader and fellow kin in Consciousness, I appreciate the time you have taken to read this.

With Love all ways,
Vicki.

www.ingramcontent.com/pod-product-compliance
Lightning Source LLC
Chambersburg PA
CBHW060351080526
44583CB00012B/269